THE PULSE OF ENTERPRISE

TimeFrame AD 1800-1850

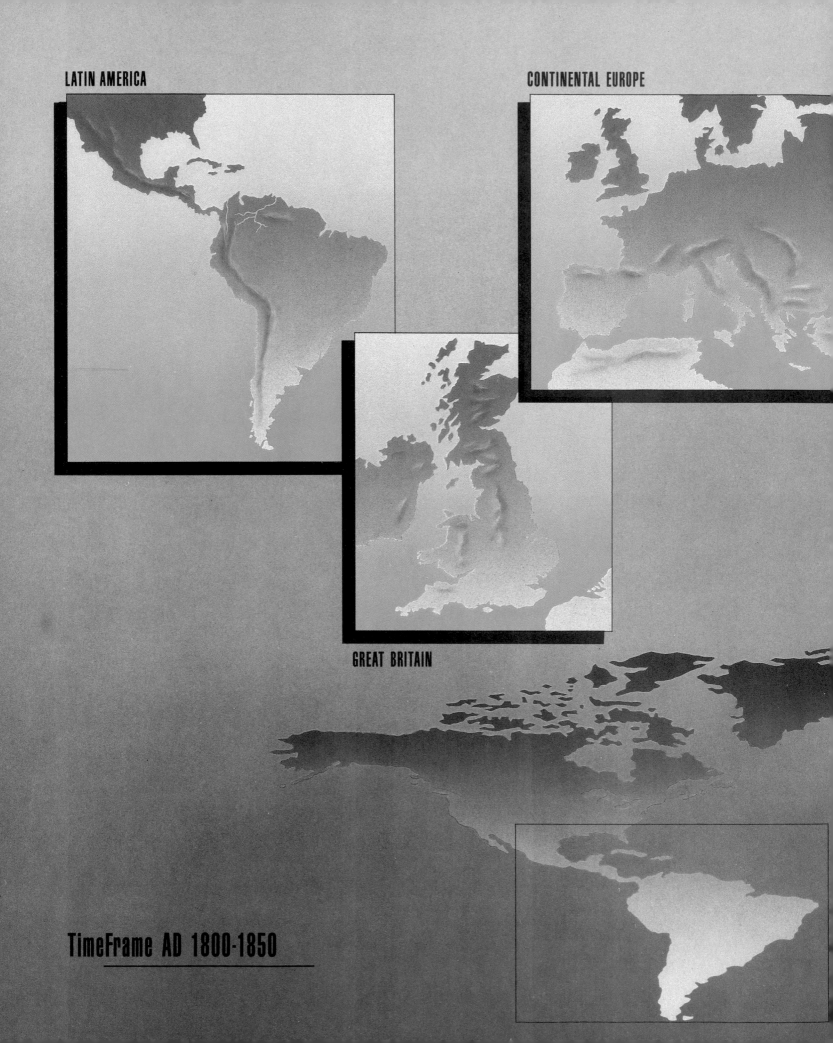

LATIN AMERICA

CONTINENTAL EUROPE

GREAT BRITAIN

TimeFrame AD 1800-1850

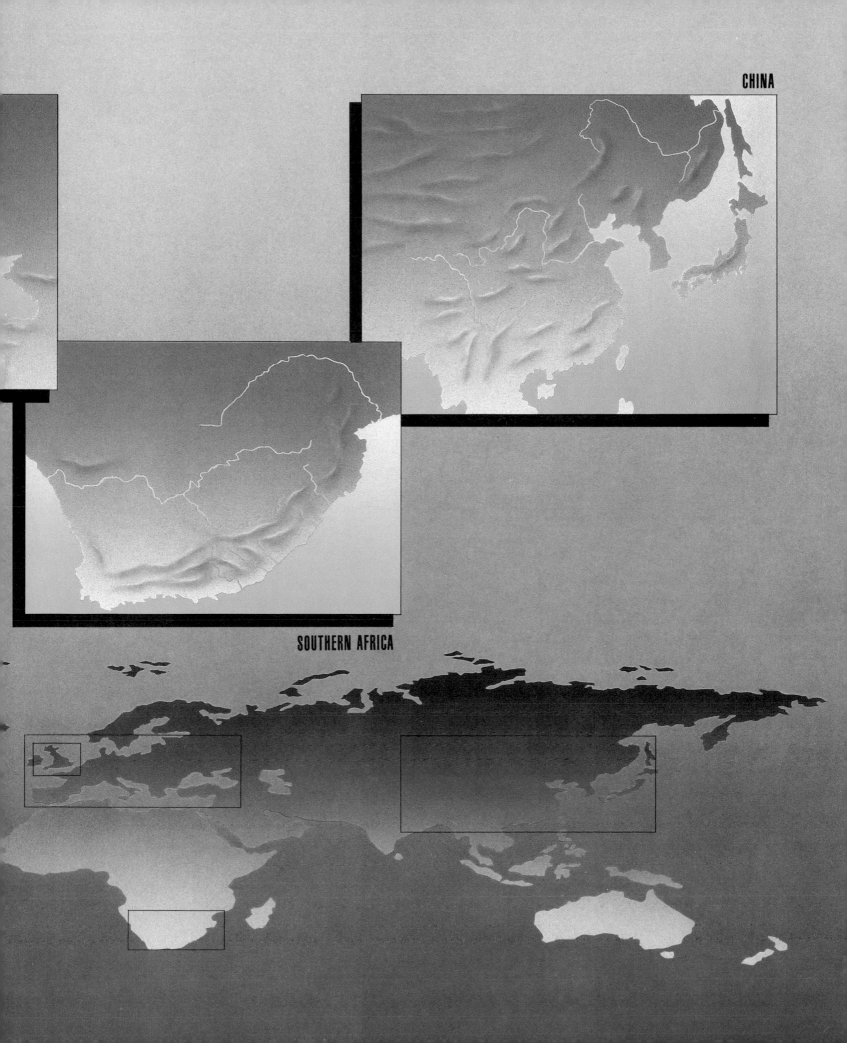

CHINA

SOUTHERN AFRICA

TIME®
LIFE
BOOKS

THE PULSE OF ENTERPRISE

TimeFrame AD 1800-1850

BY THE EDITORS OF TIME-LIFE BOOKS

TIME-LIFE BOOKS, ALEXANDRIA, VIRGINIA

Time-Life Books Inc.
is a wholly owned subsidiary of
THE TIME INC. BOOK COMPANY

President and Chief Executive Officer:
Kelso F. Sutton
President, Time Inc. Books Direct:
Christopher T. Linen

TIME-LIFE BOOKS INC.

EDITOR: George Constable
Executive Editor: Ellen Phillips
Director of Design: Louis Klein
Director of Editorial Resources:
Phyllis K. Wise
Director of Photography and Research:
John Conrad Weiser

EUROPEAN EDITOR: Ellen Phillips
Executive Editor: Gillian Moore
Design Director: Ed Skyner
Assistant Design Director: Mary Staples
Chief of Research: Vanessa Kramer
Chief Sub-Editor: Ilse Gray

PRESIDENT: John M. Fahey, Jr.
Senior Vice Presidents: Robert M.
DeSena, Paul R. Stewart, Curtis G.
Viebranz, Joseph J. Ward
Vice Presidents: Stephen L. Bair,
Bonita T. Boezeman, Mary P. Donohoe,
Stephen L. Goldstein, Juanita T. James,
Andrew P. Kaplan, Trevor Lunn, Susan J.
Maruyama, Robert H. Smith
New Product Development: Yuri Okuda,
Donia Ann Steele
Supervisor of Quality Control: James King

PUBLISHER: Joseph J. Ward

Correspondents: Elisabeth Kraemer-Singh
(Bonn); Christina Lieberman (New York);
Maria Vincenza Aloisi (Paris); Ann
Natanson (Rome). Valuable assistance
was also provided by: Ed Holland (Cara-
cas); Sharon Stevenson (Lima); Trini Ban-
dres (Madrid); Patricia Strathern (Paris);
John Maier (Rio de Janeiro); Ann Wise
(Rome); Robert Kroon (Switzerland);
Traudl Lessing (Vienna).

TIME FRAME
(published in Britain as
TIME-LIFE HISTORY OF THE WORLD)

SERIES EDITOR: Tony Allan

Editorial Staff for *The Pulse of Enterprise:*
Editor: Fergus Fleming
Designer: Mary Staples
Writer: Chris Farman
Researcher: Susie Dawson
Sub-Editor: Christine Noble
Design Assistant: Rachel Gibson
Editorial Assistant: Molly Sutherland
Picture Department: Amanda Hindley
(administrator), Zoë Spencer (picture
coordinator)

Editorial Production
Chief: Samantha Hill
Traffic Coordinator: Emma Veys
Editorial Department: Theresa John,
Debra Lelliott

U.S. EDITION

Assistant Editor: Barbara Fairchild
Quarmby
Copy Coordinator: Elizabeth Graham
Picture Coordinator: Barry Anthony

Editorial Operations
Copy Chief: Diane Ullius
Production: Celia Beattie
Library: Louise D. Forstall

Computer Composition: Gordon E. Buck
(Manager), Deborah G. Tait, Monika D.
Thayer, Janet Barnes Syring, Lillian
Daniels

Special Contributors: Neil Fairbairn,
Michael Kerrigan, Alan Lothian (text);
Sheila Corr, Tim Fraser, Deborah Pow-
nall (research); Ann L. Bruen (copy);
David E. Manley (index).

CONSULTANTS

General:
GEOFFREY PARKER, Professor of History,
University of Illinois, Urbana-Champaign,
Illinois

CHRISTOPHER BAYLY, Reader in Modern Indian History, Saint Catharine's College, Cambridge University, Cambridge,
England

Industrial Britain:
RICHARD OVERY, Reader in Modern His-
tory, King's College, University of London,
England

China:
DENIS TWITCHETT, Gordon Wu Professor of Chinese Studies, Princeton University, Princeton, New Jersey

France:
COLIN LUCAS, Fellow of Balliol College,
Oxford University, England

Latin America:
JOHN LYNCH, Emeritus Professor of Latin
American History, University of London,
England

Southern Africa:
RICHARD RATHBONE, Reader in the
Contemporary History of Africa, School of
Oriental and African Studies, University of
London, England

**Library of Congress Cataloging in
Publication Data**
The Pulse of enterprise: timeframe AD 1800-
1850 / by the editors of Time-Life Books.
   p.   cm. — (Time frame)
   Includes bibliographical references.
   ISBN 0-8094-6462-4.— ISBN 0-8094-6463-2
(lib. bdg.)
   1. History, Modern—19th century.
2. Economic history—1750-1918.
I. Time-Life Books. II. Series.
D359.7.P96 1990
909.081—dc20   90-10837
                          CIP

Time-Life Books Inc. offers a wide range of fine
recordings, including a *Rock 'n' Roll Era* series.
For subscription information, call 1-800-621-
7026 or write Time-Life Music, P.O. Box C-
32068, Richmond, Virginia 23261-2068.

CONTENTS

BONAPARTE'S EMPIRE

1

The spectacle in the old island cathedral of Notre Dame was extraordinary—even for Paris. It was 1804. Scarcely ten years had passed since the tumbrels of the Revolutionary Terror had hauled their victims through the streets, to die in the name of Liberty, Equality, and Fraternity by the guillotine that had beheaded the king of France himself. Now, despite the December weather, the same streets were jammed with crowds who had come to cheer their new emperor on the way to his coronation. For Napoleon Bonaparte, the thirty-five-year-old general from Corsica who now ruled France, was no longer satisified with the title of Life Consul of the Republic.

Draped in the robes and trappings of his new rank—including the ostensible sword of Charlemagne as well as a crown of golden laurel leaves that his ultimate heir had designed for himself—Bonaparte stood before 8,000 French and foreign dignitaries inside the cathedral and with his wife, Joséphine, was anointed by Pope Pius VII with the sacred oil of royal France. The oil was a substitute: The original had been publicly burned a few years before at the suggestion of Alexandre de Beauharnais, the zealous revolutionary who had been Joséphine's first husband. But there was nothing surrogate about the next stage in the ceremony, when Napoleon I took the crown from the pontiff's hand and placed it firmly on his own head. "*Vivat Imperator in Aeternum*," chanted the choir. France—and, indeed, much of Europe—had a new emperor.

In five years, Napoleon had transformed France from a turbulent revolutionary state into a progressive centralized republic whose domination of the Continent was unquestioned. In the years to come, his victorious armies would march across Europe, expanding the French empire with a series of campaigns that ranged from Poland to Portugal. Even the streets of Moscow, heart of the vast Russian empire, would echo to the tread of French boots. And in the wake of French troops came French systems of government and administration. Long after Napoleon had been defeated by a European coalition in 1815 and his empire dissolved, the legacy of his occupation would live on.

The half-century that saw Napolean's rise and fall also witnessed other dramatic changes. A new force was gathering in Great Britain that would have an even more devastating impact on Europe: the power of industry. In the first half of the nineteenth century, Britain emerged as the world's first industrial society, accruing such wealth with its steam-driven commerce that it would become a model for other nations.

While Britain and other Western economies were expanding, other established powers were in decline. In China, imported opium and British military might brought that powerful empire to its knees as a vassal of Western traders. Throughout the extensive tracts of Latin America, revolutionaries overthrew their Spanish overlords to form independent republics. And in southern Africa, black kingdoms were crushed by a flow of British and Dutch settlers spreading from the Cape of Good Hope.

With a commanding frown, the French emperor Napoleon Bonaparte scans a field of battle in this detail from a painting by Horace Vernet. Napoleon's inspired military prowess and political acumen swept him in twenty years from obscure origins in Corsica to personal dominance over most of Europe.

At its height, Napoleon's empire stretched from Spain to the Russian border. Areas under direct French rule *(shaded green)* included France, Catalonia, the Netherlands, the Dalmatian coast, and parts of Italy; other dependent states *(shaded yellow)* were mostly ruled by members of the Bonaparte family. For some of the countries, French occupation brought the benefits of centralized rule and liberal institutions. The Rhine Confederation, for example, which was formed in 1806 and eventually incorporated some 300 small German states, not only swept away the hidebound regimes of petty principalities but also gave the German people a greater sense of national unity. Even after Napoleon's downfall in 1815 and the subsequent dissolution of his empire, French legal codes and administrative systems were retained in most of the occupied territories.

In the West, however, the first decade and a half of the new century was dominated by Napoleon, as he used his talent and ambition, coupled with the advances in communications and warfare of the previous century, to bring most of Europe under his thrall. It would have been a great feat for even a ruler born to the purple to have achieved; but as it was, the man who assumed France's imperial mantle in 1804 was just one of the eight surviving children of a provincial Corsican lawyer. As he said to his brother Joseph on his coronation day, ''If only our father could see us now.''

The emperor-to-be was born in Ajaccio in 1769, shortly after the French Crown had purchased the turbulent island of Corsica from the Republic of Genoa. His father, Carlo Buonaparte, was a notary who claimed descent from the twelfth-century military aristocracy of Tuscany. As petty nobility, the family claimed at least some of the privileges reserved for the well-born under France's Ancien Régime. Yet by now the Ancien Régime was drawing to a close. Though practically no one at the time of Napoleon's birth envisaged the epic sweep of the revolution that was to come, most

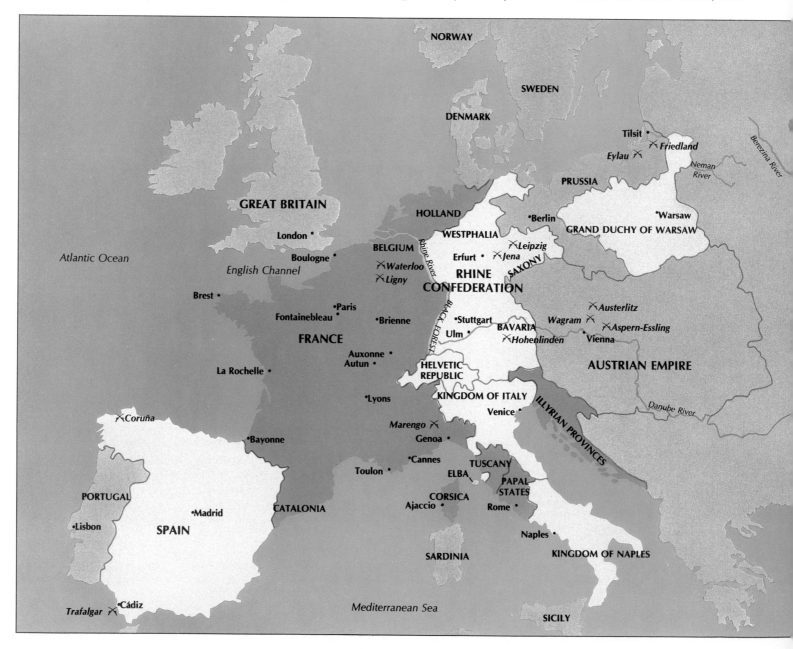

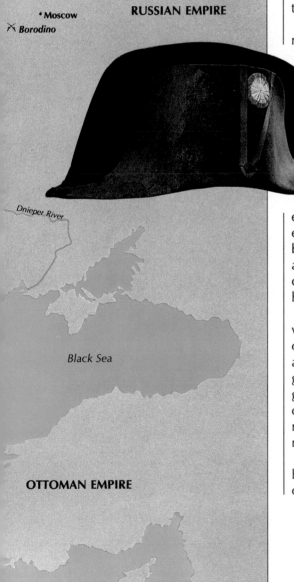

RUSSIAN EMPIRE

• Moscow

⤬ Borodino

Dnieper River

Black Sea

OTTOMAN EMPIRE

educated men anticipated at least a considerable opening up of their social world.

At the age of nine, Napoleone, as he was then known, took the first steps in his mainland career when his father used his connections to find him a place at a preparatory school at Autun. There he learned to speak French in place of Italian and lost the final e from his Christian name. A few months later, Carlo succeeded, after a lengthy struggle, in having the Buonaparte's Corsican patents of nobility recognized by the French court—a vital step for his son's military career, since the officer corps was recruited from the aristocracy. The king even offered scholarships for the sons of poor nobles, and young Buonaparte was able to move on to a more distinguished school at Brienne-le-Château in the Champagne region of eastern France.

A final report praised his conduct and his mathematical knowledge, though it noted his weakness in the "accomplishments" of music, dancing, and other social skills, and concluded: "This boy would make an excellent sailor." But the French navy never knew its loss. At fifteen, Buonaparte entered the École Militaire of Paris, and a year later—most cadets took twice as long to graduate—he was assigned as a second lieutenant in the artillery. The artillery had little prestige among France's officer nobility. Nevertheless, it was the most forward-looking arm of the French military and the one that had benefited most from eighteenth-century technical improvements.

France in 1785 was already creaking with the social strains that would erupt in revolution less than four years later. Yet even in the last days of the Ancien Régime, garrison life was leisurely, with a light work load and long leaves. Buonaparte read more than the average new lieutenant, began to write a history of Corsica, and steeped himself in the liberal ideas that were sweeping France. But he also gained a post at the Auxonne artillery depot; as aide to senior officers engaged in technical experiments, he acquired practical experience, as well as influential friends. It was here too, in 1789, that the young officer first saw active service when he and his troops were sent to quell food riots.

Buonaparte spent the earliest years of the Revolution between Paris and his native Corsica, where he contrived to have himself elected lieutenant colonel of the newly formed Ajaccio National Guard. It was an exciting command for a young man whose army rank was no higher than lieutenant, but a dangerous one, for many Corsicans had seen in France's revolutionary turmoil a chance to seize their independence. Buonaparte acted vigorously—though unsuccessfully—to suppress what he now saw as rebellion, with the result that his family had to flee to France in June 1793.

There, despite pockets of resistance, Maximilien Robespierre's radical Jacobins were now running the country. The beleaguered new republic was at war with most of Europe, and it needed all the soldiers it could get—especially if, like Buonaparte after his arrival, they wrote pamphlets with a revolutionary tone. His literary efforts gained the attention of Augustin Robespierre, brother of Maximilien and the Jacobin government's representative in the south. Robespierre's chief problem was the port of Toulon, which defecting royalists had allowed the British to occupy. A scratch revolutionary army was trying vainly to dislodge them, and when the artillery commander was wounded, young Captain Buonaparte was the obvious replacement.

It was the first real opportunity in the career of the age's greatest opportunist, and he took it. With backing from Robespierre, he forced his superiors to adopt his plan of using artillery fire to force the port's supporting fleet to withdraw, and in Decem-

Painted on a gilded Sèvres dinner plate, French scholars busily measure the massive head of the Sphinx at Giza. When Napoleon invaded Egypt in 1798, his main purpose was to threaten British access to the wealth of India; but he also hoped to inquire exhaustively into the history of Egypt, then a weak satellite of the Ottoman Empire. The stylish dinner service to which the Sphinx plate belongs—just one expression of the Egyptomania fueled by Napoleon's expedition—included sixty-six plates, each bearing a different Egyptian view accurately copied from drawings made on the spot.

ber, promoted to major, he carried it out: Toulon, an embarrassment to the republic for months, fell in forty-eight hours. Still hobbling from a leg wound he had received in the fighting, Buonaparte was promoted again, to brigadier general, and posted as senior artillery officer to Italy. There the French Army of Italy was confronting troops of the Austrian Holy Roman Empire, whose Hapsburg monarch not only controlled northern Italy and the Netherlands but claimed allegiance from the German states in between. By midsummer of 1794, his planning had gained results against the enemy. The twenty-four-year-old general seemed well set on a dazzling career.

During a revolution, though, friends in high places could prove a dangerous liability as well as an asset. When a July coup removed Robespierre's government in

In one of many portraits painted of Joséphine by her close friend Jean-Baptiste Isabey, Napoleon's first wife wears the robes designed for her part in his imperial coronation in 1804. Born on the French-Caribbean island of Martinique, Joséphine lost her first husband, the aristocrat Alexandre de Beauharnais, to the Revolutionary guillotine. But she survived to become a central figure of Parisian society. Captivated by her lively prettiness and sophistication, Napoleon married her in 1796, when he was twenty-six years old and she was thirty-two; but her extravagance and repeated infidelities, together with her failure to provide an imperial heir, brought an end to their marriage in 1809.

Paris, Buonaparte was arrested, accused of treason, and imprisoned; Jacobin heads were rolling throughout France, and his was almost one of them. Even after the charges were dropped for lack of evidence and he was released, his political backing was gone, and under the new regime, the Convention Assembly, his prospects looked bleak. For months he tramped around Paris from office to office; at one point, he was prepared to abandon everything and become a mercenary in Ottoman Turkey.

His luck changed in October 1795. Since its inception, the assembly had been troubled by outbreaks of rioting and near-rebellion in the streets of Paris. That month, a large mob threatened to storm the Tuileries palace; the man in charge of its defense, Paul Barras, found Buonaparte at hand in his hour of need. The young general rapidly assembled some artillery and coolly scattered the rioters with grapeshot. More than 200 lay dead on the capital's streets, but Buonaparte's future was ensured.

Indeed, in addition to Barras's support and a promotion (by the end of October he was a divisional general in command of the Army of the Interior) Buonaparte also acquired Barras's mistress, one Joséphine de Beauharnais, widow of a guillotined revolutionary aristocrat. In March 1796, they were married—against the advice of Joséphine's family lawyer, who warned her that her husband-to-be had nothing but "his army cloak and sword." It was an ill-fated union: He was seduced by Joséphine's beauty, breeding, and rumored wealth; she believed that her suitor's excellent prospects would lift her from her carefully concealed poverty. The match began inauspiciously: While making love on their wedding night, the general was bitten on the leg by his bride's lap dog. Soon they were being openly unfaithful to each other.

Whatever the misconceptions surrounding their marriage, Joséphine had been right about her husband's prospects. Since gaining his general's rank, Buonaparte had lobbied ferociously for a field command to match it. Barras—by this time one of the five members of the governing Directory, which had replaced the old Convention Assembly in October 1795—approved, and even spoke of an appointment coming as a wedding present. A few days before his marriage, Buonaparte received the orders he sought: Two days after the ceremony, not yet twenty-seven, he set off with a small, trusted staff to lead the Revolution's war in Italy.

There the Army of Italy was outnumbered by its Austrian enemies, badly supplied, and low in morale; its senior officers had no high opinion of their youthful leader, who—they reckoned—owed his appointment to Parisian political contacts, not military skill. Yet within a few months, Bonaparte—who now eliminated the un-French *u* from his Corsican name—had turned his ragamuffin troops into an army of enthusiastic veterans with a string of victories to their credit. In this endeavor he was aided by the very paucity of supplies available to his troops: Unhindered by cumbersome baggage trains, the French forces were able to move rapidly across the countryside, living off what they could forage or steal. By concentrating his modest but fast-moving forces against a series of points in the Austrians' extended array, Bonaparte defeated a succession of enemy commanders until, by April 1797, he had driven the Austrians from northern Italy and stood seventy-five miles from Vienna.

Having proven his worth as a military commander, Bonaparte now set out to demonstrate his political ability. On his own initiative, and with disregard for regular channels of diplomacy—to the chagrin of the Directory—he negotiated the Peace of Campo Formio by which Austria surrendered much of her Italian territory to a new, French-dominated Cisalpine Republic. The Austrians also gave up possessions in the Rhineland and the Netherlands, and Bonaparte returned to Paris and glory.

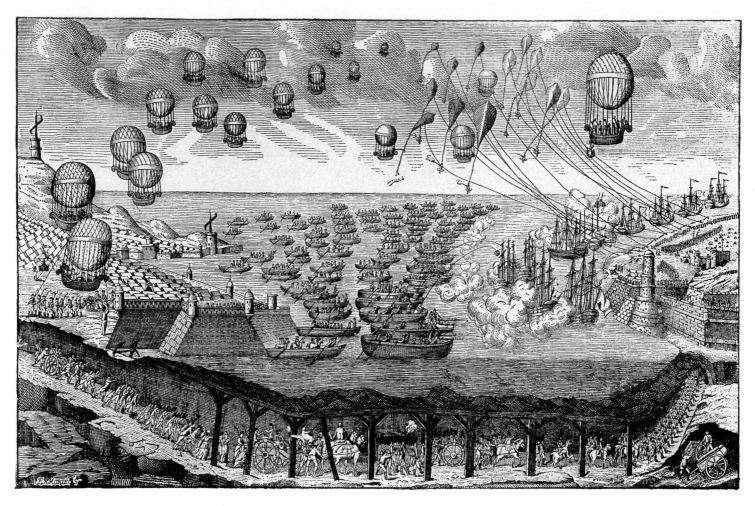

A French engraving of 1803 teems with ambitious and implausible methods for landing an invasion force in England. Balloons and squadrons of ships assail the British defenses, while French troops trundle artillery through a tunnel beneath the English Channel. Published as part of a propaganda exercise intended to fan French confidence and British fears alike, the engraving reflects ostentatious preparations for hostilities being undertaken by Napoleon on the Channel coast. British supremacy at sea—finally confirmed by the victory at Trafalgar in 1805—dashed French hopes of making a successful crossing; but France's huge and well-trained invasion force was quickly transferred eastward to campaign in central Europe.

He did not remain there long. The Directory had prepared a vague plan to discomfit Britain, France's only remaining enemy, by seizing Ottoman Egypt: Such an action, they hoped, would ruin British Mediterranean trade and might possibly even lay the groundwork for an attack on Britain's Indian possessions. With Bonaparte in command, the plan rapidly took on practical shape. In May 1798, the expedition's ships set sail, adroitly avoiding British Admiral Horatio Nelson's blockading squadrons. They captured Malta en route in June, and landed near Alexandria in early July.

Egypt's Mamluk warriors, who ruled the country under the Ottomans, were no match for the French, and Bonaparte soon had the country under his control, though the Ottoman sultan declared a holy war against the intruders. But after Nelson caught and destroyed the French fleet at its Nile anchorage in August, the expedition was cut off from reinforcement. Although Bonaparte stayed in Egypt for another year, easily defeating the Sultan's forces, the Egyptian campaign proved a waste of resources—including the troops, who lingered in Egypt when their general took ship for France.

Events in Paris were far more interesting than the sands of Egypt. The Directory government was in a state of chronic crisis, and Britain's prime minister, William Pitt, had organized and financed a new alliance against France: the so-called Second

Coalition, which included Naples, Austria, Russia, and the Ottoman Empire. Some of the Directory's members wanted military help to stage a coup that would give France a more stable regime. Bonaparte was enthusiastic. In November 1799, with the help of his troops' bayonets, a new constitution was proclaimed. Three "consuls" would rule the nation, and although their powers were ostensibly equal, there was soon no doubt as to which consul wielded the real authority: Napoleon Bonaparte.

He rapidly arranged for political appearances to match political realities. Yet another new constitution was drafted, which restricted voting eligibility to some 10 percent of the population—those placed on representative, regional "lists of confidence"—and made France's first consul a virtual dictator. A referendum in February 1800 gave Bonaparte a respectable mantle of democratic approval—of some three million votes only 1,500 were counted against him—and he set to work with his usual energy to transform a nation worn out by ten years of revolution.

Even before he moved into the former royal palace of the Tuileries, he had begun to grapple with financial problems almost as grave as those that had led to the downfall of the Ancien Régime back in 1789. By dint of borrowing (appalled at the interest rates he had to pay, he created the state-supervised Bank of France in 1800) and even a lottery, he raised enough immediate cash to keep the nation afloat until his newly recruited officials were able to collect the substantial income and property taxes on which he would ultimately rely.

Those who preferred order to chaos—the majority, as election results showed—got good value for their money. In 1799 and 1800, their first consul, with his advisers, was diligently packaging a new legal system. A decade of revolution had reformed the Ancien Régime's laws piecemeal, though often drastically; the new Civil Code—it would soon be known as the Code Napoléon—now consolidated those reforms. The old customary law of northern France was amalgamated with the Roman law of the south to form a seamless unit. And a new criminal code was introduced with judges to enforce it. The changes were sweeping, and in the years to come, the code would be extended to regulate and transform virtually every aspect of life. Indeed, one provision, insisting on the equal division of property between sons, did more than the Revolution to destroy the power of France's landed gentry.

To administer the new law and the nation, Napoleon swept away the muddled hierarchy of committees that the flawed democracy of the later revolution had left in charge of local government. Henceforth, each *département,* or province, would be supervised by a prefect appointed by the Ministry of the Interior—in effect by Bonaparte—who in turn appointed a mayor to each commune. The principle of centralized government that Bonaparte embodied in Paris was reflected throughout the administrative pyramid. France, in effect, would be his tightly organized personal fief.

Bonaparte also made peace with the Church. Since 1792, the Revolutionary government had insisted that all clergy be elected by popular vote rather than by papal authority. The majority of the French population, however, were devout Roman Catholics, and the bad relations between the pope and his loyal priests on the one hand, and the Revolution and its "constitutionalized" clergy on the other, had long been a running sore. In a concordat with the Vatican signed in 1801, orthodox Roman Catholicism was recognized as "the religion of the great majority of the French people"; its practice was authorized "in conformity with any police regulations that may be necessary for public order." In April 1802, church bells rang out for the first time since the early days of the Revolution.

By then, they were celebrating peace in Europe as well as peace between Church and state. Bonaparte needed both for his reforms to take effect. To end the war, he had taken a pause from lawmaking in May 1800 and become a soldier again. With the same speed and ingenuity he had shown in 1796, he set upon the Austrians in their remaining Italian possessions, crushing them at the decisive Battle of Marengo in June. A victory at Hohenlinden in Germany completed Austria's defeat, and the Peace of Lunéville in February 1801 ended the land war in Europe. The sea war with Britain ended shortly after: The failure of his Second Coalition forced Pitt to resign, and wearied by almost a decade of fruitless struggle, the incoming British government was happy to sign the Treaty of Amiens in March 1802.

The peace, between a deeply suspicious Britain and a France still full of expansionist vigor, was destined to be little more than a brief truce. Still, First Consul Bonaparte made the most of the fifteen-month respite, continuing his reforms with unabated energy. The whole structure of France was being rationalized. The year 1801 had seen the replacement of Ancien Régime weights and measures with the metric system. The next year witnessed the creation of a new national police force and the institution of nationwide lycées—state secondary schools. The inhabitants of Napoleon's France were to be both orderly and educated. They were also to be mobile: France was now spanned by a network of great roads lined with fast-growing poplars, which shaded the passage of both the military and an ever-larger body of merchants.

For the members of France's bourgoisie were growing in both number and wealth, their endeavors aided by judicious government intervention. The First Consul, however, had more than mere money to distribute. In 1802, the creation of the Legion of Honor, a decoration awarded for outstanding civic or military service, provided a fresh goal for the ambitions of loyal French citizens. The ablest of Bonaparte's commanders found themselves "Marshals of France," a rank that brought privileges as well as prestige. Within two years, following his coronation as emperor, Bonaparte was also dispensing titles to a new imperial nobility. The Ancien Régime may have disappeared, but France's new ruler was too wily to ignore the value of its trappings. As he remarked cynically, "It is with baubles that men are led."

Not all enjoyed Bonaparte's authoritarian rule. The Civil Code laid great importance on the authority of the male, thereby depriving women of many of the legal rights they had previously enjoyed. And while the new regime benefited the middle class, it did little for the poor. Laws introduced in 1803 required every worker to carry a registration book, stamped by his employer. Without such a pass, the worker could be treated as a vagabond. And in any case of litigation between master and servant, the employer's word was accepted without hesitation. Strict press censorship, however, coupled with an efficient secret police, silenced any with a grievance.

Nevertheless, approval for the government that had brought stability to France was almost total. Bonaparte's impregnable political position was reinforced in August 1802, when a near-unanimous referendum granted him his consulship for life. And in May 1804, a new plebiscite was held—this time to ratify Bonaparte's decision, for the safety of the state, to become a hereditary "emperor of the French." According to published figures, 3,572,329 French citizens supported him; 2,579 did not.

But by the time the votes were counted, France was at war again. In the uneasy months following the Treaty of Amiens, the British had been increasingly disturbed by Bonaparte's actions. Much of France's new-found energy seemed to be devoted

Swathed in ermine for his coronation as hereditary emperor of France, Napoleon gazes from a portrait executed by J. A. D. Ingres in 1806, more than a year after the event it records. The title of emperor was considered less shocking to republican sensibilities than that of king; it was chosen—like Napoleon's open-fronted, golden laurel wreath—to evoke classical Roman connotations of military glory and civic responsibility. Nevertheless, Napoleon's personal symbol, the bee—embroidered here in gold on his velvet robe—was taken from the tomb of a sixth-century AD French king.

to shipbuilding—not only ships of the line, but, more ominously, flat-bottomed invasion barges. At the beginning of 1803, Bonaparte annexed the Italian state of Piedmont and sent his forces to impose a new government on the Swiss Confederation. And in April, to ensure, at the very least, neutrality across the Atlantic, he sold the vast area of Louisiana—ceded to France by its ally, Spain, in 1800—to the United States for a cut-rate price of $12 million. "You will fight England again," Bonaparte remarked hopefully as he shook hands on the deal.

While Bonaparte's warlike maneuverings worried the British, they were even more concerned about his determination to turn Europe into a vast market reserved exclusively for French goods. France not only controlled almost the entire European coastline from Genoa to Antwerp, it also had the effrontery to charge extortionate customs duties. For an island nation that thrived on commerce, it was an intolerable situation. Accordingly in May 1803, on the pretext that France had not yet complied fully with certain provisions laid down at Amiens, Britain declared war.

Britain had always been Bonaparte's most dangerous enemy, the fountainhead of arms and money for all of his other antagonists. But in 1803, all the omens looked favorable for a French victory. The rest of Europe was unwilling to enter into another war. And with a population of 27 million—larger than that of any other European state except Russia, and almost twice that of Britain—France had enormous resources of military manpower. The only question, it seemed, with neither side having a foothold on the other's territory, was where to start the fighting.

Throughout 1804 and early 1805, Napoleon began massing troops along the Channel—"a mere ditch," he insisted. But the Channel was no ditch: It was an arm of ocean. Napoleon himself estimated that 20,000 of his 120,000-strong Armée d'Angleterre would drown in the crossing. ("One loses that number in battle every time," he argued in justification.) And launching an invasion in the teeth of every warship Britain could find was not the same as forcing a river crossing under artillery fire. Still, even temporary control would be enough. "Let us be masters of the straits for six hours and we shall be masters of the world," declared the emperor, who knew that Britain had too few home-based troops to oppose him on land.

First, though, he had to get there. Ever since 1793—apart from the brief respite following Amiens—British ships of war had swept French merchantmen from the oceans and sealed the survivors up in their harbors. These tactics had not only allowed profitable British trade to flow freely everywhere, but had also turned Britain's Royal Navy into a remarkable instrument of war. Its officers and men hated their long spells of blockade duty—their quarters were cramped and verminous, the food was infested with weevils, and scurvy was rife—but constant sea duty in all weather had brought them to a peak of efficiency, while France's outnumbered and undermanned fleet, trapped in its harbors, had declined in skill and morale. Although reports of Napoleon's invasion preparations—some of them plainly visible from the English coast—caused public panic, professional naval officers were ready for the challenge. Most, no doubt, shared the view of Admiral Sir John Jervis, who in 1803, had said, "I don't say the French can't come. I say they can't come by sea."

Napoleon thought differently. With the same boldness that had earned his reputation as a fighting general on land, he issued the French fleet the most aggressive orders it had received in years. Pierre de Villeneuve, its chief admiral, would break through Admiral Nelson's blockade of the Mediterranean port of Toulon to join up progressively with other blockaded French and allied Spanish squadrons. The com-

A napoleon—at twenty francs the largest denomination of the gold coinage issued in France beginning in 1804—pays homage to the emperor. The franc itself had been introduced in 1795, but during the chaos of the Revolutionary decade the constant issue of paper money had fostered crippling inflation. Napoleon's quick monetary reforms and his insistence on strict official auditing restored the currency to a sound footing.

Napoleon's own head and title appear in the center of his new meritorious order, the Legion of Honor. Instituted by decree in 1802 as a reward for citizens who strove for the good of the nation, the medal was first awarded in 1804. Initially, Napoleon's proposal for a single honor open to all Frenchmen faced stiff opposition: Committed egalitarians considered any distinction to be against the spirit of the Revolution, while senior military officers shunned sharing a decoration with lower ranks. But the emperor's belief in the award's value was soon justified by the secure place it gained in French affections. During his life, Napoleon made 30,000 awards—mostly for bravery in battle—including this one, which he bestowed upon himself.

bined fleet would then sail not for the Channel but for the West Indies, drawing the British to the defense of their valuable Caribbean possessions and making rendezvous with the blockaded Brest squadron, which would use the diversion to make its own escape. Then the armada would turn around and recross the Atlantic, sweeping the last British reserves from the Channel and allowing the passage of the French army.

The plan was partly successful. Villeneuve reached the West Indies, though without the Brest contingent—and with Nelson in hot pursuit. But when Villeneuve returned to Europe, he failed to force his way into the Channel. Instead, he retreated before a smaller British fleet, and as autumn came, he found himself blockaded once more, this time in the Spanish port of Cádiz.

Napoleon railed furiously at what he considered the incompetence and cowardice of his admiral—who had in fact been given a near-impossible task. But long before Villeneuve's ships had sought safety in Cádiz, the emperor had already postponed his great invasion. British diplomacy—backed, as ever, by British gold—had not been idle. In May and June, Prime Minister Pitt had persuaded Sweden, Austria, and Russia to join the Third Coalition against France. The coalition had invasion plans of their own: coordinated attacks in Italy and Bavaria, which the allies hoped would end in a joint Austro-Russian army's grinding through the Black Forest and destroying France's Bavarian ally before crossing the Rhine and entering France itself.

Napoleon acted with characteristic dispatch, long before the coalition's plans were mature. Late in August, the Armée d'Angleterre, renamed the Grande Armée, struck its Boulogne encampment and marched east to deal with the new threat.

The campaign that followed was probably the most brilliant of Napoleon's career—although he was greatly helped by the incompetent staff work of his enemies, whose "coordination" did not even take account of the twelve days' difference between the Julian calendar used in Russia and the Gregorian version employed by the rest of Europe. In fact, the Russians played no part in the first phase of the fighting. Without waiting for Czar Alexander's armies to arrive, Austrian Archduke Ferdinand led an unhurried invasion of Bavaria. But he was advancing into a well-planned trap.

While 50,000 French troops held northern Italy, and Marshal Joachim Murat led a feint on the Black Forest, Napoleon's main force aimed straight for the Danube. He had not forgotten the lessons of the Italian campaign: The Grande Armée, divided into a series of semi-independent corps and unhindered by cumbersome baggage trains, moved with frightening rapidity. The French crossed the Rhine on September 26, marching with paralyzing speed and briefly violating the territory of neutral Prussia to save time; by October 7, they were already astride the Danube crossings north of Ulm. The Grande Armée's separated corps closed in on the town and the Austrians who occupied it. Ferdinand escaped with most of his cavalry, but the rest of his army was forced to surrender by October 20. By the end of the month, the French had mopped up the remaining Austrian units, including Ferdinand's cavalry.

After Ulm, Napoleon wrote home, "I have been rather overdoing things, my good Joséphine. Eight days spent in the soaking rain and with cold feet have told on me a little; but . . . I have accomplished my object." Without fighting a major battle, Napoleon had disposed of one enemy. Now he set off to crush the Russians, who were advancing from Vienna under the elderly, one-eyed General Mikhail Kutusov. But the tough old commander—a notoriously heavy drinker who seldom traveled without his three favorite concubines—fell back adroitly. Although Murat seized an abandoned Vienna (and got a savage reprimand from Napoleon for wasting time),

A FLAIR FOR STRATEGY

Much of Napoleon's success was a result of his startling military talent. Even before 1789, French artillery had been the finest in Europe, and it was here that Napoleon received his early grounding in military theory. The Revolution itself provided him with the raw materials he needed to put his ambitions into practice by introducing the idea of a nation under arms, fighting for shared beliefs; and notwithstanding their initial disarray, France's untrained Revolutionary forces proved ideally receptive to Napoleon's charismatic leadership.

Although he closely studied the works of earlier military authorities, Napoleon refused to be bound by any set rules—indeed, he once declared "I have never had a plan of operations." It was this willingness to adapt his actions to the situation at hand that underpinned his success. The army was organized into small units, coordinated under his own direct command, that were ideal for flexible response in battle. Each was able to operate independently, with its own cavalry scouts and artillery; and by living off the land, rather than being delayed by lumbering baggage trains, the separate corps could move with terrifying speed. At a time when received wisdom dictated that soldiers should advance in a line, Napoleon instructed his troops to move in columns, thus enabling them both to negotiate broken country more easily and to achieve combat formation quickly. Rapid forced marches, combined with meticulous reconnaissance, allowed surprise and deception to play large parts in French victories—as did the skillful use of artillery, which Napoleon developed to a fine art.

At first, the cumbersome armies that faced Napoleon were baffled by their elusive enemy. The allies hastened to imitate their foe; but losses such as those suffered by the Russian and Austrian armies at Austerlitz—present-day Slavkov in Czechoslovakia—*(right)* served as potent reminders of Napoleon's military genius.

ANATOMY OF A VICTORY

The Battle of Austerlitz on December 2, 1805, was not only a milestone on Napoleon's march to European domination but also a tactical masterpiece. He reconnoitered the field with care, concealing a large part of his army behind high ground at the center of his line. The Russian and Austrian allies were then lured into attacking his artificially weakened right flank, at which moment Napoleon's hidden troops pounced. The painting by Simeon Fort (below) shows the scene as the French began to encircle the enemy, many of whom met a watery doom as Napoleon's artillery pounded the frozen lake across which they tried to flee. With the allied line broken, it was then easy for Napoleon's men to rout their disorganized opponents. During the day, the allies lost 27,000, the French only 9,000.

Russian and Austrian forces

French forces

Kutusov managed to join with a second Russian army approaching from the north.

The campaign had reached its crisis. The Grande Armée was now dangerously overextended. Constant detachments had reduced Napoleon's main force to little more than 50,000 men, whereas the Russians, with some Austrian support, numbered at least 85,000 and would soon be joined by fresh Austrian troops withdrawn from Italy. Worse, British subsidies were still at work: The gold that Napoleon declared had conjured a Russian army "from the extremities of the earth" had reached Berlin, where Prussia's King Frederick William III, stung by France's uninvited passage across his territory, was ready to join the coalition and add another 200,000 men to its armies. For Napoleon to hold his ground in the face of such opposition would be to court utter disaster, yet a French withdrawal would amount to a French defeat.

Once more, the emperor prepared a trap. By exaggerating his army's weakness, he determined to draw the allies into a premature assault northeast of Vienna, at a carefully reconnoitered position near the village of Austerlitz. The young czar, overruling old Kutusov's advice, marched headlong for the French. But the French had been marching, too: By December 1, enough of the Grande Armée's distant corps had rejoined Napoleon to give him more than 70,000 troops.

It was the first anniversary of his imperial coronation. That night, on the eve of battle, the army staged an improvised celebration, while Napoleon strolled informally among his men, sharing coarse jokes, patting whiskered cheeks, and tugging the earlobes of favored veterans. To the troops, it seemed their emperor—their "little corporal"—knew every one of them by name. Tired and ragged though their constant marching had made them, their morale had never been higher.

The next day, they showed what they could do. As Napoleon had anticipated, the Russians launched a massive attack—into a carefully prepared gap in the French positions. By noon, they were fighting desperately to escape encirclement; by 4:00 p.m., the battle was over. A few weeks later, Austria signed the humiliating Treaty of Pressburg under which Austria renounced all claims to possessions in Italy, as well as ceding extensive German territory to Bavaria. Pitt's Third Coalition had ended.

News of Austerlitz echoed around Europe. "I have defeated the Russian and Austrian army commanded by the two emperors." Napoleon triumphantly informed Joséphine. But he added plaintively, "I am a little tired; I have been camping in the open for eight days and as many freezing nights." The wife of the Austrian emperor received a terser account from her husband: "A battle was fought today which did not turn out very well." For their part, however, the British were assured by their ill-informed prince of Wales that "all was over with the French and that they had been sent to the Devil." When the truth dawned, it was a mortal blow for Prime Minister Pitt. Despairing, he died early in 1806. "Roll up that map of Europe," he told his niece on his deathbed. "It will not be needed these ten years."

But Britain, too, had a great victory to its credit. Back in October, even as the French were counting the spoils of Austria's debacle at Ulm, Nelson had intercepted the combined Franco-Spanish fleet off Cape Trafalgar near Cádiz. In a battle that cost

Their refined attitudes exaggerated by an engraving in a satirical journal, three fashionable ladies linger over the menu at a favorite café. As political stability returned after the chaos of the Revolutionary decade, Paris bourgeois society thankfully turned to a life of social pleasure. The luxury consumption that had long been central to the economy and the prestige of France reappeared in new forms: fashionable dresses in a high-waisted classical style; a social round of salons, theaters, and dancing; and a craze for eating out, as restaurants were opened by skilled chefs who had been displaced from their occupation in aristocratic households.

the British admiral his life, Napoleon's navy was decisively smashed. Thenceforth, British sea power was unchallenged: There could be no invasion of England, and the British felt confident enough to turn down a French peace offer in 1806.

For despite his military success, Napoleon desperately needed peace. Not only was there work still to be done on the Civil Code but, more important, the British blockade was beginning to pinch. Ways of producing synthetic saltpeter for gunpowder had been developed, indigo dye was being produced locally, alternatives to silk and cotton were being investigated, and attempts were being made to provide a substitute for Caribbean sugar that would eventually lead to the introduction of the sugar beet as a major crop. This ingenuity notwithstanding, the French economy was beginning to founder. When Napoleon returned from Austerlitz, he found the country in crisis. Several banks had collapsed and unemployment was acute. The emperor immediately instigated several grandiose public projects to provide work, while at the same time freely doling out prison sentences to strikers. But just when he most needed the time to attend to internal matters he found himself once more on the battlefield.

Whatever France's domestic problems, its dominance of the Continent was unquestioned. After Pressburg, Napoleon had deposed the Bourbon king of Naples, replacing him with his own brother, Joseph. And in July 1806, France had abolished the Holy Roman Empire and formed the Rhine Confederation, which put the some 300 states of western Germany under French control. That dominance, however, was soon to lead to war. Prussia was alarmed by French control of the Rhine Confederation, and Russia, wary of Napoleon, continued to refuse French treaty offers. It was not hard for the British, lavish as ever with their subsidies, to assemble the Fourth Coalition. In September 1806, Prussia, with 200,000 men, invaded Saxony.

Within thirty-six hours, Napoleon organized and launched his own attack: A thrust from Bavaria directed at the Prussian capital of Berlin. Once again, his opponents failed to appreciate the speed with which the Grande Armée—supposedly ready to settle into winter quarters—could move. Besides, despite its army's reputation, Prussia was no longer the military superstate that Frederick the Great had made it half a century before. While Napoleon's columns hurtled along the roads of Germany, Frederick William's generals wrangled over their plan—a sluggish advance on Stuttgart that would cut the French from their Rhine communications.

Long before Prussian operations could get seriously under way, French cavalry patrols had reached the Prussian border, with the fighting mass of the Grande Armée close behind. On October 14 at Jena, southwest of Leipzig, Napoleon met the bulk of the Prussian army and virtually destroyed it. The emperor had been lucky: The Grande Armée had not fully assem-

In a drawing of about 1810, flaring floodlights illuminate exhibits for the admiration of Napoleon and his entourage on an evening visit to the galleries of the Palais du Louvre. The national museum, founded in 1793 with works taken from the monarch and dispossessed nobles, benefited after 1798 from countless treasures appropriated during Napoleon's campaigns. The emperor took a keen interest in the collection; even while campaigning in 1806, he found time to pen a note inquiring "if it is true that the museum was late in opening yesterday, and the public was obliged to wait."

RULERS
BY APPOINTMENT

Napoleon's relatives served him well in the task of controlling his ever-growing empire; he appointed them without hesitation to the thrones of kingdoms throughout the continent of Europe.

By 1809, three of Napoleon's brothers sat on royal thrones: Louis had since 1806 been king of Holland; Joseph, after ruling the kingdom of Naples for two years, had been appointed king of Spain in 1808; and Jérôme had become king of the newly created state of Westphalia in 1807. Nor were the rest of the family forgotten: Napoleon's sister Caroline married Marshal Joachim Murat, who ascended the throne of Naples in 1808, succeeding Joseph; another sister, Elisa, whose husband was prince of Lucca, was made grand duchess of Tuscany in 1809; and from 1805, Napoleon's stepson Eugène de Beauharnais held sway as viceroy of the Kingdom of Italy.

In many cases, marriage into ruling families gave an air of legitimacy to the appointments and liberal reforms put through by the new rulers helped endear them to their subjects. But their names—which all bore the suffix Napoleon—were an unforgettable symbol of subjugation.

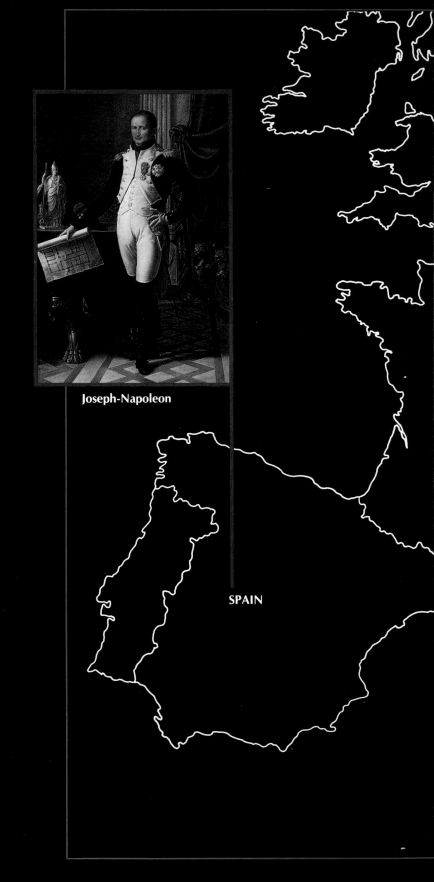

Joseph-Napoleon

SPAIN

Louis-Napoleon

KINGDOM OF HOLLAND

WESTPHALIA

Jérôme-Napoleon

FRANCE

Eugène-Napoleon

KINGDOM OF ITALY

TUSCANY

ELBA

CORSICA

KINGDOM OF NAPLES

SICILY

Joachim-Napoleon

Elisa-Napoleon

bled for the battle, and while Napoleon was fighting at Jena, another part of the Prussian army, led by the king, had been defeated by Marshal Louis Davout's outnumbered corps a few miles away at Auerstädt.

After Jena-Auerstädt, it seemed that a vigorous pursuit was all that was needed to finish off the campaign. By mid-November, most of Frederick William's troops were dead or prisoners, the French tricolor flew above the royal fortresses, and the king himself had fled for his life to the wastes of East Prussia. But in fact the war was far from over. The czar's new, post-Austerlitz army was marching to Frederick William's aid, and subsidies continued to flow from London. Despite Napoleon's victories, the combination of British gold and Russian bayonets kept the Fourth Coalition alive.

Determined to force a decisive outcome, the emperor pressed east into Poland and took Warsaw. Poles flocked to enlist in his army: The country was partitioned between Russia and Prussia, and most Polish patriots saw Napoleon not as another conqueror but as a heroic personification of French revolutionary ideas. Polish contingents had fought for Napoleon since the time of the Army of Italy, and the fresh recruits were welcome; but after a few inconclusive skirmishes with the wary Russians, the worsening weather drove even the Grande Armée into winter quarters.

It was soon in the field again. One corps, forced out of shelter to seek supplies, blundered into a Russian army attempting a surprise attack. Napoleon ordered his troops out into the snow in pursuit. The Russians retreated quickly, abandoning depots. At Eylau on February 8, they gave battle to the pursuing French. Blizzard conditions hampered cooperation between French units, and only a charge by Murat and more than 10,000 cavalry saved the French from an annihilating defeat. Even so, Napoleon lost more troops than the Russians, and he could hardly claim victory.

The battle ended the winter campaign, with both sides too exhausted to do anything other than return to warmth and shelter until the spring. It was June 1807 before Napoleon had his revenge for Eylau. At Friedland, about ten miles from his February humiliation, he defeated the Russians and captured most of their cannon. As Murat's cavalry surged eastward toward the Neman River, the czar asked for an armistice; two weeks later, Napoleon met a chastened Alexander at Tilsit, on a raft floating on the Neman. The Fourth Coalition had gone the way of its predecessors.

On July 9, 1807, both Alexander and Frederick William signed peace treaties with France. For Prussia, the terms were crushing: Its western territories became the Kingdom of Westphalia for Napoleon's twenty-three-year-old brother Jérôme, its Polish dominions were turned into the equally new Grand Duchy of Warsaw, and the remnant had to endure French occupation until a heavy cash indemnity was paid. Russia received gentler treatment: Napoleon, hoping for a future alliance, was satisfied merely with the czar's recognition of his existing conquests.

Despite his commanding position in Europe, Napoleon still had one implacable enemy: Britain. The emperor, however, already had plans for his foe. British power, he realized, was rooted in British trade. If France could choke off that trade, Britain's military might would vanish and the war would be won. Napoleon therefore decided to turn Britain's own favorite weapon of blockade against that nation.

The thinking behind the Continental System, as Napoleon called his scheme, was simple. If all Europe's ports were closed to their exports, the British would have to pay gold for imports. The cash outflow would not only diminish their ability to subsidize their allies but also, according to French economists, cause a financial crash that would trigger an industrial slump, agrarian misery, and unemployment—the perfect conditions for the "English revolution" that Napoleon was certain would come.

Naturally, the blockade would hurt France, too; but France was a self-sufficient continental power for which trade was a luxury, not a necessity, and the bankruptcy of a few French merchants was a small price to pay for the collapse of British capitalism. There were even protectionist arguments in favor of keeping out British production in order to shelter France's own infant industries: The system might conceivably do France more good than harm.

But it would not be enough to embargo British goods in French ports alone. The Continental System, as its name implied, would only work if it was applied to the whole of Europe, neutrals and belligerents alike. Of course, the same was true of Britain's maritime blockade. But the British blockade was almost invisible. A few coast dwellers might glimpse a frigate's sails on the horizon, but for most of Europe's people, it was abstract and out of sight. When it was introduced in 1806, however, the Continental System required an army of inquisitive customs officers everywhere—and usually a real army of fighting soldiers to back them up. It would take time to properly apply the system; and it remained to be seen whether Napoleon's strategy for economic warfare would create more enemies than even he could handle.

Napoleon's star was at its zenith in 1807. Britain's destruction seemed only a matter of time, once the gaps in the Continental System had been plugged—and at Tilsit, the Russians had agreed to impose the necessary embargoes. The next country on the list was Portugal—Britain's oldest ally and a useful base for the Royal Navy as well as a valuable economic partner. With Spanish acquiescence, French armies invaded.

General Andoche Junot captured Lisbon in late November 1807, but although the Portuguese regent fled with his fleet to Brazil, the campaign was far from over: Rough terrain and poor communications made it almost impossible for the French to suppress constant guerrilla attacks against them. Besides, it was becoming clear that Spain, ostensibly Napoleon's ally, was no respecter of the Continental System. Rather than admit failure, the emperor prepared to take over the Iberian Peninsula.

Murat was designated Napoleon's lieutenant in Spain, and by late February, French troops were already in position to seize key fortress towns. In March, Murat occupied Madrid. Outraged, the Spanish people rose in revolt, and forced their unpopular Bourbon monarch, Charles IV, to abdicate in favor of his son Ferdinand. Their efforts were to no avail. In April, the Spanish royal family was summoned to the French port of Bayonne, where both Ferdinand and Charles were forced to renounce their claim to the throne; and in May, Napoleon's brother Joseph was promoted from king of Naples to king of Spain. On paper at least, the takeover was complete.

In practice, the French effort had scarcely begun. With the exception of a few

In his image of Spanish women savagely resisting soldiers of the invading French army, the Spanish painter Francisco José de Goya y Lucientes indicts the barbarity of war. The work, *And They Are Like Wild Beasts,* was one of a series of sixty-five etchings evoked by the horrors that the artist saw between 1808 and 1813, when Napoleon's attempt to dominate the Iberian Peninsula was frustrated by British troops and Spanish patriots combined. Although officially employed by Joseph Bonaparte, the new king of Spain, Goya viewed the atrocities of both sides with appalled intensity.

CLASSICAL SPLENDORS REVIVED

Winged lions suggestive of ancient mythology lend their gilded forms to the arms of a throne, probably made for Napoleon in about 1805. Wings were used to support the arms of Empire chairs, their size varying with the importance of the person who commissioned the work.

In the art of France's First Empire, Napoleon's own admiration for the ancient world meshed with a prevailing international enthusiasm for the classical mode. Under the emperor's patronage, the Empire style, as it became known, combined shapes and motifs drawn from antiquity—whether Egyptian, Etruscan, Greek, or Roman—in a severe and stately symmetry that was nevertheless luxurious and often replete with allegory.

The vogue pervaded France, finding expression in such diverse fields as those of the cabinetmaker and couturier, and reaching its apogee in the work of architects Charles Percier and Pierre Fontaine, who decorated Napoleon's splendid state apartments at Château Malmaison, just outside Paris. Indeed, when Percier and Fontaine's designs were published in 1812 under the title *Recueil de Décorations Intérieures,* the book rapidly became a manifesto for the fashion conscious.

As French rule spread across Europe, so too did the new style. Long after his death, Napoleon's tastes continued to influence designers as far afield as Russia and the Western Hemisphere.

Shaped like a Greek ewer, a jug from a tea service created by Napoleon's favorite goldsmith, Martin-Guillaume Biennais, bears the low-relief decoration of repeated garlands and palm leaves that delighted users in the Empire period.

Made in 1811 for Napoleon's newborn son, a gilded cradle features several symbolic details. Cornucopia legs stand for prosperity, a winged victory and laurel wreath evoke triumph, while bees and an eagle denote the emperor.

liberals, who hoped that Napoleon would bring to their archaic society some of the benefits of the French Revolution, the Spanish people were outraged at the insult to their independence. Madrid rose in arms even before Joseph was given his crown, and by June, the whole nation, led by a provisional junta, was in ferment. Although 120,000 French troops, organized into flying columns, sought to crush resistance, they managed only to inflame it, and in July, one luckless general was forced to surrender three divisions to a Spanish army.

By the autumn of 1808, Spanish troops had pushed the French back behind the Ebro River, which flowed southeast across the country from the northern Cantabrian Mountains to the Mediterranean. Joseph was forced to leave Madrid with undignified haste, and worse was to come. Responding to Spanish pleas for aid, Britain landed 14,000 men in Portugal. Under the command of Arthur Wellesley, who had won a reputation fighting in India, they defeated Junot and forced the evacuation of Portugal. Hitherto, Britain had expended its efforts on a series of futile raids; now, Napoleon had opened a theater of war where a substantial British army, securely supplied by Britain's invulnerable fleet, could inflict real damage upon him.

At once, the emperor began to transfer 100,000 veterans from central Europe to the Spanish front. It cost him a high political price: In two weeks' negotiation at Erfurt, Czar Alexander gained a string of territorial concessions. But it seemed that victory in the Iberian Peninsula was ensured, for by November, there were 200,000 first-class French troops in Spain, led by the emperor himself. The junta could field a similar number, but in training and organization their forces were no match for the French, and a great offensive was soon sweeping the Spaniards from its path.

Madrid fell early in December. By January 1809, the British had fallen back through icy winter passes to La Coruña on the northwest coast, whence they evacuated the peninsula. Although they were victorious in the north, the French had been drawn away from their planned drive south. Napoleon's conquest of Spain was far from complete when events in central Europe compelled the emperor to leave the campaign to Joseph and his marshals and return to Paris. Austria was mobilizing.

Emperor Francis I of Austria and his government had waited years for the opportunity to revenge Austerlitz, and the Spanish imbroglio provided it. Napoleon spent three frantic months raising new troops to reinforce his depleted forces in Germany, cutting his Italian army to the bone, demanding 100,000 new levies from his increasingly reluctant allies, and conscripting an entire class of young Frenchmen a year in advance of the usual age of eighteen. Even so, when the Austrians invaded Bavaria in April, he had barely 275,000 men to field against Austria's 350,000. And the Austrians were learning. Their new army, well supplied with artillery, was organized in a system of semi-independent corps that was modeled on Napoleon's.

Their generalship was not yet up to the same standards, however. Although they made good progress against Alexandre Berthier, Napoleon's chief of staff—"I greatly desire the arrival of your Majesty," he wrote nervously to his master—the presence in the field of the emperor proved their undoing. A series of rapid maneuvers and confused skirmishes left the Austrians dispersed and defeated, creating a clear road to Vienna, which fell on May 13.

But as in 1805, a steady stream of detachments to secure the conquered territories had reduced the Grande Armée's fighting power, whereas Austrian reinforcements were on the march from the empire's far-flung provinces. On May 20, when French combat engineers threw a pontoon bridge across the Danube River, near the villages

In a painting exhibited in 1812, Napoleon—now more than forty years old—affectionately cradles his infant son, brought by his nanny to play with his father after a meal. Following the annulment of his marriage to Joséphine in 1809, Napoleon took as his second wife Princess Marie-Louise, daughter of the Austrian emperor. In March 1811, almost a year after the marriage, she provided him with the heir he desired, who was christened Napoleon and immediately designated king of Rome. The new empress, shown here sitting opposite Napoleon, was a timid soul compared with the self-reliant Joséphine: According to a lady-in-waiting, she was too afraid of hurting the child to hold him herself.

of Aspern and Essling, they were overwhelmed by vastly superior forces under the Austrian Archduke Charles and forced to withdraw. Charles, though, did not exploit his victory. A month later, Napoleon crossed again, this time with careful preparation. The outcome was the three-day battle of Wagram, which ended in an Austrian retreat and the Treaty of Schönbrunn in October. Once more, Austria ceded territory and indemnities; and once more, Napoleon had shown himself master of Europe.

But his mastery was under heavy and increasing pressure. The great battles of 1809 had been painfully more expensive in blood than the battles of 1800 or even 1805. The reason was partly the ever-increasing scale of the fighting; but in addition, Napoleon was personally overextended. Now forty years old, he had an empire to run, in every detail, as well as his current campaign. He frequently spent twenty hours a day dictating orders and memos, often on very unmilitary matters: The day after the battle of Friedland, for example, he devoted much precious time to issuing imperial guidelines for the education of girls in France.

However much time he devoted to it, the empire was becoming harder to govern. Casualties and the huge levies needed to replace them were beginning to cause the first signs of dissatisfaction in France; in Germany and Italy, resentment was increasing even faster among those who had once seen Napoleon as the personification of progress. As in France, the taxation and conscription that fed the war were becoming widely hated. So too was the Grande Armée's habit of living off the land without an organized supply train—the main reason for the extraordinary rapidity with which it could move. Years of systematic looting (which had furnished not just supplies but also most of the contents of the Palais du Louvre museum in Paris and the comfortable homes of many senior officers) had done nothing for the popularity of the French.

And although Napoleon's increasingly costly method of warfare still brought advantageous treaties, his hard-fought battles were no more truly decisive than earlier campaigns had been. After Wagram, for example, Austria was eliminated as an opponent; but it had already been "eliminated" at Austerlitz, and before that by two campaigns in Italy. Friedland had "eliminated" Russia in 1807; yet by the end of

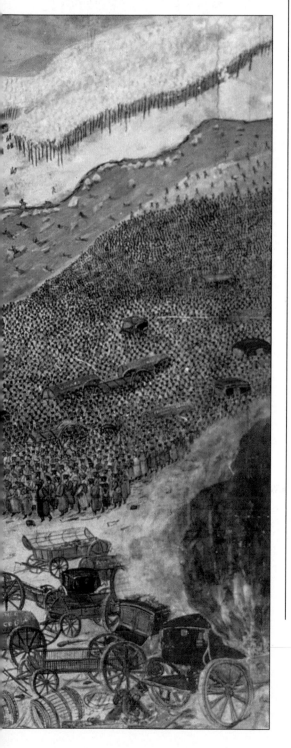

Its graphic detail testifying to eyewitness authenticity, a watercolor attributed to a French general charts French troops fording the Berezina River during their retreat from Moscow in the winter of 1812. By deceiving the pursuing Russians as to his intentions, Napoleon bought a scant twenty-four hours in which to construct a pair of pontoon bridges over the river. The task, which involved working armpit-deep in the icy waters, cost most of the 400 builders their lives. Amid heavy artillery bombardment, some 40,000 men made good their escape across the river—but 25,000 of their compatriots died in the attempt.

1809, relations between Napoleon and the czar were becoming increasingly tense, and there were already rumors of a new war.

The main reason for his enemies' ability to rise from defeat was in plain sight from the shores of northern France, and Britain was by now the object of Napoleon's most concentrated hatred. Since he had no fleet to menace her directly, he could only rely on ever-stricter enforcement of the Continental System—the prime cause of the unnecessary war in Spain, which by 1810 was already turning into what he would ruefully describe as his "Spanish ulcer."

That war was not going well. The British had returned under Wellesley—later ennobled by a grateful government in London as the duke of Wellington—and although the Spanish field armies had been smashed and scattered by Napoleon's marshals, the nationwide guerrilla warfare that took their place, at appalling cost to Spain's civil population, proved far more effective. Without the presence of the British, the French armies might just have succeeded in eliminating the guerrillas; without the guerrillas, the outnumbered British army would probably have been swept aside by the more experienced French troops. But in combination, Wellington's regulars and Spain's irregulars, both supplied by the ships of the Royal Navy, were devastating—at least to the marshals Napoleon had chosen to command.

As Wellington remarked after one narrow victory, "If Boney had been here, we'd have been beat." But Napoleon never returned to Spain; he was engaged in founding a dynasty. Joséphine, who not only had run up huge debts but also had failed to provide an imperial heir, was divorced, and almost as a postscript to the Treaty of Pressburg, a marriage was arranged with Marie-Louise, daughter of Francis I of Austria. Napoleon hoped that this union with one of Europe's oldest royal families, as well as providing an heir, would guarantee Austrian friendship. In the event, Marie-Louise gave him the son he craved: The King of Rome, as his father grandly entitled him, was born in 1811. But the marriage did not bring peace.

For the moment, at least, Austria remained docile enough. The problem once more was Russia, nervous about the substantial French forces in Poland and increasingly reluctant to support the Continental System. Throughout 1811 and the first half of 1812, Czar Alexander and Napoleon gathered their forces. By enormous effort, the emperor managed to assemble no fewer than 650,000 troops along the Russian frontier; almost every country in Europe, including a reluctant Prussia, provided a contingent. The czar could muster barely one-third as many men in the two armies he had immediately on hand. Napoleon planned one of his lightning campaigns. Marching in unprecedented strength, the Grande Armée would destroy the Russian armies in five or six weeks and impose a humiliating peace.

On June 24, the French crossed the Neman River, and their seemingly endless columns drove deep into Russia. For the first time, they were accompanied by organized supply services: Napoleon knew that the poverty-stricken Russian countryside would make living off the land almost impossible. But the supply trains acted as a brake on the Grande Armée's greatest weapon—its mobility. The Russians were able to retreat into near-limitless space, their armies converging as they did so.

By mid-August, already farther east than Napoleon had counted on ending the war, the French troops were spread over a front almost 700 miles long, their central spearhead reduced to around 150,000 men. As so often before in his career, Napoleon took a huge risk. He continued the advance and aimed for Moscow. The czar, displeased with his generals' efforts so far, entrusted the city's defense to the uncouth

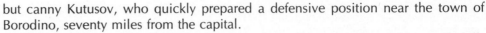

but canny Kutusov, who quickly prepared a defensive position near the town of Borodino, seventy miles from the capital.

On September 7, the battle began. Napoleon showed none of his usual skill: Frontal attacks and sheer attrition gave the French a victory of sorts, but Kutusov was able to withdraw with his surviving 90,000 men still an organized and formidable force. One week later, the French—reduced to 95,000 themselves—occupied Moscow, which had largely been abandoned by its population.

They got small pleasure from their prize. The next day, two-thirds of the city was destroyed by fire—whether by Russian die-hards or careless French looters was never clearly established. Worse, the czar simply ignored the loss of his capital, spurning all French peace proposals while reinforcements flooded to Kutusov and whole new armies began to appear from the depths of Alexander's empire.

It was too much even for Napoleon. On October 18, he ordered a general retreat. Kutusov skillfully avoided battle on Napoleon's terms, but the presence of his army forced the French to retire along the ravaged route of their own advance and the Grande Armée began to feel the first pangs of hunger—and the first icy winds of the Russian winter. By November 9, when they reached the depots of Smolensk, their discipline as well as their clothes were in tatters, and warehouses of essential supplies were looted, most of the contents being wastefully destroyed in the process.

A defeated emperor bids farewell to the ranks of the Imperial Guard at the palace of Fontainebleau on April 20, 1814. Watching from the right are commissioners of the victorious powers whose combined armies had finally overcome Napoleon at Leipzig in 1813. Forced to abdicate, Napoleon was ordered into exile on the Mediterranean island of Elba. So many of the Imperial Guard wanted to accompany their leader that the original permitted quota of 400 was increased to 1,000. Napoleon's wife Marie-Louise, however, returned to her father in Austria, taking their son with her.

The campaign now became a race for the bridges over the Berezina River, for the French the gateway to Poland and safety. The Russians got there first and destroyed them, but a brilliant rearguard action led by Napoleon held off his pursuers long enough for hastily built pontoons to allow passage for 40,000 of his men—barely one-tenth of the force that had marched toward Moscow five months before. The emperor did not stay to count them. Handing over his command to Murat, he sped homeward to Paris, where rumors of his death were daily arriving.

In fact, of the entire army, only 94,000 men returned. Not all the others were dead; but not all were prisoners. Ominously, the 20,000-strong Prussian corps had defected with its commander to the Russians. It was yet another item for the emperor to worry over as 1813 began and he struggled to raise new forces.

There was one small consolation for the disasters of 1812: Britain, too, had gotten itself into an unnecessary conflict. Britain's high-handed maritime blockade had outraged the neutral United States into belligerence, and in a succession of single-ship actions worldwide, the tiny American navy was brilliantly humiliating the world's greatest sea power. Although the new war drew scarce British infantry across the Atlantic to defend the nation's Canadian possessions, Wellington still had enough troops to inflict a succession of defeats on the weakening French in Spain.

There, Napoleon had no choice but to leave his floundering marshals to their own devices. He had a desperate new campaign of his own to fight in Germany. Prussia had joined with the invading Russians in a war of liberation; stingingly, his father-in-law's Austria was mobilizing against him too.

A contemporary cartoon satirizes the diplomatic posturing of delegates attending the Congress of Vienna in 1814. Against a backdrop of lesser committees and pressure groups, the representatives of Austria, Prussia, Russia, and Britain—later joined by France's representative Charles-Maurice de Talleyrand—met from October 1814 to June 1815 to devise a politically stable system for post-Napoleonic Europe. Their solution—achieved more at glittering social occasions than at the conference table—had as its main inspiration the desire to create strong political structures to contain France, and it disappointed liberals by its emphasis on the legitimacy of monarchical rule.

It was astonishing that he found almost 500,000 men, most of them barely trained conscripts. Horses were more difficult to obtain: The losses in Russia could not be made good without crippling the agriculture of half of Europe, and Napoleon's cavalry was reduced to insignificance. It proved a serious handicap, for although Napoleon showed his old dazzling skill against the Russians and the Prussians, the absence of cavalry reconnaissance gave much of the fighting a blundering quality. A brief armistice in June only increased the odds against him, because Austria and Sweden now formally joined the alliance. Steadily, his forces dwindled while those of the allies increased. At Leipzig in October, they were able to field more than 300,000 men against his 200,000; the so-called Battle of the Nations was a decisive Allied victory that drove the French back across the Rhine for the first time since 1796. The Rhine Confederation dissolved, and both sides readied themselves for the climactic campaign of the entire twenty-year war: the invasion of France. While Prussia, Russia, and Austria prepared a joint attack across the Rhine, Wellington's victorious Peninsular Army moved into southwest France from Spain.

Once more, Napoleon created a fresh army from almost nothing. For weeks, his skill kept the invaders at bay. But there were simply too many of them, and the war was hopelessly lost. Paris finally fell on March 31, 1814; but Napoleon, nearby at Fontainebleau with the last fragments of his army, would only admit defeat when his own marshals refused to obey him further.

The Duke of Wellington

Marshal Gebhard Leberecht von Blücher

A print of the Battle of Waterloo, fought on June 18, 1815, shows the climactic moment—at about 8:00 p.m.—when an uphill attack by Napoleon's elite Imperial Guard *(center)* was broken by steady, accurate fire from British redcoats commanded by the duke of Wellington. Shocked by this unprecedented failure and threatened by a newly arrived contingent of Prussian cavalry under the seventy-two-year-old Marshal Gebhard Leberecht von Blücher, Napoleon *(left foreground)* realized that the battle was lost and fled to Paris. Four days later, he signed his final act of abdication, accepting the end of a meteoric return to power that had begun in March when he escaped from Elba.

The empire vanished in days. Napoleon abdicated on April 4; by April 16, the allies had agreed to exile him to the tiny island of Elba, off the coast of Tuscany, where the former master of Europe could rule over eighty-six square miles of scrub-covered mountains. In his place, the victors enthroned the Bourbon Louis XVIII, whose brother's head had rolled to the Revolution twenty-one years before. On May 30, the new king signed the Treaty of Paris, imposing on France a return to the frontiers of 1792. A great congress was summoned at Vienna to set post-Napoleonic Europe in order—although predictably, the allies' wartime unity began to evaporate and within weeks their diplomats were squabbling bitterly. Still, most Europeans, whether royalist or republican, reactionary or revolutionary, heaved a sigh of relief.

The congress had gotten as far as agreeing on the creation of a moderately powerful state in the Netherlands as a bulwark against a resurgent France when it was interrupted: The wars, it seemed, had not run their course. Napoleon had escaped.

Louis was anything but popular in France: Most of Napoleon's veterans despised him, the peasants feared a restoration of the aristocracy would cost them the few privileges the revolution had given them, and the middle class railed against a reactionary regime that threatened its new importance. Chafing in Elba, Napoleon listened to reports of disaffection and risked a final throw of the dice. On March 1, with a few hundred followers, he landed near the port of Cannes. Troops sent by Louis to arrest him instead joined him, and on March 20, he reached Paris. Louis had wisely if uncourageously fled, and the city joyfully acclaimed its old emperor. Less joyfully, the allies in Vienna labeled him an outlaw. An irresistible invasion of France was planned for July; until then, 200,000 allied troops in the western Netherlands—present-day Belgium—under Wellington and the Prussian commander Gebhard Leberecht von Blücher, would have to hold the ring against him.

With time on the side of his enemies, Napoleon organized his last army, adding what veterans he could find to Louis's turncoat troops. By early June, his main force was on the march for the Netherlands in a skillful maneuver designed to drive a wedge between Wellington and Blücher. It was almost successful. On June 16, Napoleon committed the bulk of his strength to an attack on Blücher at Ligny, while Marshal Michel Ney assaulted Wellington's hastily assembled army little more than five miles away at Quatre Bras. Neither encounter was decisive: Wellington held his ground, and although the Prussians were driven back, they retreated in good order. And unknown to Napoleon, they were retreating not along their own communications, but toward Wellington. The next day, Wellington fell back to the next ridgeline, near a village called Waterloo, where, confident in a promise from Blücher that at least one Prussian corps would come to his aid, he prepared to make a stand.

A heavy overnight rainfall delayed the French artillery, and the battle did not begin until 11:30 a.m. on June 18. "Hard pounding," Wellington called it, as a series of French assaults tried to force his men from the ridge they commanded. Each attack failed, and every hour that Wellington held, the Prussians drew closer. Blücher was heavily engaged on Napoleon's right when he launched his last assault at 7:15 p.m. and the elite Imperial Guard, invincible in eleven years of combat, charged uphill at the British position. To the horror of the French, the guard broke in retreat. Wellington's men pressed forward in a general advance, and Blücher's exultant Prussians surged across from the right, turning a French defeat into a rout. It was all over.

Waterloo was very much "a near-run thing," as Wellington put it, a tribute to the steadiness of the British infantry and the resilience of the Prussians, who had made a miraculous recovery from their defeat at Ligny. But even had Napoleon won, the forces arrayed against him could hardly have failed to crush him quickly.

He was now a fugitive, like most of his army. Early in July, he reached the port of Rochefort, where he hoped to find a ship that would take him to America. But the British blockade was still in strict enforcement. On July 15, he surrendered to a British warship and sought asylum in England—"the stubbornest and most generous of my foes," as he wrote in a letter to the prince regent. But the allies were in full agreement: There would be no comfortable sanctuary this time for the defeated emperor. Without setting foot in England, Napoleon—or "General Bonaparte," the only title his British captors would ever allow him—was carried to the desolate South Atlantic island of Saint Helena, where he spent the last six years of his life. In 1821, he died of stomach ulcers—possibly poisoned by the British—attended by a handful of loyal friends.

The Congress of Vienna carried on where it had left off in March, its bickering greatly reduced by the shock of Napoleon's brief return. On the surface, the congress was a glittering social occasion, a gala of balls and receptions at which the old European order celebrated its survival. Beneath, diplomats from Britain, Austria—whose foreign minister, Prince Klemens Metternich, tried to dominate the proceedings—Russia, and Prussia worked to create a settlement ensuring that the old order survived indefinitely. Much of their effort was devoted to undoing the Napoleonic structure of Europe. To achieve a balance of power, the Rhine Confederation became a loose group of independent states, whose Federal Diet Austria could powerfully influence. The Kingdom of Piedmont was removed from French control, but Italian hopes of national unity were dashed by the restoration of the Bourbon Kingdom of Naples in the south and the return of most of northern Italy to direct rule from Vienna.

The old-fashioned balance of power was not the congress's only concern. The terrifying rise of France had been the result of revolution and revolutionary nationalism. Napoleon had exploited these forces brilliantly but he did not create them. Most of the terms of the Vienna settlement were designed equally to prevent any recurrence, and the powers of Europe, including constitutionally governed Britain, laid a strong emphasis on principles of monarchical "legitimacy."

Some changes, though, they were unwilling to abandon. The power of Napoleon's France attracted imitation as well as envy. Even during the wars, most of Europe had striven to copy his centralized, efficient administration. After 1815, the improved bureaucratic and fiscal systems were retained, and whenever they conflicted with the old feudal aristocracy and its cherished privileges, these privileges were usually set aside. The old order, in fact, had been thoroughly, if quietly, modernized.

That was only a part of Napoleon's legacy. The Civil Code he devised in 1800 continued to provide the underpinning for the legal systems not just of France but also of Holland, Belgium, Italy, and wherever in western Europe the Grande Armée set foot. To Germany and Italy, the emperor had taught a twofold lesson. First, he had come as a liberator, carrying the Revolution's ideas of liberty, fraternity, and equality to some of the most reactionary states in Europe. And in his tyranny, he gave them the experience of a national uprising against him. Neither would be easily forgotten.

In France itself, he was the yardstick by which his far lesser successors were judged. Louis XVIII's ignominious flight from Paris was long remembered, and the king was always careful to stay within the constitution he had granted, as if by royal favor, in 1814. His successor, Charles X, had more grandiose ideas of a return to an Ancien

Leaning against a cannon on the quarterdeck of HMS *Northumberland,* Napoleon stares moodily into the future on his way to exile. This print was based on a pen-and-ink sketch done by one of the Englishmen who accompanied him on the ten-week voyage to Saint Helena, an isolated island set in the middle of the South Atlantic. After his surrender in July 1815, four weeks after Waterloo, Napoleon had hoped for asylum in the United States or Britain, and he strongly objected to his banishment to this remote fastness. During his exile, he spent most of his time dictating his autobiography. Napoleon died in 1821, at the age of fifty-one, without ever again seeing his country, his wife, or his child.

Régime monarchy; in 1830, he responded to an unsatisfactory election result by dissolving his assembly, disenfranchising the electorate, and provoking a revolution. Charles's timing was far from Napoleonic: Most of his army was far from home, engaged in the conquest of Algeria. The insurgents soon seized Paris and drove him into exile. But their political objectives were limited, and they settled for the installation of Louis-Philippe, duc d'Orléans, his cousin, as a constitutional monarch.

Even a limited rebellion in France caused alarm elsewhere, and 1830 saw revolutionary agitation sweep through much of Europe. In Brussels, an uprising against the Dutch-led Kingdom of the Netherlands led to the creation of an independent Belgium, whose neutrality was guaranteed by Europe's most powerful states. In Italy, Austria violently suppressed a rising in Bologna. An insurrection broke out in Poland when the czar mobilized against a possible threat from France, leaving the country ruined by six months' fighting and firmly under Russian rule. In Britain, unrest was adroitly contained by reforms in 1832, which allowed the middle class, made wealthy by the nation's new industry, a share in the constitutional exercise of power.

Elsewhere, discontent smoldered quietly. For a few years, the forces of Metternich's Europe were too strong to be resisted. But they were negative forces: The Vienna settlement had been designed neither to accommodate nor to harness change, but simply to resist it. That had never been Napoleon's way. And even though many still thought that Metternich's goals were desirable, as the century of industrial progress continued, there were fewer each year who believed them to be possible.

On December 15, 1840—nearly twenty years afer his death—a funeral cortege of operatic magnificence conducts Napoleon I's remains to a hero's resting place in the Hôtel des Invalides in Paris. Following the overthrow of the reactionary King Charles X in 1830, France entered a prosaic period of bourgeois stability, during which a growing nostalgia for the grandeur of the Napoleonic era began to manifest itself. In 1848, Napoleon I's nephew, Louis-Napoleon, was able to exploit his uncle's fame to win power for himself.

1848

THE YEAR OF REVOLUTIONS

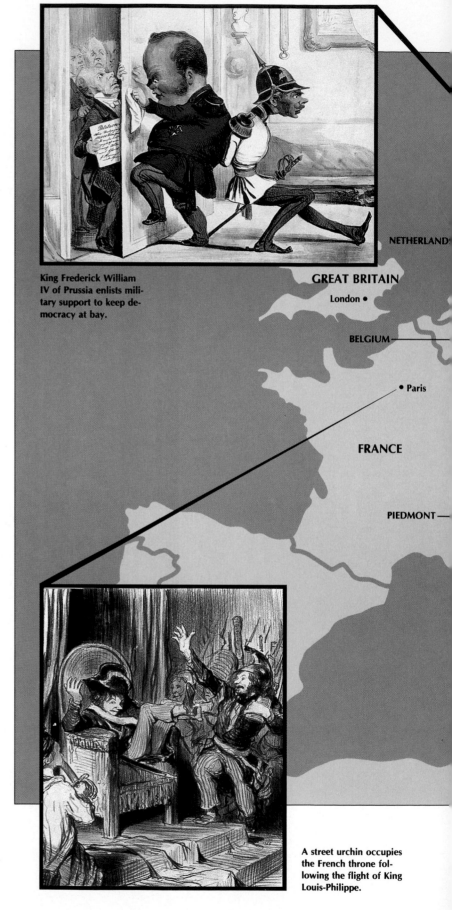

King Frederick William IV of Prussia enlists military support to keep democracy at bay.

After the turmoil of the French Revolution of 1789 and the quarter-century of warfare that ensued, the world that emerged from the Congress of Vienna, which marked the end of the Napoleonic Wars in 1815, seemed in many ways a throwback. Although France had won a constitution, a Bourbon monarch was once more on the throne; and most of the rest of Napoleon's enormous, short-lived empire had been parceled out among the authoritarian monarchies of Prussia, Russia, and Austria, where the subversive ideas that had fueled the Revolution were stifled by a potent combination of troops and secret police.

But by the 1840s, Restoration Europe—as it was known—was feeling the strain. Although Napoleon had been defeated, French revolutionary ideals lived on. In France, the populace was becoming increasingly disenchanted with the corrupt officials and limited suffrage of their

In 1848, the boundaries of Europe resembled those of today only in the west. Europe's eastern lands, from the Baltic to the Balkans, were controlled by three great empires: Romanov Russia, Hapsburg Austria, and the Ottoman domains. The center of the continent was fragmented: Germany comprised a confederation of some thirty-nine states, dominated by Austria and the powerful nation of Prussia; and Italy, similarly, was split between its own rival rulers and an encroaching Austrian empire. The thwarted nationalism underlying these divisions fueled the revolutionary spirit of 1848.

A street urchin occupies the French throne following the flight of King Louis-Philippe.

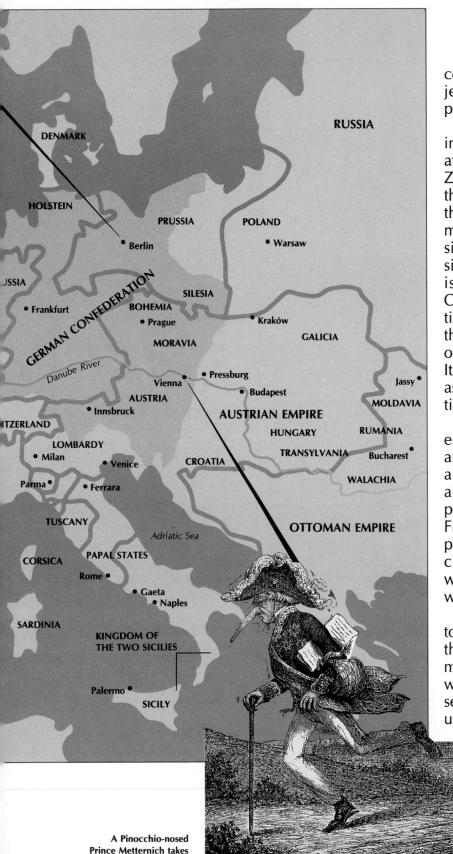

A Pinocchio-nosed
Prince Metternich takes
flight from Austria.

constitutional government. Elsewhere, the subjects of Europe's absolute monarchs were pressing for more representative constitutions.

At the same time, nationalist sentiment was increasing throughout the continent. The creation in the early decades of the century of the Zollverein, a customs union designed to reduce the expense and complexity of moving goods through Prussia and the many states of the German Confederation, had already raised the possibility of all German peoples being united in a single nation. In the Austrian empire, nationalist movements were growing among the Czechs of Bohemia, the Croatians on the Adriatic, and the Transylvanian Rumanians, while the Hungarians were openly demanding autonomy. And an ever more vociferous nucleus of Italians was following the lead of such writers as Giuseppe Mazzini in espousing the unification of Italy as a single republic.

In addition, Europe was experiencing another revolutionary process against which police and soldiers were helpless: the steady industrialization of the continent. By midcentury, Britain was still the only country with more than 20 percent of its population living in cities, but France, the Low Countries, and Germany were progressing down the same smoky road. A new class of urban workers was in the making, whose efforts in forge and factory created a wealth in which they rarely shared.

Overcrowded and undernourished, groping toward a political consciousness of their own, the urban proletariat provided a dangerous mass of concentrated discontent, and they were already learning how to organize themselves. Socialist ideas were forming, and in January 1848, the twenty-nine-year-old Karl Heinrich Marx and his wealthy collaborator, Friedrich Engels, published their *Communist Manifesto,* calling on the world's workers to unite against their masters.

A series of bad harvests that afflicted Europe from 1845 onward tightened the screws of misery in town and countryside alike. Riotous protests became increasingly frequent—especially after the potato crop failed both in 1846 and in 1847. On February 19, 1846, the peasants of Austrian Galicia rose against the local nobility, slaughtering some 1,000 people in a single night of butchery; and three days later, the free city of Kraków declared itself a socialist republic. Austrian troops lost no time in quelling the unrest and annexing Kraków. But in 1847, Europe's peace was once again shattered, as a month of civil war in Switzerland concluded with radical forces winning power. As 1848 approached, it seemed to many that Restoration Europe was teetering on the brink.

The first sign that 1848 might bring more than a little disorder came from Sicily, early in January, when a successful revolt against the corrupt Bourbon Kingdom of Naples installed a provisional government in Palermo. Southern Italy, admittedly, was far from the European mainstream, its monarchy long considered even by reactionaries as incompetent. But the next month, rebellion broke out in France itself, the revolutionary tinderbox of Europe.

The immediate cause was almost ludicrous: the banning by King Louis-Philippe of a banquet organized by Parisian journalists and politicians to rail at government policies. The streets, however, were full of unemployed and hungry dissidents, and the thwarted supper trig-

FRANCE

February 22: King Louis-Philippe bans a banquet meeting scheduled to be held by reformist journalists and politicians. His action triggers a popular uprising in Paris.

February 23: Louis-Philippe dismisses his unpopular chief minister, François Guizot. The move fails to satisfy the rioters, and street disorders increase.

February 24: Louis-Philippe abdicates in favor of his grandson, ten-year-old Louis-Philippe-Albert, comte de Paris. His decision comes too late: As mobs approach the royal palace, he is forced to escape in a carriage for England. That afternoon a republican provisional government is formed under the moderate Alphonse de Lamartine. At the insistence of the mob, three socialists—among them Louis Blanc—are later included.

February 25: France's Second Republic is proclaimed.

February 27: A government commission for workers is formed under Louis Blanc. Government-subsidized national workshops, providing manual labor, are set up to relieve unemployment in Paris and to prevent the possibility of further uprisings. Workers begin to flood into the capital. Public order is placed in the hands of a predominantly middle-class, civilian national guard.

March 2: The provisional government introduces universal manhood suffrage.

King Louis-Philippe of France poses in this early photograph.

March 5: Lamartine's *Manifesto to Europe* is published, accepting the sovereign rights of all peoples.

March 18: Gold reserves fall to one-quarter of their February level. The financial crisis leads to increased taxation and a moratorium on all bills.

April 23: Elections held for a new constituent assembly return a majority of moderate, property-owning delegates.

May 5: The constituent assembly meets. Power is transferred to a five-man executive council, from which socialists are excluded.

May 15: Workers storm the assembly and proclaim a new provisional government, which is immediately suppressed with the assistance of the national guard.

May 28: Organizers of a new "people's banquet," modeled on the one banned in February, are arrested.

June 21: The government dissolves the national workshop scheme in the hope of dispersing Paris's 120,000 workers.

June 22-26: The June Days uprising by Parisian workers leads to civil war and brutal suppression by General Louis-Eugène Cavaignac's troops. Approximately 3,000 die; an additional 3,000 are deported to the French colony of Algeria. Further repressive measures curb press freedom, ban secret societies, and limit the right of political association. Cavaignac becomes president of the executive council and continues to purge radicals.

November 4: A republican constitution is proclaimed, providing for a strong president and a single-chamber assembly, elected by universal manhood suffrage.

December 10: Prince Louis-Napoleon Bonaparte, nephew of the former emperor, defeats Cavaignac in the polls by a huge majority to become president of the Second Republic. The following month the National Assembly announces its own dissolution.

THE ITALIAN STATES

January 12: A successful revolt in Palermo, Sicily, against the rule of the Bourbon kingdom of Naples, installs a provisional government.

February 10: The events in Sicily provoke a revolt in Naples. King Ferdinand II concedes a constitution.

February 15: Grand Duke Leopold II of Tuscany grants a liberal constitution.

March 4: King Charles Albert of Sardinia-Piedmont proclaims a constitution for his country.

March 11: Pope Pius IX appoints a Roman governing ministry with a lay majority.

March 15: The pope grants a constitution in Rome.

March 23: With the support of Naples and the Papal States, King Charles Albert assumes leadership of the Italian war of liberation from Austrian rule.

April 13: Sicily declares its independence from the kingdom of Naples.

April 29: Pius IX, alarmed by popular unrest, withdraws his support from the Italian national movement.

May 15: The Bourbon monarchy's Swiss Guards crush the Neapolitan revolt. King Ferdinand II deserts the nationalist cause.

June 4: Pius IX refuses to accept the separation of the powers of church and state, demanded by liberals and nationalists, and appoints Count Rossi as papal prime minister.

September 11: Bourbon Naples accepts an armistice with Sicily.

November 16: Count Rossi is assassinated.

November 24: Pius IX flees Rome, escaping to Gaeta in the kingdom of Naples. Three months later the Roman Republic is formed as a nucleus for a united Italy, only to be overthrown the following July by French troops who restore the pope to power.

Following his restoration in 1849, Pope Pius IX removes the mask of Christ to reveal his true reactionary nature.

gered demonstrations. When nervous soldiers fired on the crowds, the demonstrations turned into uncontrollable rioting. Within two days, a republican provisional government had formed itself. By the end of February, national workshops had been set up to relieve unemployment, Louis-Philippe was in exile in London, and France's Second Republic had been proclaimed. Meanwhile, the regular army was kept out of Paris and public order was entrusted to a people's national guard.

News of the events in France lighted the fires of insurrection throughout Europe. One after another, the small princely states of Germany granted constitutions, almost daily it seemed, and usually without bloodshed. In Berlin, after a clumsy attempt at armed suppression, King Frederick William IV of Prussia withdrew his troops from his own capital and agreed to the election by universal manhood suffrage of a national assembly. At the same time, the king announced his support for a united Germany. In May, delegates from all over Germany gathered at Frankfurt to decide the future of their new nation.

In Vienna, Emperor Ferdinand I ordered his troops from the city and agreed to summon a national assembly, while his hated chancellor, Prince Klemens Metternich, fled for his life to London. Elsewhere in the great, shabby patchwork of the Austrian empire, events followed a similar course: The Milanese drove the imperial army, under the command of eighty-three-year-old Field Marshal Joseph Radetzky, out of the city; revolt flared in Parma; Venice declared itself an independent republic; the Hungarian Diet in Pressburg began to pass its own laws; a delegation arrived from Prague demanding Bohemian home rule; and Rumanian nationalists in Transylvania clamored for autonomy—a sentiment that was shared by their compatriots across the border in the Ottoman principalities of Wallachia and Moravia.

The situation in Italy was further complicated by King Charles Albert of Sardinia-Piedmont, who had already granted his own people a constitution and who now accepted the mantle of leadership of a new, independent, and united Italy. On March 24, he declared war on Austria and sent his troops into Lombardy to support the rebellious Milanese; his army was soon winning its first victories.

Throughout March and April, the revolutionary cause was everywhere triumphant. National assemblies and provisional governments issued ringing proclamations, while the Declaration of the Rights of Man, the creed of the French Revolution, was given an airing it had not had since 1789. As a distraught Czar Nicholas I wrote to Britain's Queen Victoria: "What remains standing in Europe? Great Britain and Russia."

Already, however, opposition to the new world that seemed to be in the making was growing. Appropriately, it was the French who, having started the tumult, showed how it might conclude. In mid-March a catastrophic financial crisis alarmed most of the provisional government's supporters: In April, elections for the new constituent assembly returned a solid majority of prosperous moderates, who at once set about blocking any further reform. Socialists were specifically excluded from the five-man executive council formed in early May, and the less-than-revolutionary government eyed with increasing fear the swirling underclass of Paris,

Viennese students enlist in the revolutionary guard.

AUSTRIAN EMPIRE

March 3: At Pressburg (present-day Bratislava), nationalist leader Lajos Kossuth leads the Hungarian Diet in a call for a separate constitution.

March 12: Imperial troops clash with Viennese students and workers demanding an Austrian constitution.

March 13: Chancellor Prince Klemens Metternich resigns and flees to London.

March 15: Emperor Ferdinand I promises to allow a constituent assembly and permits the agitators to form their own civilian national guard.

March 15: The Hungarian Diet passes a series of constitutional laws, which are sent to Vienna for confirmation.

March 17: After receiving news of the successful revolts in France, Vienna, and elsewhere in Italy, former political prisoner Daniele Manin leads a revolution in Austrian-controlled Venice.

March 18: Milan rises against Austrian rule in Lombardy. Five days of street-fighting force the Austrians, under eighty-three-year-old General Joseph Radetzky, to flee the city. A provisional government is proclaimed.

March 19: A delegation is sent from Prague to Vienna demanding reform.

March 20: The Venetian Republic is proclaimed.

March 24: King Charles Albert of Sardinia-Piedmont declares war on Austria and enters Lombardy.

April 8: A representative diet (parliament) is created for the three provinces of Bohemia, Moravia, and Silesia. A new constitutional government gives equal status to Czechs and Germans living in those provinces.

April 11: The imperial government in Vienna accepts the Hungarian Statute, granting constitutional autonomy to the kingdom of Saint Stephen—the historical kingdom of Hungary, including Croatia and the Rumanian principality of Transylvania.

April 25: The imperial government proclaims a new constitution for Austria itself, but makes no provision for a representative assembly.

April 26: A rising of the Polish nobility in Kraków is suppressed.

May 9: The imperial government grants a greater degree of suffrage in Austria. The vote, however, is still denied to workers and servants.

The Rumanian nationalist
Avram Iancu bears arms
for freedom.

May 15: The government tries to disband the national guard. A second uprising in Vienna, led by radicals, forces the repeal of the new constitution.

May 15: In defiance of Vienna, Bohemia forms its own national council.

May 15: Transylvanian nationalists repudiate union with Hungary and form their own assembly. Their leaders, including Avram Iancu, call for an autonomous Rumania united with Wallachia. Hungary denies the request.

May 17: Rioters seize a Viennese armory, and Ferdinand flees to Innsbruck with his court. There he agrees to convoke a constituent assembly. At the same time, however, he instructs Windischgrätz to drill his troops in preparation for retaking Vienna.

June 2: The Pan-Slav Congress meets at Prague. It rejects a proposal from Frankfurt to incorporate Bohemia into Germany and calls for greater recognition of Slav nationalities.

June 12-17: Windischgrätz's troops overwhelm street-fighting students to take Prague. The Pan-Slav Congress is dissolved, and Prague is placed under military rule.

July 22: The Austrian constituent assembly—the Reichstag—agrees to a new, more liberal constitution.

August 9: An armistice is arranged between Austria and Sardinia-Piedmont. Piedmont agrees to surrender Lombardy and to recognize the status quo in Italy outside Venice.

August 11: Piedmontese troops, already expelled from Milan and Lombardy, are driven from Venice.

August 12: His prestige and security restored by events in Italy, Ferdinand I returns to Vienna.

September 4: The Hungarian government rebels against the empire.

September 7: Serfdom in Austria ends.

September 23: The imperial high commissioner is murdered by a Hungarian mob. Lajos Kossuth is proclaimed president of the Committee for the National Defense of Hungary.

October 6: As the imperial government moves to crush the Hungarian revolt, a third uprising breaks out in Vienna. Five thousand die in the October Days fighting, including the minister of war, who is beaten to death in the streets. Ferdinand flees to Olmütz.

October 25: Rumanian nationalists take up arms against Hungary.

October 31: Using the death of the minister of war as a pretext, Windischgrätz bombards Vienna and regains the city. Radical leaders are executed, and the members of the constituent assembly are exiled to Moravia.

December 2: Ferdinand abdicates in favor of his nephew, Franz Josef I.

The Hungarian leader
Lajos Kossuth gazes sternly
from this portrait.

reinforced by thousands of poverty-stricken provincials drawn there by the national workshops. As the contemporary French historian Alexis de Tocqueville described it: "Society was cut in two: Those who had nothing united in common envy; those who had anything united in common terror."

Matters soon came to a head. On June 21, the executive council, confident of army support, abolished the national workshops. The workers' reaction—barricades in the streets and outright insurrection—was just as expected. But whereas Louis-Philippe had at once packed his bags, the new republic sent in regular troops under General Louis-Eugène Cavaignac and slaughtered the radicals wholesale: At least 3,000 died.

As far as France was concerned, the revolution of 1848 was over. Just like those of 1789, the revolutionaries of February had been divided between the haves and the have-nots. And just as in 1789, their early alliance had turned into an increasingly bitter conflict that in the end was resolved by armed force—which was the monopoly, or near-monopoly, of the haves.

The situation was the same in other French-inspired revolutions. The middle class and intellectual reformers who sought to extract constitutional rule were at least as fearful of socialists and newly conscious Communists as they were of absolute monarchists. Moreover, virtually all the old rulers had retained their thrones, and military force was still almost exclusively in their hands: Berlin, Vienna, and Milan had been evacuated by their troops, but the troops themselves were ready and waiting.

Although the Prussian army was absent from Berlin, it was not idle. In mid-May, some of its units had invaded Denmark: Despite the revolution, Frederick William was engaged in a dynastic war over the province of Schleswig-Holstein. Meanwhile other Prussian troops were helping to crush a rebellion in Warsaw. Moreover, the troops were far from sympathetic to the revolutionaries: When the Prussian assembly ordered the army to swear its allegiance to the new constitution, it flatly refused. Finally, in October, large-scale Berlin riots caused Frederick to declare his throne in danger—his senior officers had begged him to do so for months—and the army took over the capital. There was very little bloodshed, but the revolution was over in Prussia, too.

Events in the Austrian empire marched in parallel. In June, the veteran Field Marshal Alfred Windischgrätz brought a permanent end to the nascent revolution in Prague, and old Radetzky turned the tide against the Piedmontese. Although Charles Albert of Sardinia-Piedmont declared a union between his kingdom, Lombardy, and Venice, his troops were decisively defeated, and Austrian control was reimposed on Milan. The final act came in October, when Windischgrätz returned to Vienna and bombarded it into submission.

It had all been too much for Ferdinand. Before the end of the year, he abdicated in favor of his tough-minded nephew Franz Josef. The dynasty, at least, had survived everything the revolutionaries of 1848 could do to it.

There were a few loose ends, of course. Hungary was still in full revolt—unlike other revolutionaries, the Hungarians had raised a 100,000-strong army of their own—and only with Russian help would the uprising be brutally suppressed the following year. Lacking the

A Berlin student dies for liberty on March 18.

GERMAN CONFEDERATION

March 5: A meeting of liberals at Heidelberg appeals for formation of a *Vorparlament*—pre-Parliament—as an assembly to represent all Germany.

March 15-19: Rioting breaks out in Berlin. King Frederick William IV of Prussia grants reforms, convoking the Prussian Diet and ceding it the right to draw up a new electoral law. In the ensuing two weeks, revolutionary coups take place throughout the monarchic states of central Germany.

March 20: King Ludwig I of Bavaria is forced to abdicate by his subjects, who are scandalized by his relationship with the dancer Lola Montez.

March 21: Revolutionaries force Frederick William to join a street parade of Berlin radicals.

March 21: King Frederick VII of Denmark incorporates the duchy of Schleswig into his kingdom.

March 24: The German population of Schleswig and neighboring Holstein form their own government, recognized by Prussia.

March 31: The German Vorparlament meets at Frankfurt and arranges the election of a national assembly to draw up a German constitution.

April 8: The Berlin Diet votes for universal suffrage.

May 2: Prussia invades Denmark over the Schleswig-Holstein question.

Lola Montez displays the haughty beauty that cost the infatuated King Ludwig I of Bavaria his throne.

May 7: Prussian troops suppress a Polish uprising in Warsaw.

May 18: The German national assembly meets at Frankfurt, suspends the existing German Confederation, and prepares a constitution.

May 22: The Prussian national assembly meets at Berlin.

June 29: Archduke Johann of Austria is elected regent of the new Reich, or empire, that will replace the German Confederation.

August 26: The Treaty of Malmö is signed between Denmark and Prussia, confirming Danish control over Schleswig and Holstein.

September 17: Rioting in Frankfurt against the Malmö treaty becomes an insurrection.

September 18: The Frankfurt insurrection is crushed by Prussian troops.

September 23: The Prussian assembly proposes that the army swear an oath of allegiance to the new constitution. The army refuses.

October 11: During constitutional debates in the Prussian assembly, Berlin workers and released convicts riot, destroying factory machinery.

October 30: Frederick William declares the Prussian court and throne in danger.

November 9: Count Brandenburg is appointed chief minister. The assembly refuses a royal order to dissolve itself.

November 10: Troops surround the assembly.

November 13: The assembly is forcibly dissolved.

December 5: Frederick William grants Prussia a limited constitution, in which he retains ultimate authority. He refuses, however, to join the new German Reich. Within six months, for lack of a powerful leader, the Frankfurt assembly disperses.

THE OTTOMAN EMPIRE

April 10: An uprising breaks out in the Moldavian town of Jassy, calling for a representative assembly. It is quickly suppressed.

May 24: Moldavian revolutionaries draw up a program demanding the abolition of feudal obligations and the union of Moldavia and Wallachia as an independent Rumanian state. Liberal propaganda produces widespread unrest among Moldavian peasants.

June 26: Wallachian rebels declare a provisional government at Bucharest and begin to implement a program of reforms.

July 6: Commissars recruited from Bucharest's radical intelligentsia are sent to incite revolt throughout Wallachia and Moldavia.

July 10: At the request of the Ottomans, Russian forces occupy Jassy and suppress the Moldavian revolution.

September 25: Ottoman troops enter Bucharest. After heavy fighting they crush the rebel forces and resume control of the province.

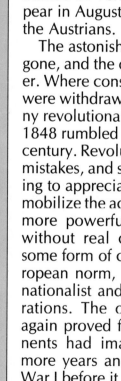

support of either Prussia or Austria, the Frankfurt assembly dissolved itself ignominiously in June 1849. In November 1848, when elsewhere the fires of revolution seemed extinguished, the pope was driven from Rome by nationalist forces, and three months later a new Roman Republic was formed. But that too was short-lived: In July, French troops, equally republican in name, returned the pope to his Vatican throne. They were obeying the command of their new president, Louis-Napoleon, nephew of Napoleon Bonaparte himself, who had imperial ambitions and wanted to ensure Catholic support. The last spark of Italian revolution burned in Venice, but even that was to disappear in August, following a five-week siege by the Austrians.

The astonishing year of 1848 had come and gone, and the old order was still firmly in power. Where constitutions had been granted, they were withdrawn or modified to specifically deny revolutionary principles. Still, the lessons of 1848 rumbled on through the remainder of the century. Revolutionaries would learn from their mistakes, and so would rulers: Most were coming to appreciate that a government that could mobilize the active support of its people was far more powerful than a monarch who ruled without real consent. Within a generation, some form of constitution had become the European norm, catering—albeit grudgingly—to nationalist and, increasingly, to socialist aspirations. The old order, however, had once again proved far more durable than its opponents had imagined. It would take seventy more years and the final cataclysm of World War I before it was swept away, and even then it would not go entirely unmourned.

The adaptable Prussian monarch rides at the side of German nationalists on March 21.

INDUSTRIAL BRITAIN

"We are credibly informed," London's *Times* newspaper told its readers on July 8, 1808, "that there is a Steam Engine now preparing to run against any mare, horse, or gelding that may be produced at the next October meeting at Newmarket; the wagers at present are stated to be £10,000; the engine is the favorite." "The most astonishing machine ever invented," exclaimed the *Observer* the following week, "she will gallop from 15 to 20 miles an hour on any circle." In subsequent weeks, sightseers could satisfy their curiosity by watching the miraculous engine, devised by the Cornish engineer and steam enthusiast Richard Trevithick, performing its trial runs on a track off Gower Street, north London; if sufficiently intrepid they could even go for a ride. Admission cards for Trevithick's railway showed the engine's motto as "Catch me who can," and boasted of "Mechanical Power Subduing Animal Speed."

In fact, the promised Newmarket outing was never to take place: The track shifted in the marshy ground of the Gower Street site, and the engine left its rails and crashed. By that time, however, eyewitnesses such as John Isaac Hawkins had seen the engine put through its paces. "I rode, with my watch in my hand, at the rate of twelve miles an hour; . . . Mr. Trevithick then gave his opinion that it would go twenty miles an hour, or more, on a straight railway." The inventor had made his point, and the public had been impressed. The engine was, indeed, the favorite.

The speculators who bet such large amounts on Trevithick's locomotive, and the crowds who flocked to see its London trials, had already had ample experience of the capacities of mechanical power. For by the beginning of the nineteenth century, Britain was in the throes of a dramatic—and at times harrowing—change, as the technological advances of the previous 100 years were incorporated into the nation's economy with explosive results.

Industrial Britain was on the march, its rural quiet shattered by the clattering din from new factories, its night sky illuminated by the eerie glow of furnaces, its landscape crisscrossed by canals and straddled by awesome bridges and tunnels. Chimneys trailed smoke across its skies; around them clustered new towns and cities, teeming with the members of a new, industrial working class. Within a very few decades, Trevithick's successors would have established a network of railways that spanned the nation and brought metropolis and province together. By the middle of the century, Britain's commercial dominance would be secure, her manufactured goods sought after throughout Europe, the Americas, and her new, expanding empire.

Alongside the triumphs, however, would come tribulations. The most prosperous society the world had ever seen would be built on suffering, as men, women, and children worked appalling hours in unspeakable conditions, lived packed together in verminous, disease-ridden cellars and tenements, and went hungry through periodic

An 1846 lithograph depicts the locomotive Acheron belching smoke as it triumphantly emerges from the gloom of a tunnel. Railway engines—first perfected in 1829—were just one manifestation of the steam-powered technology that, during the first half of the nineteenth century, helped to make Britain the world's first industrial nation. In an age when nothing seemed impossible, the locomotive, or "great steam horse," became a symbol of the driving force of British enterprise.

recessions. Nonetheless, Britain's achievements were the envy of the world, and as the century drew on, other countries would be striving to emulate her industrial revolution—and, if possible, to surpass it.

Perched off the northwest coast of continental Europe, at the rim of the Atlantic Ocean, Britain might have seemed an unlikely setting for such momentous changes. London, its capital, was a bustling center for trade with the continent and with Britain's colonies in North America and the Caribbean. Beyond the city boundaries, however, the rich undulating farmland counties of southern England and East Anglia stretched away, punctuated by small, sleepy market towns and villages where, in

The industrial revolution of the first half of the nineteenth century reshaped the face of Great Britain. New enterprises grew up around the coal fields *(shaded green)* or upland rivers that provided sources of power. Following the work, the nation's labor force began to move from the countryside into the new, factory-dominated manufacturing centers that sprang up around the country. As British business boomed, so the population increased: Between 1800 and 1850, the number of Britons more than doubled to 21 million. Some 60 percent of them were urban dwellers—a ratio higher than that of any other country in the world.

1700, the majority of England's five million people worked the land just as they had done for centuries. Farther away the countryside grew wilder and more sparsely populated, with vast areas of uncultivated wasteland and marsh, as the traveler journeyed west toward Wales, or north to where the Pennine hills, running all the way up to the Scottish borders, split the country between east and west.

Wild as they were, such wastes were not without resources. For centuries, iron had been dug and smelted by small parties of charcoal-burners working in the valleys of south Wales, the West Midlands, and the southern foothills of the Pennines. The rain-drenched northern moors, and much of the West Country, too barren to support cattle or wheat, proved ideal for the rearing of sheep. Here the cottagers built their own small-scale industry, spinning and weaving wool in their homes. And the people in the county of Lancashire, on the western side of the Pennines, found that their moist climate favored the spinning and weaving of brittle cotton strands imported from the Mediterranean.

In the early eighteenth century, such industrial activity was in its infancy and did little to diminish the overwhelming importance of agriculture in the British economy. Even in the more prosperous southeast, however, farming provided little more than subsistence for much of the existing population. Thoroughly idiosyncratic patterns of land use, evolved since medieval times, had turned the typical parish into an anarchic patchwork of small plots, unfenced and marked out only by boundary stones. Larger holdings were frequently not continuous but scattered around the district. The cottagers and small tenant farmers who tended such lands usually also had the right to graze their few animals and gather fuel on the extensive areas of common land found throughout the countryside. The poorest families had no land at all, but scratched what living they could from the commons where they built their shacks. Little was known about crop fertilizers or scientific stockbreeding. And since most animals were slaughtered every autumn for want of winter feed, large herds could never be developed, and cattle and pigs seldom reached optimum size.

Any region that did succeed in producing a surplus found itself faced with the problem of getting its produce to likely buyers: The roads were worse now than they had been under Roman occupation 1,500 years before. For much of the year they became streams of mud, impassable for wheeled traffic. In 1731, one John Metcalf raced a Colonel Liddell from London to Harrogate in the northern county of Yorkshire. Although blind and on foot, Metcalf completed the journey in six days, arriving two days before the colonel, who had traveled by coach. Men had been known to drown in East Anglian potholes, and so completely did the roads fail around the city of Lincoln that an inland lighthouse was erected to guide night travelers over the surrounding plain. Money to fund improvements, whether in agriculture or communications, was extremely hard to come by in an age that recognized no form of currency other than ready cash. It was a system that condemned the economy to sluggish inactivity.

In the course of the eighteenth century, however, much was changed as progressive landowners swept aside traditional agricultural practices. The selective breeding of livestock produced new varieties of farm animals that grew more quickly and to a greater size. In 1710, the average sheep sold at London's Smithfield market weighed less than forty pounds; by 1795, average weight was more than double that. Other breeds of sheep were developed to yield longer, thicker wool, and cows were bred to increase both milk and meat production. New strains of grass, along with recently introduced root crops such as turnips and rutabagas, provided fodder that allowed livestock to survive the winter months. Arable farming improved as landowners popularized the Norfolk system, developed by generations of farmers from that county, which got the best out of the soil by the heavy use of manures and other fertilizers, and by effective crop rotation—cultivating each field with a series of different crops, and allowing it regular breaks for lying fallow.

"Great farms are the soul of the Norfolk culture," remarked the pamphleteer Arthur Young, chief advocate of the new techniques. The improvers shared this opinion, and the landed gentry and aristocrats who dominated Parliament began passing Acts of

A haven of order on a crowded Thames River, the half-completed London Dock at Wapping is shown in an aquatint of 1803. Until the nineteenth century, all London's maritime trade came to riverside wharves. But as industrial output swelled, the Thames soon clogged—mostly with ships plying between Britain and its overseas empire—and pilfering became rife. From 1802, a series of specially built docks with high boundary walls was constructed to speed trade and protect goods from looters. The first to be built, the West India Dock, was also the largest, enclosing a space more than six times larger than London Dock's forty-five acres.

Enclosure, which reorganized parishes into larger holdings and fenced off the commons as the property of the local landowner. Such legislation had been sponsored, on and off, for centuries, but during the second half of the eighteenth century the rate increased dramatically: The decade between 1740 and 1749 brought sixty-four enclosure acts; that between 1800 and 1809 saw 574.

The new agricultural order presented exciting possibilities, but it was no place for the small farmer. Heavy investment in fertilizers and machinery was required, as well as large acreages for efficient cultivation. Those who had lost common lands and rights under the acts were given some compensation, but few could afford the higher rents the larger holdings required. Many became hired laborers on what had been their own land; others were left unemployed. Often rural communities were destroyed by the enclosures. Country life, never idyllic, was becoming intolerable.

By 1800, even Arthur Young was losing some of his enthusiasm for the enclosures he had earlier championed so vigorously. A visit in that year to a cottage inhabited by one of the rural dispossessed did a good deal to dampen his ardor. "On a bed which was hardly big enough for a hog," he recalled, "was the woman very ill and moaning; she had been lately brought to bed, and her infant was dead in a cradle by the bedside. . . . My heart sank within me at the sight of so much misery, and so dark, cold, tattered, and wretched a room."

Despite such wretchedness, Britain's population expanded, nourished by better, more reliable food supplies. By 1801, the population of England and Wales had risen to more than nine million. Nationally, agriculture was prospering; the big landowners were richer than they had ever been, and their wealth helped enrich the doctors, lawyers, land agents, and shopkeepers of the market towns.

Throughout the country, a network of banks and financial companies sprang up to look after the new agricultural wealth. The Bank of England, founded in 1694 to raise money to reduce the national debt, had gradually become the main regulatory body of the British economy. It now coordinated what was beginning to be, despite local differences and inefficiencies, a national banking system. England alone had more than 100 country banks by 1784. Ten years later that number had tripled.

New financial instruments were also growing in popularity; people were becoming less suspicious of credit, and stocks and shares of various sorts began to proliferate, giving business more flexibility than it had had in the old cash-only days. The stock exchange, founded in a London coffeehouse in 1762 as an informal trading club for stock dealers, had grown apace. By 1800, it was a respected national institution. For those shrewd enough, there were gargantuan fortunes to be made in the world of finance, and speculation on the stock exchange became a popular sport, indulged in by citizens from all but the humblest walks of life. Some grew wealthy overnight; many more lost all they had. In the meantime, however, capital was being accumulated for reinvestment.

Loans from both banks and private individuals helped bring much-needed improvements to the roads through the late eighteenth century, as engineers such as Thomas Telford and John McAdam found ways of making firm, durable surfaces that would remain stable in bad weather. Turnpike trusts set up private roads across the country, their careful maintenance funded by tolls levied on their users. Journey times were dramatically reduced: The stagecoach ride from London to Carlisle, which had taken four and a half days in 1750, took only three days by 1773.

Much of the money now being saved by the richer public was also going toward

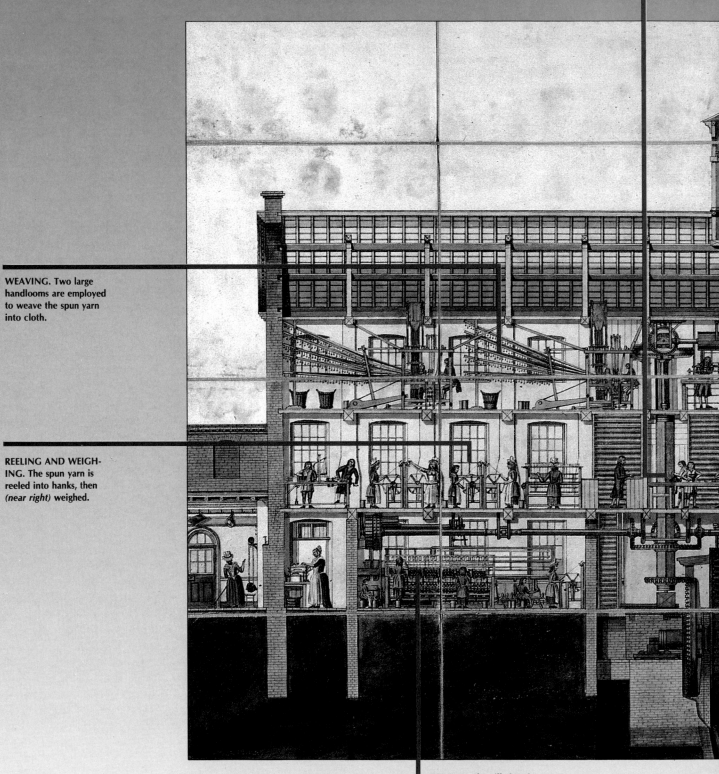

BOBBIN WINDING. The hanks of yarn are wound onto bobbins prior to weaving.

WEAVING. Two large handlooms are employed to weave the spun yarn into cloth.

REELING AND WEIGH-ING. The spun yarn is reeled into hanks, then *(near right)* weighed.

ROVING. The gilled and drawn slivers are further drawn out and lightly twisted, in preparation for spinning.

GILLING AND DRAW-
ING. Thick ropes of wool
fibers, or slivers, are
drawn out to lengthen and
straighten them.

THE MECHANICS OF PRODUCTION

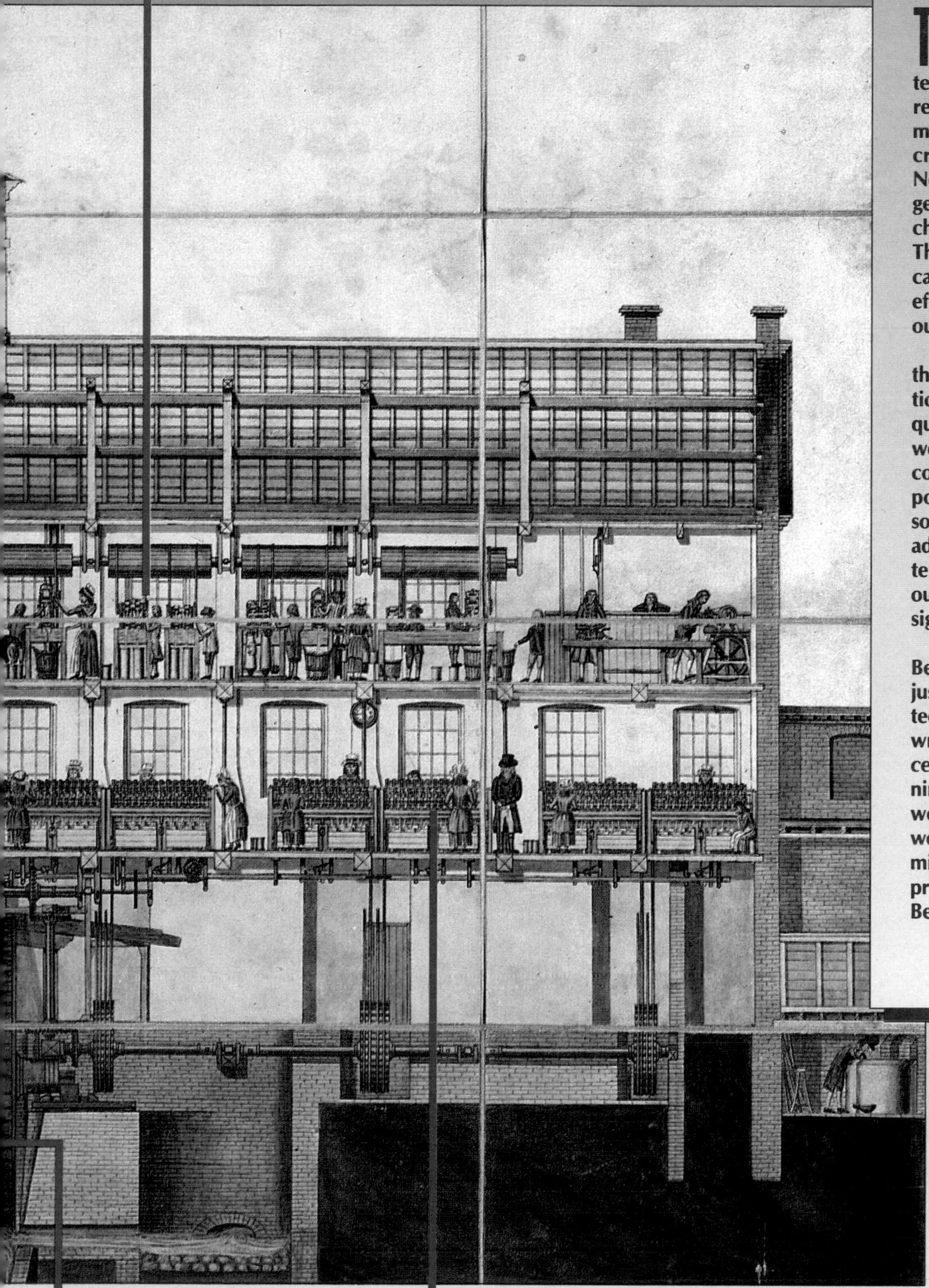

The development of large, power-driven technology in the late eighteenth century revolutionized British industry. Previously, manufacturing had been performed by craftsmen working in their own homes. Now, however, workers were brought together in large buildings, to operate machinery driven by a central power supply. The manufactories, or factories, as they became known, made possible a degree of efficiency and scale of production previously undreamed of.

Nowhere was this trend more striking than in Britain's textile trade. Early inventions improved both the quantity and the quality of yarn produced by the dispersed wool industry—which, in the 1750s, accounted for 50 percent of the nation's exports. As demand rose, entrepreneurs sought ever-greater productivity. With the advent of larger, more powerful machines, textile workers were increasingly forced out of their homes and into specially designed, three- and four-story factories.

The worsted mill at the Midlands town of Bedworth, shown here in about 1800, was just one of many that incorporated recent technological advances. Sir Richard Arkwright's water frame, for example *(right, center story)*, greatly speeded up the spinning process—although not until the 1820s would new machinery ease the task of weavers *(left, top story)*. Like many early mills—particularly those involved in cotton production, which needed a wet climate—Bedworth was powered by water.

WATER WHEEL. Turned
by water from a canal, the
wheel drives all the factory machines via a system
of cogs and pulleys.

SPINNING. The fibers are
drawn out to their final
thickness and twisted to
give the yarn consistency
and strength.

In a contemporary cartoon, Britons react with a mixture of awe and skepticism to the introduction in 1807 of gas streetlighting in London's Pall Mall. The novelty was pioneered by a German-born entrepreneur, Frederick Albert Winsor, who at first made his own gas supply in a nearby house. But he had foreseen public gasworks with underground pipes supplying whole cities, to replace the much dimmer oil lamps then in use. In 1812, he set up the Gas Light and Coke Company to supply central London, which in three years boasted almost 125 miles of gas mains. Initially, the operation was primitive: The gas ran through underground pipes constructed of bored elm trunks, and then to houses via modified army-surplus musket barrels, which were abundant after the Napoleonic Wars.

the building of Britain's inland waterway system. The use of canals for transportation, introduced in 1761, spread rapidly. The economics were simple: While eight horses were needed to haul a wagon weighing six and one-half tons, a single horse could tow a loaded barge weighing almost thirty tons. By the dawn of the nineteenth century, thousands of miles of man-made waterways traversed the country, linking all the major rivers and cities.

The newly available capital could also finance the nation's burgeoning industry. During the second half of the eighteenth century, as Britain's older American colonies matured and overseas wars brought much of India and North America into the imperial fold, British entrepreneurs discovered a vast market for manufactured goods. This development, added to the demand created by newly wealthy farmers and a growing rural population, triggered a burst of commercial activity. At the same time, productivity was boosted by a series of technological breakthroughs. Edmund Cartwright's power loom, introduced in 1785, was just one of a steady flow of inventions that boosted cotton output. And Henry Cort's reverberatory furnace had, since 1784, allowed puddling (the stirring of molten metal at high temperatures to burn off impurities), making possible the mass production of high-quality wrought iron.

Rising demand, ready finance, cheap bulk transport, a growing pool of job-hungry workers, technological advance—these were the building blocks of Britain's industrial growth. But above all, the nation's new prosperity arose from the harnessing of steam power. Experiments with steam engines had been conducted since the seventeenth century, when gentlemen of a scientific inclination had recognized the propulsive force of steam confined within a small space. The collaboration of one such amateur, Captain Thomas Savery of London, with the West Country blacksmith Thomas Newcomen succeeded in bringing the engine out of the laboratory and into the workplace as early as 1712. But it was Scottish engineer James Watt who, from 1773, virtually reinvented steam power in a series of new, constantly improving engines. More than four times as powerful as Newcomen's earlier machine, and far more adaptable, Watt's engines made the advantages of the use of steam too obvious to be ignored. Developed at the Birmingham foundry of Watt's sponsor, Matthew Boulton, these devices worked mechanical looms, rolling mills, hammers, and pumps cheaply and tirelessly. For the first time, manufacture was possible, on a truly industrial scale.

Heavy engineering was revolutionized in 1839 with the introduction of the steam hammer, painted here by its inventor, James Nasmyth. In response to a request from Isambard Kingdom Brunel, one of Britain's greatest civil engineers, Nasmyth sketched out the principles of the hammer within a bare half-hour. The concept was simple, employing steam pressure to power the downward movement of a giant iron block. The forces now available far outstripped those of the traditional smith's hammer, yet the machine could be easily adjusted to deliver taps so gentle as to crack the shell of an egg placed in a wine glass.

Among the first to benefit from steam power were the textile barons of the North. Technical advances had already led to the erection of manufactories, or factories, as they came to be known, where workers toiled in a single building over machines operated by a central power source. The industry, however, had remained dependent on water power, and thus severely limited in scale and geographical location. Now the Boulton and Watt engines allowed factory owners to exploit their systems to the full.

They were not alone. Innovators in every field were quick to see the exciting opportunities presented by the new technology. In 1779, ironmaster John Wilkinson demonstrated the benefits of cheap, high-quality iron when he built the world's first iron bridge, and later had barges, a chapel, and—finally—his own coffin built out of the material. And colossal fortunes were made by men such as brewing magnate Samuel Whitbread and Josiah Wedgwood of Staffordshire, who introduced steam power to the manufacture of pottery.

By 1801, Britain was exporting goods in unprecedented quantity. In that year, more than two million tons of commercial shipping left Britain's ports—triple the amount of just forty years earlier. By then, however, Britain was also at war, as the French

An oil painting captures distinguished guests banqueting in a half-completed tunnel designed to link London's riverside districts of Rotherhithe and Wapping. The tunnel, started in 1825 under the direction of Sir Marc Isambard Brunel and his son Isambard *(left foreground)*, was the first to be built under the Thames and was funded by public investors. The banquet—held in 1827 as a publicity stunt to reassure shareholders after a series of disasters that included cave-ins, flooding, and gas explosions—did not interrupt work, which continued apace behind a vast mirror. Despite the optimism expressed at the banquet, the project was dogged by setbacks and not completed until 1840.

leader Napoleon Bonaparte led his troops on a rampage of conquest across Europe.

For the next fifteen years, the nation endured almost constant conflict. But while the fighting may have been arduous for those at the front, it was a godsend for Britain's industrialists. Despite Napoleon's preeminence on land, it was the British Royal Navy that ruled the waves, not only protecting the island kingdom from invasion but also keeping the ocean lanes open for British exports. It was the navy, too, that enforced the orders in council, a series of legislation that declared France and her allies in a state of blockade and permitted neutrals to trade with the enemy only if they were carrying British goods and only if they paid duty on their cargoes. As well as defending the nation, Britain's armed forces were also giving her youthful industries the secure environment they needed in order to grow.

In addition, military victory was expanding Britain's empire. French possessions in the Caribbean and Mediterranean soon joined the captive imperial marketplace. When Holland fell to France, Dutch territories in southern Africa and Asia were promptly seized. The growth in colonial demand helped compensate for a decline in trade with continental Europe, squeezed by French economic sanctions. Even so, when Napoleon's troops marched toward Moscow in 1812, it was British overcoats that protected them against the Russian cold.

Guns, badges and buttons, boots and uniforms, hammers, nails, pots, pans, and axes flowed in a seemingly inexhaustible stream from Britain's ports. The heady combination of war and the manufacturing boom fired every aspect of the nation's economic life. Agricultural production swelled, buoyed by high prices; coal miners delved deeper into the earth, struggling to provide fuel to power an ever-growing number of steam engines; and giant iron foundries sprang up across south Wales, south Yorkshire, and the west Midlands Black Country—wherever coal and iron ore were found together—lighting up the night with their lurid glare. There were, it was true, years when the harvest failed, or demand unaccountably slackened, but on the whole the economy was getting steadily richer, and the wealth began to percolate further and further down the social scale.

Few were prospering as much as the cotton lords of the North. Raw cotton, by now imported from the slave-worked plantations of America's southern states through Lancashire's booming seaport of Liverpool, was being transformed into finished cloth at a tremendous rate. In 1800, £56 millions' worth of cotton had been handled by Britain's mills; ten years later, £123 millions' worth was being processed. Light to wear, easy to wash, and straightforward to dye and pattern, cotton goods found a ready market, not only at home but also, even more important, in the hot lands of Britain's eastern empire.

The process of producing woven cloth from raw cotton had never been simple. The bolls, or pods, it came in had to be opened and spread out; then the fibers had to be cleaned and separated from the seeds and combed out before being wound first into coarse yarn, then into finer thread. Complex as cotton preparation was, for all these processes human labor could now be replaced by that of machines. As one observer later wrote, "It is by iron fingers, teeth, and wheels, moving with exhaustless energy and devouring speed, that the cotton is opened, cleaned, spread, carded, drawn, roved, spun, wound, warped, dressed, and woven."

This was the strength of the factory system, which replaced the skilled manual labor of a large, scattered work force with the supervision of a few hands tending a range of machinery driven by a central power source. Men and women were still required to see that the machines were working properly, and their small children were needed to crawl underneath to remove blockages and to clean the less accessible parts. But as spinners and weavers, human workers were becoming obsolete; and as the old crafts died out, a new working class, or industrial proletariat, began to take shape, swelled by the flood of people fleeing the hardships of the land. Their attitudes and values were to be very different from those of the old agricultural poor.

Long hours and hard labor were nothing new to the poor, but those who had worked the land had at least had slack periods as well as busy ones. Throughout the winter, bad light had curtailed the number of hours during which it was possible to work. And those who had worked at home as weavers had enjoyed some limited freedom to establish their own hours.

Now the work rate was unvarying and relentless, as factory owners sought to maximize the output from their expensive machinery. The operatives—men, women, and children—toiled for up to fifteen hours a day, their rest breaks few and scrupulously timed. Rigid schedules were enforced with fines and, for the children, beatings from the overseer for any unpunctuality or mistakes in their work. All too often this strict regimen resulted in needless brutality. One apprentice, Robert Blincoe, whose memoirs were later published, recounted how his scalp had become infected from constant blows about the head. He was then "cured" by having hot pitch poured over his head; when it had cooled into a solid cap, the pitch was ripped off, taking with it all his hair.

A pair of engravings depict a flax mill built by William Marshall of Leeds, which, when it was completed in 1841, stood at the forefront of factory design. The main floor *(below, left)* covered an area of more than 86,000 square feet; conical skylights maximized natural lighting. The basement housed steam engines to drive the machinery and to heat warehouses and hot baths for the employees. On the roof *(below, right),* an eight-inch-thick layer of turf served not only to insulate the building and maintain an ideal temperature for flax-milling but also to provide grazing for a flock of sheep. Rainwater ran off by means of gutters in the internal iron pillars supporting the roof.

THE COMING OF THE RAILROADS

Steam engines had been set on rails as early as 1808, but the use of such conveyances on a large scale came with George Stephenson's Rocket, a replica of which is pictured below. With its pistons and cylinders, the Rocket embodied the design principles of all the steam locomotives that were subsequently built.

Obsessed by a vision of steam-powered rail transport, Stephenson built his first engine in 1814. In 1825, his Locomotion Cap 1 made the inaugural trip on Britain's first passenger railway, running between Stockton and Darlington. But the line, which was owned by a stagecoach company, contin-ued to run horse-drawn trains, and it was not until 1829 that Stephenson's efforts fully paid off. In that year the Rocket was chosen over three competitors to serve the Liverpool to Manchester Railway, which opened the following year.

The success of that venture sparked a massive railroad-building boom: By 1850, Britain boasted more than 6,200 miles of track (right). Unsuccessful experiments with other modes of propulsion—such as Brunel's Atmospheric Railway, driven by pneumatic power—only reinforced the fact that locomotives such as the Rocket were the transport of the future.

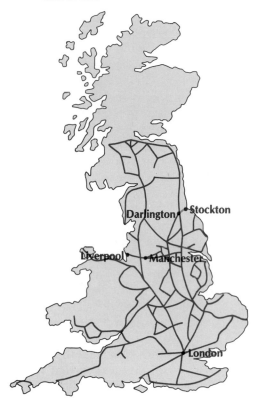

Gas lighting, which was first installed in factories in 1805, meant that the length of the working day was now dictated by man rather than nature. Artificial illumination enabled laborers' hours to be stretched to the limit—and frequently well beyond it. The distorted figures of those who worked in the textile industry bore horrible witness to long days spent in ceaseless, repetitive movements involving the use of all their limbs. One fifteen-year-old Bradford boy, permanently deformed by having worked more than ten years at a worsted mill, was only three feet nine inches in height. He had worked fourteen- and fifteen-hour shifts, and "got my knees bent with standing so long," as he told a commission of inquiry. After inspecting conditions in Manchester, Sir James Phillips Kay-Shuttleworth observed, "Whilst the engine runs, the people must work—men, women, and children are yoked together with iron and steam. The animal machine . . . is chained fast to the iron machine, which knows no suffering or weariness."

Those who endured such conditions often developed a collective spirit of discipline and militancy, and a much stronger sense of grievance than their forebears. Not all suffered the hardships of life in a cotton mill. In the metal, pottery, and leather trades, for example, different traditions prevailed, and conditions were often better. In all the new industries, however, employees could see evidence of their exploitation as their employers grew richer year by year before their very eyes. As a result, ever since the middle of the eighteenth century skilled workers had been forming combinations—the forerunners of modern trade unions—to bargain, with strike action if need be, for better pay and working conditions. And in 1793, legal recognition had been given to workers' friendly societies, which, in return for a small weekly subscription, would support a member in times of illness or unemployment and might even bear the cost of a funeral.

While friendly societies flourished, combinations soon met with difficulties. Powerful employers resented having to pay higher wages, and the British Parliament regarded the associations as a possible source of political agitation. The French Revolution of 1789, which had resulted in the overthrow of the monarchy and the subsequent execution of thousands of aristocrats, still weighed heavy in the minds of Britain's rulers. Accordingly, the government passed the Combination Acts of 1799 and 1800 to outlaw such groups. The legislation was sweeping, and there were frequent prosecutions. Nevertheless, workers still joined forces and took strike action to better their conditions. Many combinations survived by disguising themselves as friendly societies. One such, the Cotton Spinners' Association, was even able to organize a strike in Manchester in 1810, paying out £1,500 a week in strike money.

For many workers, however, better conditions within the factories would provide no solace. The thousands of handloom weavers of Lancashire and Yorkshire had always resented the advent of machinery, realizing that it would reduce their importance and lead to unemployment and low pay. As early as the seventeenth century, attempts at technological advance had been resisted when rioting London weavers had broken new Dutch looms that promised to increase efficiency. And sporadic outbreaks of machine breaking continued, with mounting intensity, throughout the eighteenth century.

In the Luddite revolt of 1812, hostility to the new technology reached a fresh pitch of intensity. Named, it was said, after Midlands apprentice Ned Ludd, who had taken a hammer to a loom—not in fact in any considered act of resistance, but in a temper after a beating from his master—the Luddites rose in rebellion against the mill

A fanciful but grim cartoon in an 1850 edition of the humorous magazine *Punch* depicts a drop of London water as seen through a microscope. The cartoon drew attention to the appalling pollution of the city's water supply, which the year before had caused an outbreak of cholera that, at its peak, claimed 400 victims a day. As a result of the city's rapid expansion, few people except the very rich had private water supplies in their homes; the majority had to use street standpipes. The water that issued from them was mostly drawn from the Thames, itself polluted by the outfall of the sewers. Not until 1852 did the government force London's private water companies to clean up their lucrative, but poisonous, monopolies.

owners and the factory system. Organized gangs of men smashed textile-manufacturing equipment and attacked their masters' homes. One manufacturer, who had expressed a desire to ride his horse up to its girth in Luddite blood, was murdered. Troops were mobilized and magistrates given sweeping powers in a flurry of legislation that placed much of northern England under virtual martial law. The revolt sent shock waves through the country before it was finally put down in January 1813, and seventeen of its ringleaders were hanged.

Even for those who did find a place in the factory system, there was no guarantee that the work would last; periods of recession and unemployment regularly followed spells of growth in the new economy. When in 1815 the combined forces of Britain's Arthur Wellesley, Duke of Wellington, and Prussia's Marshal Gebhard Leberecht von Blücher finally defeated Napoleon at the Belgian village of Waterloo, the battle ended not only the French war but also the accompanying economic boom. Distress was general throughout the country, affecting industry and agriculture alike. With food imports—which had been interrupted by the war—restored, and the demand from the armed services falling, the price of farm produce slumped. In response to anguished complaints from the big landowners, draconian laws were introduced to maintain high grain prices. Under the Corn Laws of 1815, foreign imports were barred until the price of domestic grain reached the elevated figure of ten shillings per bushel—about four shillings above the normal tariff. Effectively, the landed interest that dominated Parliament had awarded itself a monopoly.

The Corn Laws may have protected the landowners, but they worsened the lot of the poor and caused widespread discontent. A series of radical meetings that took place in the postwar years drew ever-larger attendances, to the concern of industrialists and landowners alike. On an August afternoon in 1819, a crowd of 60,000 men and women gathered at Saint Peter's Fields, Manchester, to hear a popular radical, Henry "Orator" Hunt. Alarmed, local justices sent in the militia to have the speaker arrested. When the crowd prevented this, the mounted yeomanry charged, sabering and trampling indiscriminately. In all, 11 spectators were killed and more than 400 people were wounded.

The Peterloo Massacre, named in ironic memory of England's great victory, served only to strengthen the working-class movement, which steadily gathered momentum. Combinations, supposedly abolished, flourished so vigorously underground that in 1824 the government decided to legalize them in the vain hope of reducing their appeal. The law, however, remained unclear about their right to strike—a battle that would be fought in the years to come.

It was not only the working class that was mobilizing its forces. Others, too, were seeking a greater stake in the new order. Over the years, an increasingly affluent middle class had arisen, whose ranks embraced Britons from the wealthiest industrialist to the humblest shopkeeper. More even than the working class, the new bourgeoisie was the product of the nation's industrial prowess. It was the members of this class who, on either side of the counter, filled the shops that bridged the gap between factory and home; it was they who bought the wide range of manufactured goods now touted by advertisements and made accessible by ranks of salesmen; and

The crowded houses and tall factory chimneys of Sheffield are pictured in a lithograph of 1855. The introduction of steam-powered manufacturing to this northern town, which had long been known for the quality of its cutlery, ensured its prominence as a center of the steel industry. Throughout the first half of the nineteenth century, Britain's new industrial centers grew dramatically in size: In that period Sheffield's population rose by 500 percent to reach a figure of 135,000. Except on the upwind side of the factories, where the wealthy built their houses, conditions were squalid, with workers crammed into cheap, jerry-built housing. Nevertheless, beyond the slums, the countryside was still readily accessible.

it was they who both used and provided a growing service sector in law, estate agency, and banking. Now, with the industrialists at their head, they sought to make their voices heard amid the clamor of industrial Britain's politics.

As champions of the new system to which, in 1821, political economist James Mill had given the name capitalism, the industrialists found themselves increasingly at odds with the aristocrats who ran the country from Parliament. The capitalists espoused the doctrine of laissez-faire—of minimizing government interference, maximizing competition, and allowing market forces the freedom to attend to themselves. Economists such as Adam Smith and David Ricardo provided intellectual ammunition for the fight against what was increasingly perceived as a reactionary landed interest. The Corn Laws in particular could obviously benefit none but the big landowners. Increases in the price of bread brought hardship to the poor and pushed up wage bills for industrialists.

In general, however, the wisdom of any form of protective restriction was coming into question as industry found its imported raw materials going up in price, and other nations unable to afford its products, as a result of such sanctions. With its lead in industrialization firmly established, Britain could best be served, it was argued, by the removal of all possible restrictions on commerce. "Free trade" was to become a rallying cry; and it was the cynical use of parliamentary dominance to keep the Corn Laws in place that was, more than anything, to spur on the middle class—as yet unrecognized by a political system inherited from earlier, wholly agricultural times—to demand electoral representation for itself.

The existing system did not, in its distribution of political seats, reflect the changes that had been taking place in the country over the last century. Country seats were in the pockets of the local landowners, whose electors were well-to-do farmers who knew better than to rock the boat. And many boroughs, despite having neglible electorates, were represented in Parliament on equal terms with much more populous areas. The representative of one such rotten borough, as they were known, announced after the 1802 election:

> Yesterday morning, between 11 & 12, I was unanimously elected by one Elector to represent this Ancient Borough in Parliament. . . . There was no other candidate, no Opposition, no Poll demanded. So I had nothing to do but thank the said Elector for the Unanimous Voice by which I was chosen. . . . On Friday morning I shall quit this Triumphant Scene with flying Colours, and a noble Determination not to see it again in less than seven years.

Where two or more candidates did stand for election, bribery was commonplace, and hired ruffians were frequently employed to beat up the opposition—and the electorate who, unprotected by a secret ballot, were forced to vote aloud at public meetings. When not corrupt, the system was simply cumbersome and outdated. In the country towns, the voting qualification varied enormously, and confusingly, although

An engraving from a parliamentary report on child labor in mines shows a "trapper" opening an underground door to allow a "hurrier" to push through a coal-laden truck. Ventilation in pits depended on doors being mostly closed, and the trappers, usually between five and ten years of age, spent twelve hours a day sitting alone in the dark, opening and closing air doors for the hurriers. Hurriers, many of them young girls, pushed the trolleys, which weighed about 900 pounds loaded, up to three and one-half miles a day between the coal face and the pit shaft, often through tunnels no more than twenty inches high. As a result of the report, the 1842 Mines Act banned the employment in mines of children under ten and of women.

Ranks of coffinlike beds abut the central stove of a night refuge for London's homeless, in an 1859 engraving from the *Illustrated Times*. On the right, new arrivals are registered, while others wait their turn to use the washbasins. As Britain's population expanded, homelessness became a major problem in the capital. Centers such as this one offered a modicum of relief, but conditions were far from comfortable: The conventional morality of the day taught that poverty was God's will and that the poor should learn to help themselves.

there was always some sort of property-owning stipulation. Great cities, such as Manchester, Birmingham, and Sheffield, that had grown rapidly as a result of industrialization were, preposterously, still unrepresented in Parliament during the 1820s, despite their swelling populations.

As self-made men from relatively humble backgrounds, the new industrialists had little influence in the government of the country. Often they were dissenters, brought up in strict, nonconformist Protestant churches that inculcated in them the virtues of thrift, abstinence, and hard work, but that also set them apart from the Anglican majority of their countrymen. All their energies went into their enterprises—as did most of their profits. In the early years of their businesses, such men often paid themselves the most meager of salaries, plowing the remainder back into the company to pay for improvements or expansion.

Later, perhaps, they or their descendants might relax and begin to enjoy the material benefits of their success. Brewing magnate Samuel Whitbread's son would squander most of the fortune his father had built up on an unsuccessful political career—and end by committing suicide. But such extreme examples apart, the big manufacturing families were soon well-nigh indistinguishable from the aristocracy in the scale and extravagance of their homes, estates, households, and carriages, in the schooling of their children—in everything, in fact, but pedigree and power. For however rich they became, the capitalists were kept out in the political cold.

Nevertheless, pressure for reform was growing. Parliament could no longer ignore the wealth and power of the middle class. In 1830, a bloodless coup toppled King Charles X of France, reviving among the landed gentry unhappy memories of the French Revolution. When, that same year, the death of the British monarch, King

George IV, necessitated a general election, the reformists got their chance. "A democracy has never been established in any part of the world, that . . . has not immediately declared war against property," declared the outgoing prime minister, the Duke of Wellington. His successor, Lord Charles Grey, however, came in pledged to change the situation. And in 1832, the Reform Act was passed, which gave a significantly greater number of electors the right to vote and established a more rational system of electoral districts. The new manufacturing towns now gained representation in Parliament, and the manufacturers and middle-class professionals won the right to vote.

Having gained the influence they had so long craved, the middle classes were not slow to set about wielding it. They launched what was to be a long, arduous campaign to promote free trade. From 1839, the attack was spearheaded by the Anti-Corn Law League, whose speakers—the most notable of whom were John Bright and Richard Cobden—traveled the country from their Manchester base, pressing the case for an end to the landowners' monopoly. In the small market towns, they ran the gantlet of angry mobs of laborers and farmers, stirred up by the landowning interests who had persuaded them, quite incorrectly, that everyone in the country benefited from what was in fact merely a large subsidy for the rich. In reality, however, the league's campaign and the landowners' resistance were a battle for supremacy between what were now the country's two greatest power bases. The league's ultimate victory in 1846 was not only important in bringing about the repeal of the Corn Laws and the introduction of free trade, it also made plain to the country the preeminence of capitalism.

The working class, meanwhile, was still excluded from the electorate by qualifications requiring sole occupation of a building worth at least £10. The capitalists had strict ideas about where political reform should end. Workers were, nonetheless, emboldened by their employers' victory

A watercolor shows an infants' dancing class in the school held in the institute opened in 1816 at New Lanark by Robert Owen (inset). Holding that character was formed by influences in a child's early years, Owen insisted that pupils be encouraged by kindness rather than cowed by threats of punishment. Such teaching methods were far in advance of their time.

An Apostle of Reform

The human misery caused by the factory system and the explosive expansion of British cities attracted the attention of many wealthy philanthropists. But few achieved such international fame as Robert Owen.

Born in 1771 in Newtown, Wales, Owen quickly rose through the ranks of industry to become a partner in a large Manchester cotton mill. It was not his business acumen, however, but his vision of a new industrial society that brought Owen distinction. Deeply sensitive to the plight of the disadvantaged, he believed that good character could be achieved only in a favorable social environment.

Accordingly, in 1800, Owen purchased a mill town of some 2,000 inhabitants called New Lanark, near Glasgow. There, at considerable expense, he set about creating an industrial utopia of good housing, social order, and education. The mill thrived, and soon New Lanark became a place of pilgrimage for social reformers, statesmen, and even royalty.

On the back of this success, Owen began propagating the creation on a world scale of villages of unity and cooperation as a cure for poverty and unemployment. At the same time, he tried to organize British workers on a national basis, with the creation in 1834 of the Grand National Consolidated Trades Union.

Neither enterprise flourished, but Owen continued to preach his ideas. Long after his death in 1858, his visionary ideals would influence social reformers.

and began once again to flex their muscles: 1834 saw attempts to establish a Grand National Consolidated Trades Union—a federation of unions intended to combine all workers, industrial and agricultural.

This development was fiercely resisted by the upper classes, who seemed to share activist James Bronterre O'Brien's view that this union, if successful, would bring "a change amounting to the complete subversion of the existing order of the world." In Tolpuddle, Dorset, six farm laborers attempting to enlist members to the union were arrested and convicted of the crime of administering secret oaths. The transportation to Australia in 1834 of the "Tolpuddle Martyrs"—as the unfortunates became known—broke the Grand National Consolidated, whose organizers were unprepared for this line of attack. But the popular outrage felt at their fate was to be a potent source of strength for the union movement for many decades to come.

Other workers sought to improve their position by direct emulation of the industrialists. Among the old skilled trades—those whose traditional ways had not yet been swamped by the factory system—increasing numbers began to feel that representation in Parliament offered the only real prospect for a better life. In 1838, cabinet-maker William Lovett and Francis Place, a London tailor, drew up a People's Charter calling for universal male suffrage without any property requirement, and a secret ballot to end intimidation of the electorate.

The Chartist movement gained widespread support within the working class, and a petition taken at their rallies had, by 1839, assembled nearly 1.25 million signatures. When the reformed Parliament dismissed the petition without ceremony, the backlash was angry and immediate. Rioting and strikes flared across the country, but they eventually died down when the government remained unyielding. The most determined of the Chartists kept up their fight through the 1840s, although by 1848, when the last Chartist rally—a dismal failure—was held, the working-class movement seemed to have lost much of its militancy.

However plodding the rate of political reform, industrial progress was continuing apace throughout the 1830s and 1840s. Each cotton worker was "performing, or rather superintending, as much work as could have been done by two or three hundred men sixty years ago," trumpeted one admirer of the factory system in 1835. And in 1830, engineer James Nasmyth gazed spellbound as the west Midlands blast

A note drawn on a Birmingham exchange offers the bearer items to the value of five hours' work. Owen believed that labor should be the only measure of worth and in 1832 set up the first labor exchanges, where goods could be bought or sold according to the time taken to make them. The idealistic project soon failed.

furnaces were put through their paces: "I saw the white-hot iron run out from the furnace; I saw it spun, as it were, into bars and iron ribbands, with an ease and rapidity which seemed marvellous." But Nasmyth was shocked, at the same time, at the impact iron founding was making on the rural landscape: "The earth seems to have been turned inside out. Its entrails are strewn about; nearly the entire surface of the ground is covered with cinder-heaps. . . . When it became dark . . . the horizon was a glowing belt of fire, making even the stars look pale and feeble."

Even greater changes were heralded that same year with the opening of the Liverpool and Manchester Railway. In quarries, collieries, and iron foundries, trucks carrying heavy loads of rock, coal, and ore had for some years been hauled along wooden or iron rails, sometimes by fixed steam-powered engines or by simple locomotives like Trevithick's. But it was George Stephenson's Rocket, runaway victor at trials held in 1829 to choose a locomotive for the new railway, that ushered in an age of railway building that would transform the country and the lives of its inhabitants. Actress Fanny Kemble, given a ride on Stephenson's vehicle a month before the railway's official opening, described "how strange it seemed to be journeying on thus, without any visible cause of progress other than the magical machine, with its flying white breath and rhythmical, unvarying pace, between these rocky walls . . . I felt as if no fairy tale was ever half so wonderful as what I saw."

There was, of course, nothing supernatural about Liverpool's Edge Hill cut, through which she was traveling at the time. Like other great civil engineering achievements

A contemporary engraving shows a Chartist petition, bearing more than three million signatures, being taken in procession to Parliament in 1842. Although Britain's political system had been overhauled in 1832, when the Reform Act extended the franchise to the middle classes, the Chartists enlisted the support of workers who felt the measure had not gone far enough. Three petitions were presented, whose demands included the provision of universal male suffrage and annual parliaments. All were ignored. The movement finally crumbled in 1848 when a mass rally proved a fiasco, with more policemen attending than demonstrators.

of the age, it was the work of an army of navvies—so called after the navigations, or canals, on which such gangs had first worked. Wild, ragged bands of laborers, often from Ireland—which had, since 1801, been united with Britain—the navvies led nomadic lives, moving from one construction project to the next. Everywhere they were feared and resented by the resident populations, who regarded them as little better than animals. Their work was hard and performed under atrocious conditions, their safety cynically disregarded by corner-cutting contractors determined to save time and expense. The building of the Woodhead Tunnel in Cheshire claimed dozens of lives. Indeed, one observer calculated that the casualty rates among men employed on the project were—at more than 3 percent dead and 14 percent wounded—greater than those for the British army at Waterloo.

Despised and unprepossessing as they may have been, the navvies blasted and dug their way across the countryside, realizing the most daring dreams of civil engineers, chief among them the constructor of the Great Western Railway network, Isambard Kingdom Brunel. By 1838, approximately 500 miles of track had been laid in Britain. In 1843, about 2,000 miles of railroad snaked from town to town, traversing mountains, crags, marshes, and rivers, with trains bowling along at speeds of more than thirty miles per hour. Every businessman wanted a share of the profits, and a plethora of small lines were put down, financed by local money, catering to regional needs, and constructed according to the standards of individual engineers. Not until 1846, by which time there were approximately 200 separate rail networks in the country, was a national standard gauge of 4 feet 8½ inches adopted—to the chagrin of those in the West Country, who had opted for the 7-foot gauge favored by Brunel. By 1851, mergers had reduced the number of lines to twenty-two major ones, but even then the building did not stop. Four years later, the nation could boast more than 8,000 miles of track.

Iron and coal industries worked flat out to meet the new demand for their products. For other businesses, transport costs gradually fell as the monopoly of the canals was challenged. Food prices, too, dropped as newly accessible agricultural districts began to compete with farmlands surrounding the towns. Passenger travel was transformed beyond recognition. Wherever the railway went it galvanized social and commercial life. In 1848, writer Charles Dickens described the changes wrought in a former slum district: "Crowds of people and mountains of goods, departing and arriving scores upon scores of times in every four-and-twenty hours, produced a fermentation in the place that was always in action. The very houses seemed disposed to pack up and make trips." If commerce was the lifeblood of industrial Britain, the railways were its veins and arteries.

The new energy that pulsed through the nation did not bestow its benefits evenly. As they brought the rail network into the heart of each city, the engineers took the line of least resistance, remorselessly plowing their way through low-grade, rented housing, and rendering thousands of workers homeless. While the landlords received compensation, it was, for the evicted, just another cross to bear. For as bad as conditions in the factories were, employees must often have felt more comfortable there than in their homes. Packed together in the burgeoning industrial towns, they

Surmounted by a dove of peace, an industrious tableau adorns a membership certificate of the Amalgamated Society of Engineers, Britain's first enduring trade union. Although its membership was strictly limited to skilled craftsmen—a very small proportion of the total work force—the ASE nevertheless became the model for all subsequent labor organizations. Designed in 1851, the year the union was founded, the certificate reflects the pride that workers took in harnessing the new forces of production.

found the hardship of the country replaced by the unimaginable squalor of city life. Average life expectancy for the urban lower classes was shockingly low: seventeen years for the Manchester laborer and fifteen for those born in Liverpool, as opposed to thirty-eight for farmhands in the rural county of Rutland. Infant mortality rates were to a great extent responsible for these harrowing figures: More than 52 percent of children born in Liverpool died before their fifth birthday, according to records kept in the 1840s—although many deaths went unreported.

The young American writer Herman Melville, ashore in Liverpool after his first voyage as a merchant seaman in 1839, was horrified by what he saw. "Poverty, poverty, poverty, in almost endless vistas: and want and woe staggered arm in arm along these miserable streets," he later wrote. Melville recalled walking down an alley past an open grating, hearing a dismal "soul-sickening" wail, and peering down into the darkness, "there, some fifteen feet below the walk, crouching in nameless squalor, with her head bowed over, was the figure of what had been a woman. Her blue arms folded to her livid bosom two shrunken things like children, that leaned toward her, one on each side. At first I knew not whether they were alive or dead."

Such scenes were all too common in Britain's cities. Slums of narrow alleys and unventilated courtyards crowded against each other, constructed of the poorest materials by speculative builders cashing in on the new housing boom. Often there were no foundations; walls might be only one brick thick; and the upper stories were made of such flimsy timber that their inhabitants commonly fell through to the floor below. Overcrowding was rife: Reformer Joseph Adshead found thousands of people living in damp, airless cellars in Manchester; one four-room house in London rented out to Irish tenants in 1847 accommodated fifty people from eight families—not counting the eleven lodgers who rented beds in the cellar.

The promiscuity, filthiness, and drunkenness fostered by such living conditions appalled observers such as Adshead, at a time when the middle classes were acquiring an ever-stricter regard for cleanliness, sobriety, and respectability. Some wondered whether it might be an innate lack of breeding that accounted for the repellent nature of the lower orders. Others blamed industrialism itself for creating conditions under which sobriety and respectability could not possibly be maintained. For many workers the "gin temple" was a regular source of relief from a day's drudgery—and a yawning chasm of solace in times of unemployment. Nor was alcohol the only addiction. Babies left at home with children or with elderly neighbors were routinely sedated with "quietness," a patent opium preparation that prevented them from being too lively and troublesome.

Cleanliness and hygiene, too, were beyond the reach of the poor. "Where there's muck, there's money," ran one Yorkshire saying, and indeed, filth seemed an inescapable facet of economic growth. Urban sanitary arrangements were hopelessly inadequate, even for the well-to-do. Sewerage systems, designed only for draining off rainwater, signally failed to cope with the demands made upon them by the massive growth in population and by the water closets that were now appearing in the homes of the wealthy. For the poor, crammed together in their cellars, courts, and tenements—often built on top of boarded-up cesspits—it was much worse. Earth privies were all that was available, and they were often few and far between. Some streets in Manchester, it was discovered, had no facilities at all; in the city's Oldham and Saint George's roads, more than 7,000 residents shared thirty-three privies. Very often, human excrement was simply thrown into the street, there to be collected for manure—although, on occasion, the waste was so noxious that it poisoned the meadows on which it was spread.

Water was a scarce commodity for most. While the affluent could pump their supply in the home, the poor depended on standpipes in nearby streets, or on water carriers, who peddled the precious fluid from large pails. In either case, the supply was at best unreliable, at worst a serious menace. Londoners of all classes relied on the Thames River both for the disposal of sewage and for drinking purposes. Elsewhere, sewers routinely leaked into people's homes, as well as into the wells and streams that supplied their water.

Typhus was an ever-present threat that struck at all, regardless of wealth. Most of the royal family suffered from its ravages at one point or another, while the youthful Queen Victoria, who had ascended the throne in 1837, would later lose her husband to the disease. And fearsome cholera epidemics killed thousands.

Confronted with such squalor, many began to wonder whether capitalism's successes were not hollow ones. Thomas Carlyle, stern critic of industrialism and its materialist values, voiced the thoughts of many: "We have more riches than any Nation ever had before; we have less good of them than any nation ever had before. . . . In the midst of plethoric plenty, the people perish."

William Powell Frith's 1856 painting *Many Happy Returns of the Day* pictures a Victorian family at home for a birthday celebration. Preaching—and often practicing—the virtues of industry and thrift, the middle classes were the main beneficiaries of Britain's economic expansion. Much of their wealth was expended on the home, which, run with the help of several servants, usually housed an extended family. Its comfortable surroundings not only displayed status but also provided a sanctuary from the filth and human degradation beyond the front door.

The plight of the poor was receiving growing attention from outside their ranks, as a wave of religious evangelicalism swept the nation. Christian compassion now began to rival laissez-faire as a force in society. An increasingly large and vocal element among the middle and upper classes read horrific accounts of poverty as depicted in the so-called Blue Books—hugely popular government publications containing statistics on every conceivable facet of British social life—and, rather more vividly, in popular novels such as those of Charles Dickens.

Slavery had been abolished in the empire in 1830—but in the debate leading up to abolition, the conditions of near-slavery existing in British factories and mines had been highlighted. Through the 1830s and 1840s, investigations were held into public health, sanitation, housing, criminal law, education, and almost every other imaginable aspect of life in the country, and reforms followed. By 1843, conditions in the factories had been eased somewhat by the passing of a series of Factory Acts. Within the next decade the ten-hour maximum working day and the provision of schooling for children would be mandatory.

While many capitalists fiercely resisted such reforms as these, other industrialists took the lead in proposing and supporting them. Since the beginning of the century, one such benevolent magnate, Robert Owen, had been attempting to build a new, just order of cooperation between capital and labor at his New Lanark mill in Scotland. In other areas, working-class laborers and craftsmen worked to establish

their own self-sufficient cooperative communities. Although such drastic measures proved too radical for most, affluent Britons had at least, by 1850, become far kinder to their poorer compatriots.

Although enemies of reform proclaimed that tighter regulations were stifling trade and enterprise, industrial output gave no indication of it. By the middle of the century, Britain boasted 1,800 cotton factories, employing 328,000 workers and using steam engines with a total power of almost 53,000 kilowatts to produce more than 1.75 billion yards of cotton per annum—an eightfold increase in production since the end of the Napoleonic Wars. The annual output of coal had more than quadrupled over the century to stand at more than 60 million tons, while that of pig iron had risen twentyfold and, at more than two million tons, comprised half the global output. Britain had indeed become the workshop of the world.

But its most important export was industrialism itself. British finance found rich investment opportunities in Belgium—where abundant coal and iron supplies and a tradition of textile manufacture provided conditions much like Britain's own—and later in Germany and the northern departments of France. Expertise, too, crossed the sea, as engineers and technicians brought British industrial skills to the Continent, building railways and factories and mechanizing industry wherever they went.

It was the same story in the United States: By 1840, Cunard Line's steamship *Britannia* had crossed the Atlantic in a staggering fourteen days, and by 1846, a regular passenger service had been established. Factories sprang up on the East Coast, and railways spread with astonishing speed, pushing into the interior and carrying westward the benefits—and evils—of industry. By 1860, there would be more than 28,000 miles of track. The head start with which Britain had begun its industrial revolution was soon being whittled away by her foreign competitors.

Nevertheless, at the middle of the century, Britain remained the showpiece of industrialism. The nation's achievements in the course of the nineteenth century had been extraordinary; the changes it had undergone immense and breathtakingly rapid. At the same time, the accompanying social and political reforms seemed just sufficient to enable Britons to accept the new order. When, in 1848, continental Europe was gripped by revolutionary tumult, arising partly from a reaction against industrialism, no equivalent cataclysm occurred in Britain.

On the contrary, 1850 found the nation more self-confident than it had ever been before. And the following year, the triumph of its progress was demonstrated to all at a trade fair in London's Palace of Industry. From May 1 to October 15, in the Great Exhibition, as it was known, 13,000 exhibitors attracted six million visitors from all over the world to view the marvels of free trade and British enterprise. One visitor was so impressed that she attended the exhibition thirty times, and in recording her impressions, summed up the buoyant mood of the British people: "We are capable," wrote Queen Victoria in her diary on April 29, 1851, "of doing anything." ▬

A lithograph by Joseph Nash shows the machinery hall in the British section at the Great Exhibition of 1851. The show was housed in a giant structure of cast iron and glass known as the Crystal Palace *(inset)*—itself a marvel of its time—in London's Hyde Park. The stated aim of the event was to show the achievements in trade and industry of all nations. In fact, Britain's command of the world's sea trade and her technological superiority ensured that the Great Exhibition was mainly a paean to her own industrial paramountcy.

Perched high on a mountain crag, a solitary figure communes with nature in Caspar David Friedrich's *The Wanderer above the Mists.* Rejecting the ordered conventions of eighteenth-century landscape painting, Friedrich once declared that "Every true work of art must express a distinct feeling."

ROMANTICISM: THE SPIRIT UNFETTERED

"I do not like crooked, twisted, blasted trees," says Edward Ferrars in Jane Austen's 1811 novel *Sense and Sensibility*. "I admire them much more if they are tall, straight, and flourishing. I do not like ruined, tattered cottages . . . and a troop of tidy, happy villagers please me better than the finest banditti in the world." Edward's common-sense views won him scorn and disbelief. For the early years of the nineteenth century had seen a revolution in attitudes that refuted accepted thought as profoundly as industry was changing traditional ways of life. Rational, orderly, respectable "sense"—the creed of the industrial world's new middle class—was now considered dull and unimaginative; instead, convention was scorned, and intense feeling, or "sensibility," was prized. The proponents of this new order—Romantics, as their half-admiring, half-suspicious critics called them—spread a message that would transform the Western world.

The roots of Romanticism lay not so much in rebellion against the developing industrial world as in reaction to the previous century's rationalism. Since 1687, when Isaac Newton published his discovery of the physical laws governing the solar system, a new world view had come to dominate intellectual life. All now seemed ordered and logical: The earth, it seemed, was a component in a complex but smoothly running machine.

As reason swept away old superstitions, faiths, and certainties, this age had become known as the Enlightenment. The order that Newtonian mathematics had found in the natural world could, it now seemed, be applied to all aspects of life. Poetry, art, drama, philosophy, theology, and morality—all sought to embody the perfect balance of creation. Any imperfections in nature could be tamed by humankind's artists and architects, all mysteries cleared away by its scientists and philosophers, for everything had its place in the machine of nature. As one of England's greatest poets of the period, Alexander Pope, expressed it in his *Essay on Man:* "All Nature is but art, unknown to thee; / All chance, direction, which thou canst not see; / All discord, harmony not understood; / All partial evil, universal good: / And, spite of pride, in erring reason's spite, / One truth is clear: Whatever is, is right."

But such ideals of order and civilization were not shared by all. From the 1760s on, the Geneva-born French philosopher Jean-Jacques Rousseau—himself a son of the Enlightenment—began preaching his gospel of the "natural man." Man was naturally good, argued Rousseau, but civilization de-

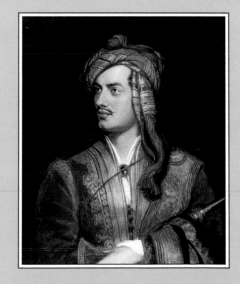

Portrayed here in Albanian national costume, Lord Byron reflects the Romantic fascination with exotic cultures. Idolized for his poetry, brooding looks, and scandalous lifestyle, Byron was, for many of his contemporaries, the epitome of Romanticism.

Mariners struggle with the elements in *Fishermen at Sea,* by the English artist J. M. W. Turner. The son of a London barber, Turner won fame and fortune with his atmospheric depictions of nature in all its various moods. He frequently depicted some human disaster to heighten the drama of his works.

based and enslaved him. The "noble savage"— living close to nature, uncorrupted by the artificiality of civilized life and the institutions of the modern state—was the ideal. Rousseau's writings sounded a note of dissent that would rise to a clamor as it was taken up by his followers toward the end of the eighteenth century.

Another discordant tone was struck in 1774 when the twenty-five-year-old German writer Johann Wolfgang von Goethe published his novel

The Sorrows of Young Werther. Maddened by his love for the unattainable Charlotte, the hero, an acutely sensitive youth, shows so little respect for rational behavior that he kills himself. No savage, but nevertheless an outsider to respectable society, Werther, with his spontaneity and intensity of emotion, quickly became a role model for young men across Europe. Thousands emulated his agonized postures and his defiantly outrageous costume; some even copied his suicide.

As the nineteenth century began, the spirit of Rousseau and Werther triumphed. While some espoused Enlightenment values, many of the younger generation sought to overturn what they saw as the stifling restrictions of eighteenth-century conventions. In 1802, when German composer Ludwig van Beethoven wrote, "I will seize fate by the throat," he reflected the creative community's increasing desire to become master of its destiny.

In reaction to the artificiality of civilized modernity, some artists and writers looked to the more savage—and, they thought, nobler—past, finding in the imagined ways of the so-called Dark Ages an ideal refuge. The period was falsely seen by them, as it had been by their eighteenth-century predecessors, as one of blood feud and revenge, religious fervor, and ungovernable passions. But while the Enlightenment had deplored such lack of restraint, the new century gloried in it. The poems and novels of the Scottish baronet Sir Walter Scott, with their elopements, warring clans, and duels to the death, were thrilled to and sighed over by genteel readers from London to Moscow. In Russia, tales of Crimean khans, Circassian amours, and gypsy folklore were to inspire the verse of Aleksandr Pushkin. And throughout Europe, a craze for exuberant folk-based dances such as the mazurka and schottische reflected society's yearning for the unfettered ways of yore.

Interest in the past was not confined to literature and music. Architects rediscovered the soaring glories of medieval cathedrals, whose riot of spires, buttresses, traceries, and gargoyles had for centuries been regarded as the essence of bad taste. Where eighteenth-century design had expressed the ascendancy of logic and clarity, the revived gothic style celebrated the triumph of feeling and faith, and the defeat of intellect in the face of the universe's mystery.

The Romantics found geographical distance as attractive as historical remoteness, and a fashion for Orientalism accompanied the medievalist vogue. Its appeal was similar: Exotic places, like distant times, were seen as natural settings for passionate lives. Artists turned for inspiration to Arabia or the Asian steppes, whose nomadic societies were unfettered by institutions and constricting social rules. They portrayed in lurid colors the lives of Eastern rulers, imagined as opulent and sensual despots whose slaves and harems stood in flagrant violation of Western decorum.

This view of the East came vividly alive in the paintings of the French artist Eugène Delacroix, as well as in the verse of the British aristocrat George Gordon, Lord Byron. Byron's brooding poems, with their misanthropic, guilt-ridden heroes, always outcasts and often outlaws, took Britain and the Continent by storm—one poem, *The Corsair,* sold 10,000 copies in one day after its publication in 1814. A compulsive violator of taboos and a moody, cynical heartbreaker, Byron seemed to be one of his own heroes. After 1816, however, when it emerged that he had had an incestuous relationship with his half sister, the similarity between art and life became unacceptably close, and Byron was forced by public outcry to leave Britain. He wandered the Continent until 1824, when he died of a fever at Missolonghi. He had gone there to join the Greeks in their fight for independence against the Ottoman Turks, a Romantic to the last in his dedication to freedom.

For the passion of nationalism was another brand that fired the Romantic imagination. The ideals of the French Revolution and the subsequent disruption of Europe's old order by Napoleon's campaigns had aroused strong feelings of national identity. From Russia and Hungary to Spain and Scandanavia, writers, artists, and musicians now rejected the universal ideals embraced by the Enlightenment and strove to emphasize the uniqueness of their own cultures. By the middle years of the century, operagoers could appreciate works as diverse as *Tannhäuser* by the German composer Richard Wagner and *Rigoletto* by a contemporary, Giuseppe Verdi. While Wagner evoked the glories of his people's heritage with tales of Teutonic legend, Verdi, in a no-less-brilliant but completely different style, sought to capture the fire and spirit of his Italian homeland.

And increasingly Romantic art impinged on politics. Aleksandr Pushkin and his compatriot, writer Fyodor Dostoyevsky, were both exiled for subversive activities. *La Muette de Portici,* composed by Daniel Auber, sparked an uprising in 1830 that eventually saw Belgium gain its independence from the Netherlands. And the works of both Wagner and Verdi were to become potent sym-

bols for the unification of their fragmented nations in the second half of the century.

While freeing the spirit of national identity, the Romantics also strove to liberate the mind from the fetters of rationalism. The great Spanish painter Francisco José de Goya y Lucientes entitled one of his engravings *The Sleep of Reason Brings Forth Monsters*. Yet Goya, like many of his contemporaries, had an unwilling fascination for such monstrous forms, born of the essentially irrational nature of things, and took a perverse delight in depicting them. It was a taste he shared with others of the time. The English writers Samuel Taylor Coleridge and Thomas De Quincey, for example, were addicted to opium, finding that its effects liberated the mind from its ordinary, hidebound, rational course. The French composer Hector Berlioz, who fantasized his own death in opium dreams, depicted his nightmares in the "March to the Scaffold" and "Dream of a Witches' Sabbath" movements of his 1830 *Symphonie Fantastique*.

Others tried to explore the realm of unreason without narcotics. The genesis of Mary Shelley's novel *Frankenstein*, published in 1818, was an evening's ghost-storytelling competition with Byron and Mary's poet husband, Percy Bysshe Shelley. Her work, which brought her fame at the tender age of nineteen, has proved one of the most enduring monuments of the so-called Gothic school of fiction, which reveled in dungeons, castles, murder, madness, and the supernatural.

Literature's settings could be as fantastic as its plots: "But oh! that deep romantic chasm which slanted / Down the green hill athwart a cedarn cover! / A savage place! as holy and enchanted / As e'er beneath a waning moon was haunted / By woman wailing for her demon lover!"

So wrote Coleridge in his opium-inspired fantasy-poem *Kubla Khan,* in 1816. Like his friend and fellow poet William Wordsworth, Coleridge was fascinated by the wilder aspects of the natural world, but also felt that nature could be a nurturing force: While the spirit of man struggled to breathe in cities, the untamed landscape of the mountains could, both poets felt, foster a better, more natural state of being.

For Wordsworth and other Romantic artists, nature also evoked deep religious sentiments. "One in everything and everything in one, God's image in leaves and stones, God's spirit in men and beasts, this must be impressed upon the mind," wrote the German novelist Friedrich Novalis. His compatriot, the painter Caspar David Friedrich, linked Man and the Divine in landscapes of awesome majesty. His masterpiece, *The Cross in the Mountains,* transcended Christian sectarianism in its assertion of the link between religion and nature. "Evergreen, enduring through all ages," he wrote, "the firs stand round the Cross, like the hope of mankind in Him, the Crucified."

By the middle of the nineteenth century, the Romantic message pervaded Europe, stirring emotions that were to affect society profoundly. As diverse as the strands of Romanticism were, one common impulse suffused the movement: the striving for uniqueness and originality. In place of the dogmatic rigidity of the previous century, there was a sense of the value of the individual, whose personal fulfillment, whether artistic, political, or religious, seemed of central importance. Increasingly, virtue was seen as lying not in laws that defined but in the cause that defied.

In the years to come, conditions would provide a backdrop for that defiance. At a time when the Industrial Revolution was spreading across the Continent, bringing new social problems and a coarsely materialistic set of values, more and more people would come to share the Romantic longing for unsullied wildernesses and the ways of a less-complicated past. Simultaneously, the reactionary regimes of Europe's old order would serve as potent stimuli for the burgeoning spirits of nationalism and liberalism.

And increasingly, it would be the artist, rather than the statesman, philosopher, or scientist, who influenced the way mankind thought. No longer a hired servant in a salon, creating beauty at the behest of often unappreciative patrons, the creative spirit was now as likely as not portrayed as a bohemian garret dweller, ahead of his time in the profundity of his vision, whose insights would be recognized for their worth only by generations that were yet to come.

"Dare to know!" the Enlightenment philosopher Immanuel Kant had declared. The Romantics went one step further: They dared to imagine. And in so doing, they helped free the spirit of mankind.

The tricolor of revolutionary France is brandished above a Parisian barricade in Eugène Delacroix's *Liberty Leading the People*. The painting was inspired by the rebellion of 1830, which deposed France's King Charles X in favor of his cousin Louis-Philippe.

LIBERATION FOR LATIN AMERICA

In the summer of 1805, a young Venezuelan aristocrat, on a walking tour of Italy with his tutor, ascended Monte Sacro and gazed toward the ancient monuments of Rome. It was on this hill, more than 2,000 years earlier, he recalled, that oppressed plebeians had first rallied in their successful struggle to wrest political equality and economic justice from an arrogant patrician minority. Overcome by emotion, the young man sank to his knees and, clasping his tutor's hand, vowed to free his own country from the oppression of Spanish rule. Simón Bolívar devoted the rest of his life to fulfilling this vow.

Twenty years later, in October 1825, he climbed the formidable slopes of Mount Potosí and on its desolate summit unfurled the flags of Colombia, Peru, Chile, and Argentina. An aspiring rebel no longer, he was General Bolívar, the most famous citizen of South America, known throughout the continent as El Libertador—the Liberator. President of Colombia and dictator of Peru, he now surveyed the treeless highlands of Bolivia, a country named in his honor. His vision was complete. Spain had finally lost its grasp on the South American continent. Colonial rule had given way to independent republics whose high-minded constitutions promised freedom and prosperity. "In fifteen years of continuous and terrific strife," Bolívar announced to his assembled aides on the summit of Potosí, "we have destroyed the edifice that tyranny erected during three centuries of usurpation and uninterrupted violence."

The next five years were to betray the ideals and sacrifices of Bolívar's campaigns. One by one, the newly created republics of Spanish America fell prey to disunity and violence, as despots of the New World replaced the imperial sway of Spain. Disillusioned and discredited, Bolívar was forced to witness the edifice he had erected come crashing down. "To change a world is beyond a poor man's power," he finally admitted. Yet he never lost sight of his own achievements. "My name already belongs to history and there I shall have justice," he defiantly wrote, shortly before his death.

At the time of Simón Bolívar's birth in 1783, Spain's huge American empire was more than 250 years old. Ever since the conquistadors had overwhelmed the Indian societies of South and Central America in the early sixteenth century, the Spanish rulers had laid claim to most of the southern continent. Only Brazil, a colony of Portugal, remained outside Spanish jurisdiction.

Four weeks' journey away from the mother country, this vast territory was ruled on behalf of the Spanish monarch by four viceroys, who in turn delegated administration to a string of regional captains general, governors, and lesser officials. In the southeast lay the viceroyalty of Río de la Plata, comprising the present-day states of Argentina, Paraguay, Uruguay, and Bolivia. The viceroyalty of Peru, a mountainous region bordering the Pacific Ocean, included both modern Peru and much of what is now

Waving kerchiefs, dancers reel outside an Andean water hole beneath the flag of a newly independent Chile. Formerly a Spanish colony, the predominantly rural country of Chile was just one of many Central and South American states that, during the first half of the nineteenth century, gained independence from their Iberian overlords. The often bloody battle for freedom did not, however, always produce the happiness that this illustration from Peter Schmidtmeyer's 1824 *Travels into Chile* might suggest. For much of Latin America, the cost of liberty was division and dictatorship.

UNITED STATES OF AMERICA

MEXICO

CUBA

SANTO DOMINGO

HAITI

PUERTO RICO

JAMAICA

• Mexico City

BRITISH HONDURAS

HONDURAS

GUATEMALA

EL SALVADOR

MOSQUITO COAST

Caribbean Sea

NICARAGUA

Santa Marta

Cartagena •

• Coro

• Caracas

Carabobo

BRITISH GUIANA

COSTA RICA

• Cúcuta

• Angostura

FRENCH GUIANA

PANAMA

LLANOS

VENEZUELA

DUTCH GUIANA

Boyacá

Orinoco River

Bogotá

NEW GRANADA

Magdalena River

Quito •

Guayaquil •

ECUADOR

Pacific Ocean

PERU

EMPIRE OF BRAZIL

Junín

Lima •

Ayacucho

BOLIVIA

• Potosí

• Rio de Janeiro

PARAGUAY

URUGUAY

• Santiago

• Buenos Aires

Río de la Plata

ARGENTINA

CHILE

UNITED STATES OF AMERICA

VICEROYALTY OF NEW SPAIN

SAINT DOMINGUE

SANTO DOMINGO

CUBA

— BELIZE

JAMAICA

BRITISH GUIANA

VENEZUELA

FRENCH GUIANA

VICEROYALTY OF NEW GRANADA

VICEROYALTY OF BRAZIL

VICEROYALTY OF PERU

UPPER PERU

VICEROYALTY OF RÍO DE LA PLATA

CHILE

Spanish Colonies

Portuguese Colonies

British Colonies

French Colonies

PATAGONIA

Chile, separate territories that were already virtually independent of each other. New Granada occupied the sloping northern shoulders of the continent, taking in modern Venezuela, Colombia, Ecuador, and Panama. Farther north, the viceroyalty of New Spain comprised Central America, Mexico, and much of what is now the western United States. In the Caribbean, Cuba, Puerto Rico, and Santo Domingo—today the Dominican Republic—completed Spain's American possessions.

From the very beginning, Spain had viewed her New World empire primarily as a source of revenue and raw materials. Precious metals, which had first lured the conquistadors, continued to enrich the mother country. In 1800, mines in Mexico and the region of Upper Peru—now Bolivia—in La Plata supplied 90 percent of the world's silver. It was agriculture, however, that constituted the largest portion of Spanish America's exports. Huge estates, or haciendas, in New Granada produced the coffee, tobacco, and cacao for which Europe had developed an insatiable appetite; sugar from Caribbean plantations satisfied the Old World's increasingly sweet tooth; while on the vast grasslands of Argentina and Venezuela, herds of wild cattle provided a profitable source of hides for export.

Spanish America was not encouraged to profit from any of these raw materials itself. Indeed, it was allowed to trade only with Spain, and in Spain only with the port of Cádiz. Spain's policy was to keep her colonies in a state of perpetual economic dependence, captive markets for her own manufacturing industries. When, for example, Cádiz merchants complained that sales of Spanish wine in the northern provinces were falling, vineyards in New Granada were uprooted to prevent cheap local wines from undercutting the expensive imported product.

For Spain desperately needed its New World income. Indeed, it maintained its position among the European powers only with a steady flow of precious metals and raw materials from its American possessions. Under the Bourbons, who succeeded to the Spanish throne in 1700, efforts were made to lift revenue by strengthening Spain's control over its colonies. New laws increased sales tax and tightened state monopolies on such goods as tobacco, spirits, and salt. The powers of the *cabildos*, town councils that were the only form of local representation available to colonial citizens, were restricted, and salaried officials arrived from Spain to supervise provincial government. When it appeared that locally raised militias were likely to prove rebellious, Spanish-born officers were appointed to fill most senior army posts.

While increasing their control over colonial bureaucracy, Bourbon administrators liberalized the economy. During the second half of the eighteenth century, they lowered tariffs on imports and exports and abolished long-held trading restrictions. Although colonial merchants were still prohibited from dealing directly with foreign states, they were eventually granted the right to trade with any Spanish port as well as with other Spanish or foreign colonies.

The reforms, however, came too late. The overall effect of these attempts at modernization and centralization was merely to encourage a growing demand for independence. Even the new freedom in trade did little to satisfy the colonies. Some American merchants complained that the reforms did not go far enough; others were ruined by the influx of inexpensive foreign imports. Higher taxes and officious Spanish bureaucrats offended nearly everyone. Resentment of rule from Europe continued to grow, while the social and racial tensions that had characterized South America since Spain's conquest steadily increased. The forces were already released that would plunge the region into rebellion and civil war.

In 1800, virtually all of Central and South America, with the exception of Portuguese Brazil and some small territories belonging to France, Britain, and the Netherlands, was ruled by the Spanish king through a system of viceroyalties *(inset)*. The Napoleonic Wars, however, destabilized the Iberian powers, giving their colonies the opportunity to seize freedom: By 1825, neither Spain nor Portugal controlled any part of the Americas. For a time, attempts were made to unite the newly independent states: the revolutionary hero Simón Bolívar briefly linked Venezuela, Ecuador, and New Granada under his leadership. But by 1850, those efforts had failed; as the main map shows, Latin America was divided into separate countries that have for the most part retained their borders to the present day.

Sharply polarized between Spaniards and Americans, between races and cultures, between rich and poor, Spanish-American society had long teetered on the edge of explosion. In 1800, nearly 17 million people lived in the Spanish-American colonies; of these, slightly more than 3 million were white. At the very top of this most privileged racial group stood the European-born Spaniards, or *peninsulares,* numbering no more than 40,000 in all. The remainder of the whites were Creoles, born in the New World. Although not all Creoles could boast great riches, they were immeasurably better off than the mixed-race and nonwhite people who constituted the great mass of South America's population. Chief among these were the mestizos, of mixed white and Indian blood. Next in order of status came the mulattoes, mixtures in varying proportion of European and black African races.

From their position of superiority, the whites referred to all free nonwhite people as *pardos,* or coloreds. Within the group, however, there were innumerable degrees of whiteness. Pale-skinned people of mixed race made strenuous efforts to legally establish that they were in fact white. There was more than pride at stake; their ethnic classification affected all aspects of their lives. Pardos were denied education and were excluded from public office; a pardo might be prohibited from carrying an umbrella, his wife from wearing jewels, silk, or velvet; and in some areas, even church seating was segregated.

Near the bottom of the social ladder were the free Indians and free blacks, as well as the *zambos* of mixed black and Indian blood. Finally there were the Indian laborers and African slaves, whose numbers varied from region to region. Most Indians were not officially classed as slaves, but their invaluable services in mines, haciendas, and public works were ensured by various means—including enticing them into debts that a lifetime's labor could not repay. Despised and oppressed, the enslaved underclass of blacks and Indians provided the foundation upon which the wealth and privileges of both Spain and her colonies rested.

Spain's exploitative policies provoked violent, if spasmodic, rebellion. During the first two centuries of colonial rule, slave and Indian revolts were common. But the Bourbon reforms caused even greater protests. In 1780, Tupac Amaru, a Peruvian Indian who claimed descent from the Incas, sent shock waves through South America with a rebellion demanding an end to tax oppression. The 60,000 untrained men who responded to his call to arms were, however, no match for armies under the command of experienced European officers. The uprising was crushed. Taken prisoner,

An engraving from Peter Schmidtmeyer's book sets forth the laborious business of refining silver ore in the Andes. The crushed ore is passed into water-filled pits, from which the metal-bearing sediment is removed and trampled *(center)* with an amalgam of salt, dung, and mercury. The amalgam is later washed *(right)* and heated to leave the pure silver. For centuries, the enormous mineral wealth of South America had enriched the economies of its Spanish and Portuguese overlords. In 1800, the Spanish-American highlands produced virtually all of the world's silver supply. The destructive wars of independence, however, sparked a flight of labor and capital from which the Latin American mining industry would not recover until the late nineteenth century.

Tupac Amaru was forced to witness the execution of his family, then tied to four horses and publicly torn into quarters.

In spite of such cruel and exemplary punishment, the spirit of rebellion spread like a plague up the social scale. By the early nineteenth century, the contagion had awakened sleeping resentments among the wealthy Creole classes. The rebel movement had at last found its leaders.

Throughout the continent the Creoles constituted the aristocracy of South America. They owned the great haciendas and were supported in lives of privileged ease by slaves. Their sons went to schools in Europe; their families inhabited town houses in the elegant capitals—Caracas, Lima, Buenos Aires—that were comparable to the provincial centers of Spain in the style of their public buildings and the gaiety of their social gatherings. Anything money could buy, the Creoles were free to enjoy. But they were denied the one thing that would satisfy their growing sense of identity: political power. Fearful of disloyalty, and anxious to reward its emigrants, Spain ensured that all of the best administrative jobs, as well as senior positions in the army and the Church, went to peninsulares. The arrogance of these newcomers infuriated the American-born elite. According to the German naturalist Alexander von Humboldt, who visited South America in the early nineteenth century, "The lowest, least educated and uncultured European believes himself superior to the white born in the New World."

The whiff of revolution from abroad further aroused the Creoles' political aspirations. Were they not in the same powerless state as their North American neighbors had been before they succeeded in throwing off the British yoke in 1781? Were they not slaves to a decadent, uncaring court, as had been the French rebels in 1789? Ambitious young Creoles hungrily read the works of liberal European thinkers. Incipient revolutionaries exchanged smuggled volumes of works by authors such as Voltaire, Jean-Jacques Rousseau, Adam Smith, and John Locke. Some paid dearly for daring to think. Antonio Nariño, a brilliant young Creole from Bogotá, attempted to publish a Spanish translation of the Declaration of the Rights of Man, the creed of the French Revolution. For this act of "treason" he was imprisoned for ten years.

Events in Europe helped accelerate Spanish America's hesitant first steps toward independence. In 1796, Spain allied itself with France in a costly war against Britain, provoking a retaliatory naval blockade that effectively cut it off from its principal source of wealth. This left the colonies free to trade using foreign vessels, a state of economic independence they had never previously enjoyed. Once tasted, such freedom was hard to relinquish.

Free trade, free speech, lower taxes, more political representation—the familiar cries of revolutionary movements all over the world—were beginning to be heard throughout the continent. Most of the fledgling rebels remained staunchly loyal to the king, while calling for the fall of his government. A few, however, argued that Spain would never tolerate a semi-independent South America. They advocated a clean break

The main building of a large hacienda, or estate, is shown in an 1824 engraving. More mundane than gold or silver, the agricultural output of such properties nevertheless formed a large part of Spanish America's exports. Visible at the right of the mansion is a station for preparing goods such as beef and hides for market. The proprietors of these huge landholdings—who were mostly of European descent—were as much merchants as farmers, usually retailing the hacienda's produce at their own urban outlets. They also profited from sales at the hacienda itself: Employees were forced to buy their supplies from estate stores, such as the one shown in the right foreground, usually at exorbitant prices.

with the mother country. Independence, in their opinion, was the only solution.

The winds of revolution had begun to blow in the Caribbean long before the Creoles could agree upon any single course of action. In 1804, after years of rebellion, the French island colony of Saint Domingue became the independent republic of Haiti. Led by a former slave, Toussaint-Louverture, an uneasy alliance of black slaves and mulattoes drove out a massive army sent by the all-conquering French leader Napoleon Bonaparte. The Spanish-American nationalists were both heartened and dismayed. What could be done in Haiti, they saw, could likewise be done in Venezuela or Peru. But at what cost? In Haiti the triumphant rebels had expelled all whites. Many Creoles hesitated to commit themselves for fear of unleashing the potentially awesome powers of the resentful nonwhite multitude. A volcano of their own making, they feared, was about to erupt.

Events in the south, however, took even the most radical nationalists by surprise. Ever on the lookout for markets, Great Britain had been quick to

Racial prejudice was strongly rooted in Spanish-American society, where the closer a person's antecedents were to Europe the greater was his or her access to political power. At the top were the immigrants from Spain—in 1800 just 0.23 percent of the total population—followed by the Creoles, or American-born people of European descent. Then came the enormous mass of "colored" peoples, or *pardos,* ranging in minute gradations of status from those of mixed blood to Indian laborers and African slaves.

By the dawn of the nineteenth century, there was increasing agitation against this exploitative system. The Creoles in particular—themselves often wealthy landowners—resented the control of the European-born minority and were in the forefront of the fight for independence. But liberty brought no relaxation of class divisions. A huge gap still existed between the rich Creoles who replaced the Spaniards and the poor pardos who remained in subjugation.

A SPECTRUM OF SOCIAL DIVISION

Three upper-class Mexicans sport the European dress that marks their elite Spanish descent.

A swashbuckling estate manager of mixed blood reflects the highest status enjoyed by his class.

target Spain's newly isolated South American colonies as a useful addition to its expanding trade empire. And in June 1806, a British expeditionary force from the Cape of Good Hope sailed into the Río de la Plata and confidently occupied Buenos Aires. But while the viceroy fled and official Spanish resistance crumbled, a hornets' nest of resistance broke out among the poorer classes. Within two months, the British were routed by a makeshift army of mixed races led largely by Creoles. Spanish authority was restored, but the Creoles had discovered their own power and had begun to suspect that the monster ruling over them was without teeth and claws.

In the same month that the citizens of Buenos Aires were celebrating their victory over the British, a band of 600 rebels landed in the captaincy general of Venezuela and called for their fellow citizens to rise against the Spanish. The leader of this optimistic army was Francisco de Miranda, a charismatic, swashbuckling visionary who had spent much of his life in Europe attempting to gain support for Spanish-American independence. Tall, handsome, and always impeccably dressed, Miranda was the great publicist for colonial freedom. He had dined with Napoleon, who had

Their bodies painted with plant pigment, Brazilian Indians wear lip and ear plugs—indications to supercilious Europeans of their lowly rank.

compared him to Don Quixote; Catherine the Great of Russia took him to her heart and, it was rumored, her bed. But Miranda's ability as a general was far below his genius at public relations. Out of touch with his own country, particularly with the interests of the Creole elite, he hopelessly miscalculated the mood of Venezuela. Even with the informal naval backing of Britain, his invasion was an embarrassing failure. Miranda fled to London, where his house became a center for subversive South American expatriates. "Never admit that despair or discouragement ever possessed your soul," he once advised a fellow revolutionary. Despite his military failure, his contagious enthusiasm remained an inspiration to the growing number of young Creoles who saw armed revolt as the only way forward.

In this society of high ideas and stifled ambitions, of optimism and inertia, Simón Bolívar received his early education. Born in Caracas, the principal city of Venezuela, he was the fourth child of a vastly wealthy Creole family that could trace its Spanish-American ancestry back to the sixteenth century. His father died when he was three, his mother when he was nine. Although an uncle supervised his upbringing, the man who most influenced him was a politically radical tutor named Simón Rodríguez. Under Rodríguez, Bolívar read the liberal books that were then circulating among nascent revolutionaries.

But it was in Europe, where Bolívar completed his education, that he developed a passion for politics. It was there, too, that another trait revealed itself: his love of fame. He witnessed Napoleon's imperial coronation in 1804 and was thrilled by the universal love that the huge crowd accorded their hero. To be so honored, wrote Bolívar, seemed to him the "pinnacle of man's desires."

It was now that Bolívar began seriously to entertain notions of playing a part in his nation's future. "I believe that your country is ready for its independence," remarked Alexander von Humboldt, whom Bolívar met shortly after the great scientist's return from Spanish America in 1804, "but I cannot see the man who is to achieve it." In his heart Bolívar accepted the challenge. Reunited with his old tutor Rodríguez, he went on a walking tour of Europe. In Rome, near the end of their travels, he made his vow on Monte Sacro. The course of his life was set.

Returning to South America in 1807, Bolívar assumed the life of a wealthy landowner. He managed his huge estates ably, to all appearances a model proprietor. But his main concern remained the political independence of his homeland. He was not without fellow conspirators. At regular gatherings—their true purpose masked by literary readings or even gambling—Bolívar and the radical young Creoles of Caracas debated the best methods by which to achieve their republican aims.

Dramatic events in Europe did not give them time to reach a conclusion. In 1808, Napoleon invaded the Iberian Peninsula. Intent upon closing European ports to British trade, the emperor had grown increasingly impatient with the inefficiency of his ally Spain. Taking advantage of Napoleon's invasion, the Spanish people forced their corrupt king, Charles IV, to abdicate in favor of his son Ferdinand. Napoleon wanted neither man. He deposed both monarchs and in their place, to the outrage of the Spanish people, installed his own brother Joseph.

With this clumsy act of nepotism, Napoleon had dealt the republicans of South America a winning card. Suddenly all of Creole society was united in its opposition to the unloved Joseph. "Long live King Ferdinand!" was the cry that resounded through the capitals of the continent. French emissaries were driven out. And Spanish officials, increasingly seen as puppets of a French usurper, struggled to maintain their authority. For more than a year they clung to power, but in 1810, the Creole population throughout the continent, acting in remarkable unanimity, arose in a great spasm of anger and deposed their powerless rulers. Only Peru was unready to cast off Spanish authority.

In Caracas, the mild-mannered governor stepped down almost gratefully on April 19, 1810, to be replaced by a junta of prominent Creoles. Bolívar, however, was not one of the new leaders. His position was uncompromisingly republican, while the moderate members of the junta still hoped for some relationship with King Ferdinand. Still, because he was one of the most articulate of the rebels—and because he offered to pay for his passage—he was sent as chief delegate on a mission to London.

Despite his eloquence, Bolívar failed to win either official military or economic assistance for Venezuela. Britain, now fighting on the side of Spain against Napoleon, could ill afford to support her ally's rebellious colony. But while his public reception was cool, Bolívar found a warm welcome at the house of Francisco de Miranda. This flamboyant revolutionary, now sixty, was still at the heart of expatriate activity. Smitten by the charm and patriotic passion of the "famous general," as London called him, Bolívar asked Miranda to lead the revolution in Venezuela. Although the British government tried to prevent his leaving the kingdom, Miranda slipped away in secret and returned to his native land for the last tragic chapter of his life.

The expedition got off to a promising start. On July 5, 1811, the National Congress of Caracas—an elected body of wealthy Creoles that had been created earlier that year—voted, with only one dissension, for independence from both Spain and New

In an 1835 lithograph by Johann Rugendas, African slaves newly arrived in Brazil rest around a fire on their way to the plantations where they will serve. Black slaves had been commonly used for field labor throughout Latin America since the sixteenth century, when the indigenous Indians were decimated by European diseases such as smallpox and influenza; Africans were also considered to be more robust than Indians. Brazil's plantation economy and its easy access to Portugal's African possessions provided perfect conditions in which slavery could flourish. Most Spanish-American countries had abolished slavery by the mid-1850s, but it was not made illegal in Brazil until 1888.

Granada. The country itself, however, was divided. Not all the provinces of Venezuela acknowledged the leadership of Caracas, and there were many who feared that a complete break with Spain would only lead to a tyranny of the most privileged Creoles. Indeed, the republicans themselves were soon split, with Miranda and Bolívar gradually growing to detest each other.

Beset by enemies from without and within, weakened by political squabbles and an increasingly chaotic economy, the infant republic was struggling for survival when nature delivered the *coup de grâce*. March 26, 1812, was Maundy Thursday. It was a stiflingly hot and cloudless afternoon in Caracas; some spoke of an oppressive silence. Suddenly the ground heaved and fell and rose up again, and the beautiful city—the third largest on the continent—with its spacious squares and handsome houses, its eight churches, its theater, and its wide streets, was reduced to rubble. Ten thousand people, nearly one-quarter of Caracas's population, died in the earthquake.

The more superstitious of the populace, encouraged by the clergy, saw this disaster as a divine rebuke for straying from Spain. "Mercy, King Ferdinand!" they cried among the ruins. And indeed, Spanish retribution was not far distant. From the Royalist stronghold of Coro, 200 miles away, an army under Spanish captain Domingo Monteverde advanced toward Caracas, meeting scarcely any opposition along its way. At the same time, a spate of savage slave revolts helped convince wavering Creoles that Spain would offer greater security than any republican regime.

Venezuela's First Republic was sinking fast. On July 25, 1812, Miranda agreed to an armistice with Monteverde, a truce amounting to little more than outright surrender. He also prepared for his own escape, taking care to provide himself with sufficient money for his retirement. But on his last night ashore, he was seized by Bolívar and several fellow officers and, on the accusation of treachery, handed over to the Spanish authorities. The old man died four years later in a jail in Cádiz. Bolívar fled to the Dutch island of Curaçao. The First Republic had come to an inglorious end.

Bolívar did not linger in exile. From Curaçao he sailed to Cartagena, the principal Caribbean port of New Granada. Cartagena, like several other New Granadan cities, had declared its independence, but the country was disunited and under constant threat from royalist forces. The Venezuelan émigré was warmly received by the Cartagenans and given an immediate command.

Before embarking upon another campaign, Bolívar wrote his *Manifiesto de Cartagena*, a shrewd analysis of Venezuela's First Republic. In this document emerged a theme that was to remain Bolívar's credo throughout his life. "Not the Spaniards, but our own disunity had led us back into slavery," he wrote. "A strong central government could have changed everything." The very structure of South American society militated against democracy, he maintained. A people who were so innocent of representative government could only achieve freedom and happiness under a "terrible power" that would sweep the Spaniards from the land. It was a vision of dictatorship that was fraught with consequence.

Bolívar now flung himself against the Spaniards with an energy that took both his enemies and his allies by surprise. On his own initiative, he embarked on a whirlwind campaign that took him victorious into the Andes, the daunting frontier with Venezuela. The conquest of Caracas, he argued, was essential to New Granadan security. Impressed by his achievements, if not by his willfulness, the high command in Cartagena authorized Bolívar to advance.

The ferocious conflict that ensued took Bolívar from the Andes to Caracas in three

An oil painting of 1829 shows Simón Bolívar, Spanish America's great hero of independence, clad in military uniform. Popularly acclaimed as the Liberator of South America, Bolívar harbored dreams of eventually uniting all of Spain's American colonies in a political federation, but his visionary ambitions were doomed to failure. This portrait, painted the year before Bolívar died, captures his lined and tired face at a time when he was already witnessing the lapse into political chaos of many of the countries he had freed.

months. As he advanced, his army grew from about 700 to 2,500 men, for the poor and dispossessed of rural Venezuela—mostly of mixed race—had learned that the cruelty of the Spanish counterrevolution exceeded that of the First Republic.

Both sides fought with the utmost barbarism, competing with each other in atrocities and terrorism. One Spanish general, it was said, encouraged his men to decorate their hats with the ears of republican sympathizers (and kept a trunk of these souvenirs for that purpose). Bolívar, for his part, proclaimed war to the death against any Spaniard who did not join the republican cause. "Our revenge shall equal the cruelties of the Spaniard," he announced. It was a policy of mutual destruction that would transform Venezuela into a wasteland.

For the time being, however, Bolívar was triumphant. On August 7, 1813, he entered Caracas. White-clad girls led his horse through the streets. "Long live our Liberator!" shouted the crowds. Two months later, Bolívar chose this title officially for himself. He was known as El Libertador for the rest of his life.

Determined that the Second Republic should not go the way of the first, the Liberator of Venezuela accepted the role of dictator as well. "Our administration must be reduced to the simplest denominator," Bolívar explained. From the beginning, however, the country was faced with crippling problems. The economy was in tatters, the great estates depopulated, and the cities ruined. Moreover, the republican factions were soon fighting among themselves.

In the eastern provinces of Venezuela an independent nationalist movement had finally driven Monteverde and the bulk of his army from the country. Santiago Mariño, the young rebel leader, was not a man to share power. Proclaiming himself Dictator of the East, he set himself up in opposition to Bolívar. His refusal to cooperate with Caracas contributed to the tragedy that ensued.

For a terrible new enemy had arisen to the south. José Tomás Boves was a Spanish adventurer who had spent some years in exile on the llanos of central Venezuela. These were the vast treeless plains of the interior, where grass grew as tall as a man and the cattle ran free. Only the *llaneros* lived here. Half-wild themselves, these mixed-race cowboys were uninterested in politics, but they seized the opportunity of plunder offered by the royalist cause. Armed only with knives, lances, and lassos, Boves's cavalry burned, looted, and raped a trail of devastation through republican towns and villages. Boves himself delighted in cruelty, ordering children to be dismembered or forcing men and women to walk on flayed soles over splintered glass.

A mindless brutality gripped the land, infecting republicans and royalists alike. In the desperate spring of 1814, Bolívar ordered the execution of 800 royalist prisoners, including the ill and wounded, for fear that they might rebel. Such cruelty availed his cause little. Short of armaments and totally demoralized, the republicans evacuated Caracas the following July, less than a year after Bolívar's triumphant entry as Liberator. Twenty thousand civilians now dragged themselves eastward, many to die along the way. Bolívar himself fled to Cartagena, where he again offered his services to the rebellion in New Granada.

A ceiling fresco in the Capitol at Caracas depicts the Battle of Boyacá, the decisive engagement by which Bolívar liberated New Granada—present-day Colombia—from Spanish rule in 1819. The barefoot patriots charging the royalist forces reflect the ragged state of Bolívar's army, which had just crossed the Andes, enduring terrible privations and loss of life. The battle, fought around a bridge over the small Boyacá River on the road to Bogotá, lasted only a couple of hours and claimed few casualties on either side. Nevertheless, most of the Spanish troops—including their general—were taken prisoner, and five days later, on August 10, the patriots entered Bogotá unopposed.

But one year had transformed the political situation. Napoleon was now in exile, and in Spain, a restored King Ferdinand VII was determined to discipline his wayward colonies. A Spanish expeditionary force of nearly 11,000 fighting men arrived in Venezuela in the spring of 1815, occupied Caracas, and then sailed on to Cartagena. The city fell after a terrible siege, which left most of the inhabitants dead of starvation.

The fall of Cartagena marked the nadir of the revolution. Bolívar, who escaped to Jamaica, took up the pen and purged his sense of failure with another political manifesto. In his *Jamaica Letter* of 1815, he again argued the case for strong central government. "Institutions that are wholly representative are not suited to our character," he claimed, proposing a president elected for life as a cure for the infant republic's factionalism. At the same time, he expressed a desire to see all of South America united under a "congress of representatives of the republics, kingdoms, and empires that would discuss peace and war with the rest of the world." It was an ambition he would pursue for the rest of his life.

Rejoining his fellow revolutionaries in the friendly republic of Haiti, he launched another invasion of Venezuela in the spring of 1816. It was an expensive failure, but undeterred, Bolívar set out on a completely different tack at the end of the year.

It had become increasingly clear that any invasion of the populous and heavily defended coastal strip of Venezuela was doomed to failure. Bolívar chose now to invade the valley of the Orinoco, the huge and marshy river, miles wide in places, that wound through rain forests and llanos to the Atlantic Ocean. Poorly defended by the Spanish, this impenetrable terrain offered the republicans a place to consolidate their forces and form the stable order of command that had been lacking in previous campaigns. In Angostura, a riverside town of 6,000 inhabitants situated 200 miles from the coast, the patriots made their headquarters and at last gained a permanent foothold in their native land.

Bolívar's first job was to establish himself as supreme commander. The vain and willful Mariño was once more refusing to cooperate with him. More dangerous still was a mulatto general named Manuel Piar, who now openly planned rebellion. Determined to exert his authority, Bolívar ordered Piar's arrest. He was captured, court-martialed, and to the amazement of his fellow officers, executed. Bolívar later claimed that his act saved the country. "Never was there a death," he claimed, "more useful, more political, and at the same time more deserved." Mariño, for one,

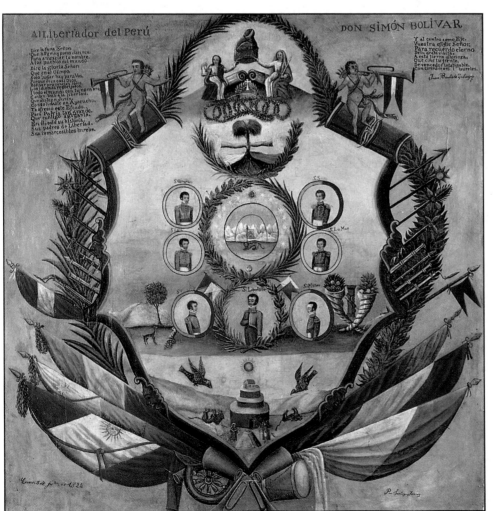

An allegorical painting of 1825, featuring a shield reminiscent of colonial heraldry, honors Simón Bolívar as the Liberator of Peru. In place of the heraldic beasts of Spain, symbols of the freedom struggle—a Phrygian cap, a laurel wreath, and the clasped hands of brotherhood—reflect Peru's pride in its newfound independence. The revolutionary heroes pictured on the shield include the Liberator himself, in the center; his favorite general, Antonio Sucre, at top right; and at bottom right, General William Miller, one of many Britons who volunteered to serve under Bolívar.

was humbled by this show of force. He arrived in Angostura and swore allegiance to the republican authorities.

General Piar's danger as an enemy had partly been his threat to divide the republican movement along racial lines. Resentful of the privileged Creoles and humiliated by the stigma of his mixed blood, he had sought to attract the great mass of pardos and slaves into a separate army. This would have been fatal to Bolívar's strategy and a blow to his idealism.

Unlike many of his Creole contemporaries, Bolívar was a sincere libertarian. A people who were fighting to be free, he argued, could not in conscience live with what he called "the dark mantle of barbarous and profane slavery." At the same time, he shared with other privileged whites a fear of an uprising from among the oppressed races. He believed that the only means of defusing the time bomb of racial injustice was political reform. Already, he claimed, liberal initiatives had transformed society in republican areas of Venezuela. "Has not the odious distinction between classes and colors been broken forever?" he asked his troops after Piar's execution. "Have I not ordered national property to be distributed among you? Are you not equal, free, independent, happy, and respected? Could Piar give you more? No. No. No."

Far below such high-flying rhetoric—as Bolívar was well aware—lay the sad reality of continued racial exploitation. Even the Liberator himself had not freed his slaves (although he would do so later, in 1821). Many of his fellow republicans would never seriously consider such a step and only reluctantly extended legal privileges to the pardos. Yet the colored masses of Venezuela were necessary to swell the ranks of the republican army. As a means of satisfying both military necessity and his genuine libertarian sympathies, Bolívar promised freedom to any black slave who enlisted with the patriots. Few rushed to join the ranks, but in offering even conditional freedom to the blacks, Bolívar helped disarm a potentially dangerous enemy. Pardos, however, responded more positively to Bolívar's promises of equal opportunity in promotion, especially since the predominantly white officer corps of the Spanish forces offered no such incentive.

A new and invaluable republican ally now emerged from the llanos to the west of Angostura. Boves had been killed in battle, but the llaneros had found another hero in José Antonio Páez, a huge, illiterate Creole who had fled to the llanos at the age of fifteen to escape the law. A genius at swift guerrilla warfare, "Uncle Antonio" exulted in violence and claimed to have killed seventy men with his own hands. Prone to epileptic fits in battle, he was attended by a gigantic black man called El Primo Negro, who carried his master's stiffened body to safety after a seizure. Páez came to an instant understanding with Bolívar when the two met in 1818.

If the wild plainsmen of the llanos represented one extreme of the republican army, red-coated recruits from Britain were another. Bolívar, who was an ardent anglophile and had long sought to attract Britain's economic and military support in the wars of independence, now launched a drive to recruit a private army from the British Isles. The time was right. Bored and impoverished by civilian life after years of continental warfare, thousands of British veterans responded to Bolívar's call to arms. Absurdly clothed and inadequately informed as to the nature of the war, many of these soldiers of fortune deserted or died of tropical diseases at an early stage. Some, however, remained with Bolívar throughout his campaigns, developing a personal attachment to the man and his cause. From Britain Bolívar also received supplies, arms, and equipment, bought on credit by his agent in London.

On February 15, 1819, a congress of elected representatives gathered at Angostura and heard Bolívar deliver a typically stirring and wide-ranging speech. He was now thirty-five years old and at the height of his powers. His face was lean and sallow, with high cheekbones and an aquiline nose. Slight in build, he stood five and one-half feet tall, but seemed to grow in stature when addressing a crowd. According to his archrival Mariño, Bolívar's eloquence was such that he "could have convinced stones of the necessity of his victory."

At the Congress of Angostura that day, Bolívar proposed a constitution for Venezuela. In keeping with his growing skepticism over popular assemblies and fear of disunity, this was to include a hereditary senate in the style of Britain's House of Lords. He went on to urge the union of Venezuela and New Granada in a state to be called Colombia—later Gran Colombia. With more than half of Venezuela still in royalist hands, this may have seemed an extravagant proposal, but Bolívar in full flight of oratory was an irresistible force. The next day, Congress elected him president of the Third Venezuelan Republic.

Bolívar now embarked upon one of the most remarkable campaigns of the war. He and Páez were making no progress against the powerful royalist army to the north. Why not change the scene of action altogether? On May 23, 1819, Bolívar called his generals to a council of war. Seated on the bleached skulls of cattle in a ramshackle hut, they agreed to invade New Granada by crossing the Andes.

It was the rainy season, the worst of all times to travel across the overflowing tributaries of the Orinoco. In order to reach even the foot of the mountains, the army had to suffer extraordinary hardships. "For seven days we marched in water up to our waists," wrote Daniel Florencio O'Leary, Bolívar's Irish aide. Hastily made cowhide boats transported soldiers unable to swim and armaments across the deeper stretches.

Then came the mountains. To the plainsmen of the tropical Orinoco valley, surmounting the Andes was a terrifying experience. Painfully trudging over sharp rocks, their boots cut to ribbons, or mounted on stumbling, dying horses, they ascended into the icy clouds. In order to increase the element of surprise, Bolívar had chosen the hardest route for his crossing: a bleak plateau, the Páramo de Pisba, that reached a height of more than 13,000 feet and was considered impassable in the rainy season. This nearly proved to be the case. All the horses and cattle died. Then the men too began to drop, some of cold, others of altitude sickness, some from sheer fatigue. Of the 3,000 men who began the journey, fewer than half reached the other side.

In early July, Bolívar's army struggled down from the heights of this savage wilderness, taking the Spaniards of New Granada completely by surprise. The peasants greeted the republicans enthusiastically, fed them, clothed them, and reequipped them with horses and mules. Many volunteered to serve with Bolívar; others were recruited at gunpoint. Thus revitalized, the Venezuelan army attacked the Spanish with a spirit that their demoralized opponents could not match. Even the European mercenaries were infected with patriotism. *"Viva la patria!"* shouted Colonel Rooke of the British legion from his deathbed, waving his amputated arm in victory.

On August 7, 1819, in the Boyacá valley, 2,000 republican soldiers met

Following Napoleon's invasion of Spain in 1808, the Mexicans, in common with most Spanish Americans, saw their colonial administrators as French puppets and began to agitate for self-government.

In 1810, a small-town parish priest named Miguel Hidalgo led tens of thousands of peasants in a bloody uprising that called for an end to Spanish rule, for racial equality, and for the redistribution of land. The revolt was put down within a year and Hidalgo was executed.

His cause lived on, however, and in 1820, the rebel movement received help from a surprising quarter. In that year, a coup in Spain forced the reactionary King Ferdinand to implement a liberal constitution. Mexican conservatives, alarmed that the contagion might spread across the Atlantic, saw independence as the only way of protecting their position. A royalist soldier, Agustín de Iturbide, persuaded a rebel leader, Vicente Guerrero, to join him in ousting the Spanish. In 1821, Iturbide entered Mexico City in triumph, where by popular acclaim, he was crowned emperor of Mexico the following year.

Independence did not bring stability. Within two years, the empire, whose arms appear above, had been replaced by a republic. And by 1850, Mexico had been forced to cede vast swaths of territory—present-day Texas, New Mexico, and California—to invading U.S. troops.

MEXICO BREAKS FREE

Dressed in martyr's white, the Peruvian patriot José Olaya is pictured in an oil painting of 1823, the year of his death. Olaya, a Peruvian Indian, carried letters between republican forces holding out in the Andes and their collaborators in the Spanish-held capital of Lima. Captured and finally executed by the Spanish, Olaya refused under torture to reveal to whom his letters were to be delivered. Not all Indians, however, shared Olaya's patriotic fervor: Most felt that the struggle for independence did not concern them.

an army of 3,000 royalists in a battle that decided the destiny of the continent. Sixteen hundred royalists were taken prisoner, along with their general and his staff. Suddenly the tide of revolution had turned. Bogotá, the chief city of New Granada, welcomed Bolívar with triumphal arches and a flower-strewn procession. The Liberator then hastened back to Angostura with news of his victorious campaign. Before leaving, he appointed General Francisco de Paula Santander as vice president of New Granada. It was to prove a fateful decision.

Later that year in Angostura, Bolívar achieved what he had described as the ambition of his life. On December 17, 1819, the Venezuelan parliament officially established the Republic of Colombia, a compound state consisting of Venezuela, New Granada, and Ecuador. None of these countries, it is true, was completely free of Spanish troops, but republican confidence was high and Europe now came to Bolívar's aid.

As the result of a liberal revolution in Spain, General Morillo, commander in chief of the royalist forces in Venezuela, received instructions to negotiate with Bolívar. The general was at first astonished by his opponent's unassuming appearance. "That little man in the blue coat and campaign hat sitting on a mule!" he exclaimed. "That is Bolívar?" But Bolívar's eloquence won him over. The two foes slept that night in the same room and parted like brothers. As a result of this encounter—one of Bolívar's most remarkable victories over Spain—Morillo asked to be relieved of his command and returned to Europe.

An armistice, agreed to last for six months, survived only five before the republicans took advantage of their growing strength to resume hostilities. On June 24, 1821, they finally won the battle for Venezuela on the plains of Carabobo near Valencia, and Bolívar once more rode victorious through the streets of Caracas.

Although Venezuela was still not at peace, Bolívar was anxious to complete his vision of a united Colombia by liberating Ecuador, the Pacific coastal territory to the south of New Granada. He had already sent his ablest general, Antonio José de Sucre, to begin the campaign. Now he hurried south to help him. Almost in passing, in the autumn of 1821, he accepted the presidency of Colombia offered to him by the newly assembled Congress of Cúcuta in New Granada. Again he chose Santander as his vice president.

Guayaquil, Ecuador's principal port, had already declared its independence. The mountain city of Quito, Ecuador's capital, fiercely resisted republican attack but fell to Sucre in May 1822. Meanwhile, Bolívar's army had forced its way south after bitter fighting in the Andean passes. In July 1822, the Liberator entered Guayaquil and again turned his eyes south—to Peru.

Bolívar's haste to liberate Ecuador was only partly motivated by his love of freedom. He was convinced that the revolution in the north would not be secure as long as the Spanish remained undefeated in the south. In addition, he was particularly concerned that the valuable port of Guayaquil, with its shipbuilding industry and excellent natural harbor, should form part of the Colombian state and not be absorbed by Peru. He was also jealous of the one man on the continent whose reputation matched his own: José de San Martín.

San Martín was an Argentine who had spent his youth in Europe and served with distinction in the Spanish army. Inspired by news of rebellion in his native land, he had returned to Buenos Aires in 1812 and offered his services to the patriots of La Plata. At that time, the country was in disarray. The viceroy had been expelled and a Creole government established two years earlier. But as a succession of short-lived dictators struggled to gain support from regional factions, the provinces of La Plata proved difficult to govern and impossible to unite. Upper Peru remained staunchly royalist; the northern region of Paraguay had repudiated all outside authority, to become a sovereign state in 1811; and across the Río de la Plata, the province of Banda Oriental—modern Uruguay—was fighting for its independence against both Buenos Aires and encroaching Portuguese armies from Brazil.

To this anarchic land, San Martín brought a selfless devotion to freedom and a genius for military organization. His value was quickly recognized by the government, which entrusted him with the task of protecting the country from Spanish

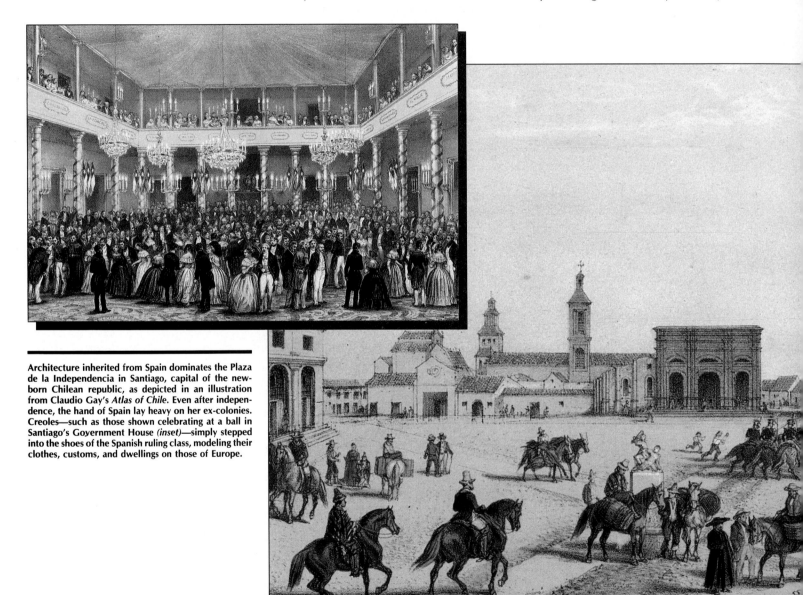

Architecture inherited from Spain dominates the Plaza de la Independencia in Santiago, capital of the newborn Chilean republic, as depicted in an illustration from Claudio Gay's *Atlas of Chile*. Even after independence, the hand of Spain lay heavy on her ex-colonies. Creoles—such as those shown celebrating at a ball in Santiago's Government House *(inset)*—simply stepped into the shoes of the Spanish ruling class, modeling their clothes, customs, and dwellings on those of Europe.

invasion. Like Bolívar, San Martín saw that his country's newborn independence—officially declared in 1816—would be perpetually threatened as long as Peru and Chile remained in Spanish hands. Accordingly, from the western town of Mendoza, in the shadow of the Andes, San Martín devoted more than two years to equipping and training what he described as "a small disciplined army." His aim was awesomely simple: to march across the Andes, liberate neighboring Chile, and then sail north to conquer Peru.

In this audacious undertaking, San Martín was aided by Chilean patriots, who had fled eastward when Spanish troops had crushed their disunited army of independence. Chief among these émigrés was Bernardo O'Higgins, whose Irish-born father, Ambrosio, had improbably risen from being a merchant-adventurer to become viceroy of Peru. At an early age, Bernardo had fallen in with Miranda in London and followed the path of revolution. As commander in chief of Chile's patriot army, O'Higgins lost decisively to the Spanish in 1814, a defeat precipitated largely by the resentment of his fellow nationalist leaders. Now he joined San Martín in Mendoza and enthusiastically prepared to liberate his native land.

In January 1817, San Martín and O'Higgins began their ascent of the Andes. The whole operation was meticulously planned and precisely carried out. An army of about 5,000 troops—along with artillery, supply wagons, and herds of cattle—crossed this formidable barrier by four separate passes in only twenty days, enduring altitudes higher than 11,500 feet and reassembling exactly as arranged on the Chilean side of the mountains. The Spaniards, who had been deliberately misinformed about San Martín's tactics, were totally unprepared when his well-equipped army suddenly descended from the wall of rock and snow that had seemed to offer such security. On February 12, the patriots routed a royalist army on the plains of Chacabuco and three days later entered the capital city of Santiago in triumph.

It was another year before the patriots finally succeeded in breaking the back of Spanish resistance. Then, with O'Higgins installed as supreme dictator of Chile, San Martín turned his attention to the second phase of his grand scheme of liberation. In 1820, his fleet of seven warships—bought, complete with mercenary crews, from Britain and the United States—sailed northward to Peru. Less than a year later, San Martín was installed in Lima.

But while the Spanish had lost the capital, they still controlled the resource-rich highlands of the interior. San Martín had no illusion that he could subdue the rest of royalist Peru as easily as he had conquered Chile. Despite the urgings of Lord Cochrane, his British admiral, San Martín chose to avoid military confrontation. "I wish to have all men think with me," he wrote, emphasizing his desire to persuade rather than coerce the population.

In the event, he could do neither. Although many Peruvians were won over to the nationalist cause, they failed to unite behind their "Protector," as San Martín described himself. Some envied the power that this foreigner had assumed; others, dedicated republicans, were angered by his avowed intention of establishing a constitutional monarchy in Peru. Moreover, his military position was growing increasingly precarious: He had broken with the chaotic leadership in Buenos Aires, which had opposed his advance on Lima, and by 1822, he had lost the backing of many of his officers, who suspected him of dictatorial ambitions. Meanwhile, the Spanish army had menacingly regrouped in the safety of the Andes. A solitary lifeline lay to the north: Simón Bolívar was campaigning in Ecuador. With the assistance of the Colombian army, San Martín hoped to crush the Spaniards and impose political order in Peru. Like Bolívar, he was tempted by the thriving port of Guayaquil. "I shall meet the Liberator of Colombia," he announced, and hastened northward.

The two men met in Guayaquil on July 26, 1822. Bolívar, who had already declared himself dictator of the city, was in no mood to grant concessions to his rival. The following evening, after another day of fruitless discussions, San Martín slipped away from a celebratory ball and set sail for Lima. Two months later, he resigned his supreme command and left the country. Taciturn and proud, he offered little explanation for his withdrawal. "I am tired of being called a tyrant," he said. He died in the French city of Boulogne in 1850.

The way was now open for Bolívar to embark upon the liberation of Peru. It was to be a lonely enterprise. By this time, San Martín's forces had dissolved, and Admiral Cochrane had taken his fleet south to harass Spanish shipping for his own gains. Moreover, in Chile, the past six years had shown O'Higgins to be a pleasant man but an incapable politician. He was a fervent egalitarian, determined to apply his principles through strong government. "If they will not become happy by their own

efforts," he proclaimed of his people, "they shall be made happy by force, by God they *shall* be happy." He abolished all Spanish titles, confiscated royalist land, and reformed the tax system to pay for improvements in education and transport. But his brand of enlightened despotism was not appreciated by all. In the underdeveloped south, resentment at high taxes resulted in continual, debilitating warfare. In addition, his reforms infuriated both the clergy and the Creole landowners. When, in October 1822, he proposed a constitution that would give him virtually dictatorial powers for ten years, it was the last straw. The next year, his opponents forced him to abdicate and flee to Peru. In the subsequent years of chaos, as a series of presidents sought to impose their control on the disunited country, Chile had little time to spare for events farther north.

Undaunted, Bolívar set sail for Lima in August 1823. He found Peru in a state of political disorientation and military collapse. "The country is afflicted by a moral pestilence," he wrote. It was also afflicted by the Spanish. By February 1824, when a desperate parliament officially appointed Bolívar Dictator of Peru, the republic retained control over only one coastal province.

Nevertheless, with the aid of General Sucre, Bolívar trained and equipped a force of nearly 10,000, and in June 1824, the generals led their army into the high Andes. Two months later, they defeated the royalists in a skirmish on the plains of Junín. Victory seemed in sight, but in October, Bolívar received an order from the Colombian parliament in Bogotá to withdraw from his command. (Vice President Santander, he presumed, was behind this spiteful move.) Sucre assumed full control, and on December 18, he forced a confrontation with the royalists at a place bearing the Indian name of Ayacucho—the Corner of the Dead.

It was a battle that broke the back of Spanish opposition in Peru. Sucre moved swiftly south into Upper Peru, defeating the Spanish in April 1825. It was the last battle Spain would ever fight on the continent. That August, Upper Peru declared its independence, adopting the name Bolívar (later Bolivia), with Sucre as president. Bolívar, who had taken no part in the final fighting, arrived and climbed Mount Potosí with Sucre and his staff to celebrate the end of the war against Spain. Although the Spanish still held their Caribbean possessions, the liberation of South America was complete.

With the fight for independence over, the battle for South America's future stability began. It was to prove one struggle the Liberator could not win.

Bolívar enjoyed playing the role of elder statesman to the newborn republic of Bolivia. He advised its leaders on a variety of matters, from agriculture and commerce to hygiene and the raising of llamas. To assist with a program of education, he even recalled his old tutor Simón Rodríguez (who was soon banished for his uninhibited sexual behavior). But Bolívar's major and most controversial contribution was the Bolivian constitution, a highly personal document that reflected his growing disillusionment with democracy. Although it guaranteed human rights and abolished slavery, this constitution called for a president for life with the power to

Circumstance rather than conflict won Portuguese Brazil its independence. In 1807, when French forces invaded Portugal, the prince regent, Dom John—along with some 2,000 members of the royal family and court—fled to Brazil. Rapturously received, the émigrés immediately began transforming the colony. A hastily glorified Rio de Janeiro became the capital of the Portuguese empire, and Brazilian ports were opened to worldwide trade.

After the death of his mother in 1815, Dom John declared himself king of both Brazil and Portugal, and four years later, he returned home, leaving his son Pedro behind as regent. But it soon became apparent that the Lisbon government was determined to restore Brazil's colonial status. In 1822, with virtually no bloodshed, Brazil declared its independence, with Pedro, pictured above dressed in his coronation regalia, as its first emperor. His son Pedro II, who came to the throne in 1831, continued the dynasty until 1889, when it was toppled by a republican coup.

BRAZIL: THE PEACEFUL REVOLUTION

appoint his own successor. Elections, Bolívar explained, "produce only anarchy." He was immensely proud of the Bolivian constitution. Under his influence, Peru adopted it in 1826, and Bolívar urged Colombia to do the same. "Everyone will consider this constitution as the ark of the covenant," he wildly claimed. To his political opponents, it bore a closer resemblance to the golden calf.

The time was now ripe for the realization of Bolívar's greatest ambition: a confederation of all South and Central American states. The entire southern continent was free of European rule. Mexico and Guatemala—including not just the present-day country of that name but also El Salvador, Honduras, Costa Rica, and Nicaragua—had achieved independence in 1821. And Brazil had peacefully declared itself a constitutional monarchy, independent of Portugal, the following year. Bolívar now proposed a league of nations that would arbitrate in disputes between states, abolish racial discrimination, and provide for mutual defense. To launch the project, he invited delegates from all the new nations, and Britain and the United States as well, to Panama, which had recently declared its independence.

The resulting Congress of 1826 was a failure bordering on farce. Now that they had achieved independence, most states were more concerned with solving their own domestic problems than initiating any joint action. Some countries declined to send delegates at all; others arrived too late to attend. The United States representative died on the way, while Bolívar himself remained in Peru. In the end, only four American states—Mexico, Colombia, Peru, and Guatemala—participated. Their resolutions were of little consequence and were soon forgotten in the turmoil that now engulfed Colombia.

In Bolívar's long absence, relations had steadily worsened between Santander and the llanero Páez, now commandant general of Venezuela. Indeed, Venezuela was in a state of open rebellion when Bolívar finally returned to Bogotá late in 1826. The Liberator hastened to settle the differences between the two men. But he had scarcely turned his back on Lima when the New Granadan troops who had stayed behind to maintain order mutinied against their Venezuelan officers and returned home. Peruvian politicians were quick to throw out the Bolivian constitution and restore their country to the chaos in which they seemed to thrive. Bolívar's dreams of unity were, it seemed, to be unattainable.

In his efforts to restore order to Colombia, Bolívar began to espouse increasingly authoritarian solutions. "Without force there is no virtue," he announced. "Give us inexorable laws." His views, however, merely alienated him further from the liberals. In 1828, constitutional government broke down, and Bolívar assumed dictatorial powers as a self-styled President-Liberator. That same year, his disappointed rival Santander, having engineered an unsuccessful plot on Bolívar's life, went into exile.

Bolívar's position, however, was growing increasingly precarious. He clung to power for another year and a half, but his popularity declined and his health deteriorated. Peru, which had already forced General Sucre out of Bolivia, now invaded Ecuador. This attack was repulsed, but Venezuela under Páez rebelled and seceded from Colombia. Bolívar's vision of union was fast receding. While Venezuelans repudiated him, in New Granada generals and politicians alike saw him as a liability. The liberals vilified him, still fearing that he would seize tyrannical powers.

Bolívar resigned from the presidency, and on May 8, 1830, he left Bogotá, determined to emigrate and escape the debilitating factionalism of South America. Further blows awaited him. Before he reached the coast, he received the news that Ecuador had declared itself independent, destroying the last remnant of the Colombian dream. Then came news that Sucre, his most loyal and capable general, was dead—murdered on a mountain road in southern Colombia.

Wasted by tuberculosis and devastated by the collapse of his life's work, Bolívar lost all hope for the continent. His last political pronouncement, written a month before his death, revealed his disillusionment. "America is ungovernable. Those who serve the revolution plow the sea. The only thing to do in America is to emigrate."

He died on December 17, 1830, in a villa near Santa Marta on the coast of New Granada. Twelve years later, when hatred for El Libertador had finally subsided in Venezuela, his body was borne to Caracas and interred at last in his native land.

The years immediately following Bolívar's death bore out his final despairing message. Any lingering dreams of international cooperation and continental unity were lost in a welter of violence and greed. Venezuela, New Granada—later to be renamed Colombia—and Ecuador were convulsed by bloodthirsty civil wars. Bolivia invaded Peru, and Chile warred against both countries. In place of constitutions, military strongmen known as caudillos cast their forbidding shadows over the politics of Latin America. Bolívar's conviction that a president should serve for life had spawned a malignant brood of dictators.

The long, hard road to independence had not led to freedom. Creoles now replaced Spanish peninsulares as the ruling political class without giving up any of their former privileges. Long-promised land reforms came to nothing. Huge haciendas continued to dominate the rural economy as a small clique of newly rich Creoles seized property previously owned by peninsulares. Few suffered more than the Indians, whose communal lands were cynically absorbed by the new elite under the pretense of integrating their traditional owners into the republic.

The economic vacuum created by Spain's departure was filled by Britain and other European powers, whose interests were equally self-seeking. In 1823, the United States had proclaimed the Monroe Doctrine, a unilateral declaration asserting that any attempt by Europe to oppress or control independent governments in the Western Hemisphere would be seen as an act of enmity. South America, however, was still within the reach of the Old World's mercantile tentacles. Indeed, Bolívar himself had once suggested to the Peruvian government that it "sell in England all its mines, lands, properties, and other government assets to cover the national debt." Now a stream of inexpensive manufactured products from Europe poured into the continent in exchange for raw materials. But while wealthy Creoles enjoyed the luxury of consumer goods from Britain's industrial centers of Manchester or Nottingham, laborers in the mines and on the farms continued to live in poverty.

For Latin American society remained profoundly divided by race and class. The fine words of abolitionists were forgotten in the wake of independence. In states such as Argentina, Colombia, Venezuela, and Peru, whose economies still had a use for forced labor, slavery was not abolished until the 1850s. Other laborers lived in virtual slavery, tied to the land by debt or despair.

But the wars of liberation were not fought in vain. Boyaca and Ayacucho, Sucre, O'Higgins and San Martín were names remembered with awe, while Bolívar became a demigod within a generation of his death. The ideals and deeds of the Liberator and his fellow revolutionaries remained inspirations to the rebellious spirits of the future, for whom the vision of a free South American people would never die.

THE OPENING OF CHINA

It was rumored that the foreigners came bearing amazing gifts: dwarfs less than twelve inches high; a songbird that consumed more than forty pounds of charcoal per day; a horse the size of a mouse; an elephant no bigger than a cat; and a magic pillow that immediately transported the sleeper to the land of dreams. These offerings were, the Chinese considered, only just and fitting tribute for their emperor, Qianlong. Accordingly, in the sweltering September of 1793, bystanders gazed expectantly at the bizarre procession that trudged northward along the dusty road from Beijing to Jehol, the emperor's summer residence. One hundred high-ranking mandarins—imperial dignitaries—on horseback led the way, then came a column of ninety or so Europeans, crowned with powdered wigs and perspiring, according to their status, into servant's livery, military uniforms, or court dress. At the rear of the column, which marched to the music of its own band, came the leader of the foreigners, riding in what appeared to the onlookers to be some kind of chariot, perched on the back of which was a small black boy in a turban. The conveyance was, in fact, an English post chaise, and its occupant was Lord George Macartney, a distinguished British diplomat who hoped to negotiate the first Western trade agreement with the Chinese.

With him Lord Macartney had brought gifts to help further his cause. They were, it was true, not exactly of the magical caliber touted in the streets of Beijing. But they were marvels in their own right, examples of Western industry and expertise, all of which were unobtainable in China. There were modern firearms and saddles, chiming clocks and Derby porcelain, crystal chandeliers and astronomical instruments. There was even a hot-air balloon, complete with pilot.

But the emperor, a shrewd octogenarian who had been on the throne for almost sixty years, was unimpressed. The ruler of the world's largest and oldest empire, regarded by his subjects as the Son of Heaven, Qianlong wished to maintain his country's seclusion from the West. He was not about to be seduced by British baubles. Indeed, he was not even sure where Britain was, nor did he greatly care. What he was sure of was that China was the Middle Kingdom—the center of the world—and the one true source of civilization. To him, as to all Chinese, foreigners were "barbarians" or "foreign devils," and the gifts presented by Macartney he regarded as no more than the tribute of an inferior people.

Thus, although treating the British mission with meticulous courtesy, he refused to discuss with its members the purpose for which it had traveled halfway around the globe. Eventually, after several weeks of mounting frustration, Macartney and his retinue set off back to the coast, their mission unaccomplished. Moreover, it had not gone unnoticed that Macartney had refused to kowtow—to perform the ritual prostration, touching the forehead to the ground, that was a traditional Chinese sign of respect and submission. "Our ways have no resemblance to yours," noted the

A guard tower looms over a bridge outside the northwestern walls of China's capital, Beijing, in a scene captured by William Alexander, official draftsman to an ill-fated embassy dispatched from Britain to China in 1793. Proud in its isolation, imperial China refused to grant the mission the trading rights sought by the British government. Within the next half-century, however, China would be brought to its knees by a potent combination of imported opium and Western military might; by the 1860s, the once-isolated imperial capital would be home to traders and diplomats from all the major Western powers.

At the beginning of the nineteenth century, China's Qing ruler held sway over one of the world's largest empires *(shaded green)*, as well as dominating the satellite states of Korea, Burma, Vietnam, and Nepal. But by midcentury, Qing sovereignty was threatened. In 1842, following a disastrous war to halt the importation of opium by Western traders—the pipe *(inset, below right)* symbolized an increasing Chinese addiction—China was forced to cede trading rights to the West as well as to grant the island of Hong Kong to Britain. A second war in 1860 brought the number of ports open to Western trade *(colored red)* to seven.

emperor tartly in an official reply to Britain's King George III. "As your ambassador can see for himself, we possess all things. I set no value on objects strange or ingenious, and have no use for your country's manufactures." After Macartney's departure, the mandarin archivists, fearful that a bad precedent might be set, recorded that he had kowtowed: In China's records, even if not in reality, Great Britain acknowledged its subordination to China. It was symptomatic of a blindness that would cost the Middle Kingdom dear.

For millennia, China had been home to one of the most advanced civilizations in the world. Its scientists had perfected the use of cast iron, paper, movable type,

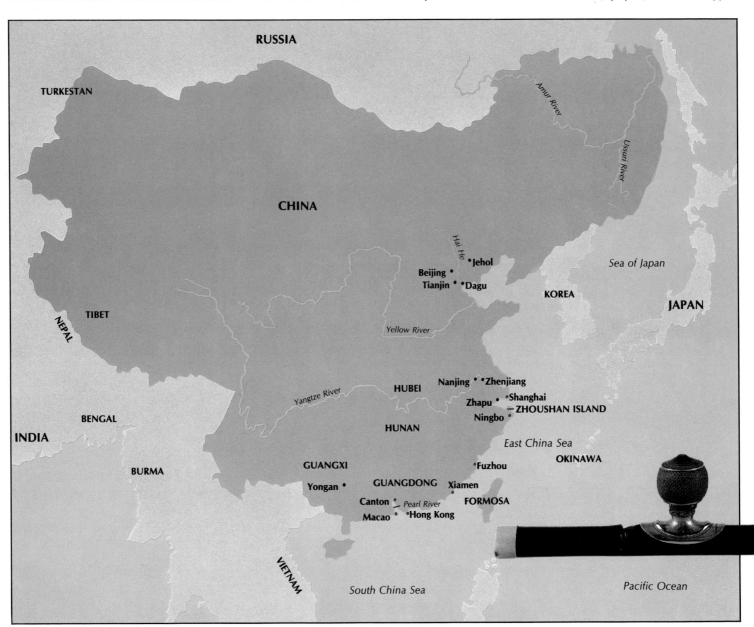

magnetic compasses, clocks, and astronomical instruments centuries before such technology had reached the West. At a time when European armies had still been belaboring each other with swords and spears, those in China were using rockets, flamethrowers, and gunpowder artillery. From time to time, it was true, less civilized invaders had swept in victoriously from the surrounding steppes and mountain ranges. But all had eventually been submerged by Chinese sophistication. It was thus with good reason that the Chinese considered all other nations inferior to themselves. By 1800, however, the rest of the world had begun to catch up. And as Qianlong had noted, their ways were very different.

A hasty sketch by a British soldier inspired William Alexander to paint this watercolor of Emperor Qianlong advancing to meet the British delegate, Lord Macartney, on September 14, 1793. To conceal Macartney's ignorance of Chinese protocol, the emperor arranged for the audience to be held in an informal setting, the Garden of Ten Thousand Trees, near the imperial summer residence of Jehol, just outside Beijing. During the encounter, the British were treated with impeccable courtesy: The Chinese even provided two cows to give milk for English-style cups of tea. But while Macartney compared the occasion to witnessing "Solomon in all his glory," the emperor was distinctly unimpressed with either the British mission or the gifts it brought.

Over the next half-century, the frenetic energy of the newly industrialized West would rudely shatter China's complacency. A massive influx of opium from British India would open the country to Western trade, plunging it into economic and social chaos, and sparking two disastrous wars with Britain that fatally undermined its independence. China's humiliation at British hands was to act as an encouragement not only to other countries—France, the United States, Russia, and later Japan—but also to indigenous opposition groups alienated by years of oppression and exploitation. By 1850, the fuse had been lighted for an explosion that would ultimately destroy the ruling Qing dynasty and with it imperial rule in China.

At the time of Lord Macartney's visit, the Qing dynasty was at its zenith. It had been 150 years since its founders had swept down from their mountain homeland in Manchuria to oust the last Ming emperor. Over the years, the Manchus had, like other invaders before them, assimilated the culture and religion of the native Chinese. The only permanent reminder of their conquest was the pigtail, the traditional Manchu way of wearing hair braided in a single plait, which they had imposed on the Chinese as a symbol of their authority.

The new rulers devoted much of their energy to imperial expansion. Burma, Vietnam, Korea, and Nepal were all forced to acknowledge Qing suzerainty. Success abroad was matched by prosperity at home. Encouraged by the long period of political stability, China developed a thriving economy, producing many goods—silks, cottons, lacquerware, porcelain, and, most important, tea—that found a ready market in Europe.

However, Europeans found trading with the Chinese far from easy. In the West, commerce was considered to be a respectable calling and the expansion of trade a desirable and worthy objective. In China, by contrast, commerce was regarded as somewhat disreputable, and foreign merchants had always been kept at arm's length. Although the emperor had sanctioned the establishment of a Portuguese trading center at the mouth of the Pearl River on the peninsula of Macao in 1557, no foreign traders were allowed to settle on the mainland itself. A caravan of merchants from Russia was occasionally given license to make its way to Beijing, but generally, Western traders could travel no farther than the port of Canton (modern Guangzhou), forty miles upriver from Macao.

Here, restricted to a small waterfront area outside the city walls, the Europeans lived almost as lepers. They were banned from bringing their wives with them; they were not allowed to row on the river; it was illegal for them to learn Cantonese; and they were barred from having direct contact with any Chinese official. All business

The flags of Spain, the United States, Britain, and the Netherlands fly above the Canton "factories" of each nation, in an oil painting by a Chinese artist. Located about forty-five miles up the Pearl River estuary, Canton was, until 1842, the only seat of commerce open to Westerners outside the Portuguese trading post at Macao. The factories, although confined to a 1,100-foot-long stretch of waterfront, extended to a depth of some 400 feet. As well as providing living quarters for European traders and their Chinese servants, each factory contained offices, warehouses, and a granite treasury.

had to be conducted with the imperial viceroy through a cartel of Chinese merchants known to Europeans as the Co-hong. The foreign barbarians, according to the regulations, were permitted to make occasional excursions outside their quarter—but not more than three times a month, not "in droves of more than ten at a time," and never without a Chinese interpreter, who was held responsible for their good behavior. And even Canton was available to them only during the tea-trading season, from April to September; for the rest of the year, they were confined to Macao.

These constraints were felt most keenly by the British East India Company, which, besides governing two-thirds of the Indian subcontinent, had the largest share of the West's trade with China. But the company's concern went far beyond the petty indignities faced by its servants in Canton. Over the years, it had built up a triangular trade, shipping British textiles to India, Indian cotton to China, and Chinese tea, silk, and porcelain to Britain. The problem, however, was that the value of the goods the company sold the Chinese was far exceeded by the value of the goods the Chinese sold the company. And these had to be paid for in silver—usually Spanish dollars—the medium upon which China's monetary system was based. With the failure of Macartney's mission to secure an extension of British trading rights, the company sought its own means of restoring the balance. Enterprising American merchants had created a small but profitable niche in the sale to the Chinese of Canadian ginseng—reputedly an aphrodisiac—and sealskins. But with what commodity could the company force its way into the Chinese market? The answer was opium.

The custom of smoking opium, long established in the East Indies, had been introduced into China by Dutch traders during the seventeenth century. After a slow start, demand for "foreign mud," as the Chinese called the drug, had gradually increased, and by the end of the eighteenth century, approximately 2,000 chests—around 140 tons—were being shipped into the country each year, most of them from Bengal, where the East India Company had established an exclusive right to cultivate the opium poppy.

The Chinese had long declared their opposition to the opium trade. As early as 1729, there had been an imperial decree forbidding the sale and smoking of opium. In 1796, Qianlong's successor, Jiaqing, had placed a complete ban on the importation of the drug, describing it as a "destructive and ensnaring vice." The new emperor, however, was a weak ruler. Timid, obstinate, and set in his ways, he wielded little control over his people. By 1807, piracy was so rife off the south China coast that one bandit fleet could muster 500 sail. And in 1813, an uprising in the south was put down only at the cost of 20,000 executions. In this atmosphere of unrest there were plenty of Chinese officials who were willing to turn a blind eye to the opium traffic in return for "squeeze"—the bribe demanded by the Chinese for services rendered. Thus, though condemned by the authorities as pirates, the opium merchants carried on their trade with virtual impunity.

By 1816, the number of chests imported each year had risen to 3,000, by 1820 to 5,000, by 1825 to almost 10,000. At first, most of the deliveries were made at Whampoa (present-day Huangpu), which lay a few miles downriver from Canton. But in 1821, the opium merchants, both Western and Chinese, set up their buying operations on the small island of Linding, northeast of Macao. It was here the Indian opium ships would discharge their cargoes, either directly into the vessels of the merchants who smuggled the opium into coastal ports, or into storage hulks kept permanently moored along the shore.

It was not the East India Company itself that fronted the opium operations in China. The company, which was perfectly content to supply opium to the ever-growing number of addicts among Britain's industrial poor, balked at jeopardizing its Chinese trade by dealing in what had been declared an illegal substance. Accordingly, the company sold the drug in Calcutta to so-called Free Traders for resale in China. Enterprising merchants, mostly Scots and Americans (who, having decimated their seal-breeding grounds, were quick to turn to opium), the Free Traders grew enormously wealthy. In 1831, the Scottish firm of Jardine, Matheson and Company was selling 6,000 chests of opium—more than the entire Chinese import of ten years earlier—at an annual profit of £100,000.

These hardheaded entrepreneurs were an unstoppable force. The ships at their command—rakish clippers to speed the opium from India, and shallow-draft coasters for dangerous inshore work—formed a much more powerful fleet than anything the Chinese could put in the water. Moreover, their vast profits could absorb almost unlimited amounts of squeeze. In 1830, a Christian missionary at Canton noted that the ships that brought the opium "are but seldom interfered with, nor are they likely to be, so long as the Free Traders can afford to pay the mandarins so much better for not fighting than the government will for doing their duty."

An attempt was made by the Chinese to cultivate opium in China, again in defiance of the emperor's edict, but it was weak stuff compared to the potent foreign mud, and imports from India continued to rise. In 1833, under growing domestic pressure to lessen trade restrictions, the British government abolished the East India Company's monopoly on opium, and within a year, the number of Western merchants in Canton had almost tripled. As well as increasing the flow of opium into the country, this move brought China into direct conflict with Great Britain. For the time being, it was Britain—represented in Canton by a trade superintendent, Lord William Napier—rather than the company, with which the Chinese had to contend. Previously, the Canton merchants had been happy to comply with Chinese regulations, provided they made a profit. Napier, however, seeking to uphold the honor of his nation, adopted a more aggressive stance. It was a foolish policy.

From the first, Napier was a figure of fun to the Chinese. Tall, rawboned, and red-haired, he was the very stereotype of a foreign barbarian. Moreover, he seemed to the Chinese to be entirely without manners, disregarding all the established rules regarding foreigners at Canton. He even had the temerity to address a letter to the imperial viceroy without the prefix *pin*, or "petition"—the written equivalent of a kowtow. How could normal business be conducted with such a person? Carefully transposing Napier's name into phonetic characters that could be read as "Laboriously Vile," the viceroy issued an edict requiring him to depart. Napier refused. The viceroy announced an embargo on all trade with the British. Suddenly the situation had become explosive.

Napier wrote home urging the government to send a naval expedition to occupy Canton, restore trade, and assert Britain's position in China. "The exploit," he claimed, "is to be performed with a facility unknown even in the capture of a paltry West Indian island." Both the British government and the Canton merchants were horrified. Such a move, they reasoned, could only do irreparable damage to profits, and a letter was promptly dispatched from London advising Napier to take conciliatory measures. By that time, however, the increasingly distraught superintendent had taken matters into his own hands. On September 7, 1835, two British frigates set

Portrayed here toward the end of his life, Wu Bing-jian—known to Europeans as Howqua—was the most prominent merchant of Canton's Co-hong association. With a membership restricted to a maximum of thirteen, the Chinese merchants of the Co-hong controlled all foreign commerce in Canton, acting as mediators between the imperial authorities and Western traders. The financial rewards attached to their position were great—shortly before his death in 1843, Howqua's personal fortune was estimated at $26 million. But the role of these mercantile intermediaries was at times unenviable: Chinese authorities held the Co-hong responsible for foreigners' wrongdoings and could impose crippling fines or even clap the merchants in chains.

An 1807 painting depicts five British sailors facing a Chinese court of inquiry held in Britain's Canton factory. After the death of a Chinese man in a quarrel involving ratings from a ship belonging to Britain's East India Company, imperial authorities declared a ban on British trade until a culprit was found. The entire fifty-two-man crew, tried in groups of five, maintained their innocence. But the embargo remained in force until the court judged one of their number to have been "the most riotous" and fined him for accidental homicide. China's insistence on applying its rigorous legal system to foreign nationals created intense resentment among the Western community in Canton. Many merchants called for armed intervention to prevent their trade being ruined by what they saw as Chinese caprice.

sail from Macao, heading for Canton and firing at Chinese coastal defenses along the way. Before they could reach their destination, however, they were halted by a hastily erected blockade between the island of Whampoa and Canton.

Full-scale war seemed the only way out of this impasse. The honor of both Britain and China was at stake. But as the two sides pondered their next move, nature intervened. Napier, the Chinese were delighted to hear from his doctor, had contracted a raging fever, and in return for a passage to Macao, he would agree to withdraw the frigates. It was the perfect face-saving solution. The British ships were ordered back to base. And amid a cacophony of drums, gongs, and firecrackers, Laboriously Vile was humiliatingly transported in a Chinese junk to Macao. There, to the relief of all, he died on the night of October 11.

In the aftermath of these dramatic events, the triumphant Chinese paid little attention when, on January 1, 1836, a small, peculiarly shaped vessel, with a draft of less than seven feet, entered the mouth of the Pearl River en route to Canton. Curious onlookers described it as "a cartwheel ship that puts axles in motion by means of fire." The Aberdeen-built paddle steamer *Jardine* was, in fact, the latest purchase by the enterprising firm of Jardine, Mattheson, which had seen the chance to augment its sizable profits by operating a rapid mail service between Macao and Canton. A Chinese admiral, who came out with an escort of 100 men to inspect the ship, admired its capability. Having gotten the *Jardine* to tow his junk back and forth, he

A profusion of intricate wave and cloud motifs decorate the summer robe of an imperial prince.

Opulently trimmed with fur, this robe served as autumn apparel for the sons of princes. Supplementing the imperial dress codes, periodic edicts ascribed dates for seasonal changes in costume.

An embroidered panel representing a four-clawed dragon indicates the lesser status enjoyed by an official of the fifth rank.

Medallions bearing the imperial five-clawed dragon embellish the dowager empress's yellow robe.

At the highly formal court of the Qing emperors, official dress reflected hierarchy through a complex code. Sartorial rules, enshrined in imperial laws published in 1759, prescribed subtle variations in color and decoration of the vestments worn by courtiers of different ranks. Some are shown painted on silk *(left)* in illustrations from a nineteenth-century album provided to guide of court members.

Under an outer garment of dark blue silk, the principal raiment for both sexes was a front-fastening, ankle-length robe embellished with dragons—an ancient Chinese motif symbolizing power. The robes of the emperor and his immediate family bore a design of writhing, five-clawed dragons, denoting superior status, and were frequently dyed a brilliant yellow—a color emblematic of kingship. Symbolic representations of cosmic and natural elements further distinguished the emperor's robes. Those of less exalted personages were usually woven of blue silk and had simpler designs.

As the century unfolded, dress codes were eroded, and unauthorized officials increasingly affected imperial dress. Europeans, such as missionaries and customs officials, were eventually granted the right to wear court apparel. And by the end of the century, Westerners were sporting Qing finery as dressing gowns.

DRAGON ROBES OF THE QING COURT

announced himself delighted with its performance. If it was up to him, he cheerfully declared, he would happily let it proceed upriver, but unfortunately the viceroy had given him strict instructions to the contrary.

The paddlewheel was duly removed from the *Jardine,* but the vessel's arrival was a portent. Able to travel into the wind, and capable of navigating easily in shallow rivers and coastal waters, a paddle steamer was a weapon of war against which China had nothing to offer. Secure in the knowledge of their superiority, the Chinese scarcely felt the first, menacing touch of Western industrial might.

The Chinese were happy with the outcome of the "Napier fizzle," as a disgruntled British prime minister called the incident. Their traditional ways had been proven far superior to those of the foreigners. Trade could now continue as normal, and the Chinese authorities asked if Britain could perhaps send a more commercially minded superintendent. "This is an affair," they said, "of buying and selling; it is not what officers can attend to." Events were to prove them wrong.

The loss of the Macao-Canton mail route did no great harm to Jardine, Mattheson. For by the time of the *Jardine*'s maiden voyage, some 30,000 chests of opium were entering the country annually, supplying the needs of an estimated 12 million addicts, including even members of the imperial bodyguard. Opium dens proliferated, ranging from the primitive to the luxurious. At the upper end of the scale, the customers would be offered upholstered couches, elegant surroundings, and courteous service—all the facilities, indeed, of a first-class private club. Often, women and gambling would also be provided. The other end of the scale was summed up by an appalled American observer, who declared that "Never, perhaps, was there a nearer approach to hell than within the precincts of these vile hovels."

So great was the opium traffic that by 1836 it was causing a serious drain on the country's silver reserves. The balance of trade, once so favorable to China, had been dramatically reversed: In the eight years preceding, $38 million had flowed out of the imperial coffers. Alarmed at the harm being done to the nation's health and economy, Emperor Daoguang, a vigorous reformer who had come to the throne in 1821 (his name meant "Glorious Rectitude") ordered that all those convicted of opium smoking should be given 100 strokes with a bamboo rod and forced to wear the cangue—a heavy wooden collar through which the hands were fastened—for two months. Raids were also carried out on some opium dens and a number of dealers executed. One such execution in Canton provoked a near-riot among the foreign merchants.

Such measures, however, proved totally ineffective, and in 1836, some of the emperor's advisers argued that the best course would be to legalize the importation of opium, tax it, and stop the outflow of silver bullion by making the drug salable only by barter. The most passionate opponent of this view was Lin Zexu, a plump, mustachioed mandarin of fifty-three, with a penchant for poetry and a reputation for honesty that had earned him the nickname of Lin-the-Clear-Sky. As governor general of Hupeh and Hunan, he had ruthlessly suppressed drug trafficking within his jurisdiction, and he urged that the same tough line should be fol-

A lush panorama, painted in the mid-nineteenth century, documents the various stages of cultivating and processing Chinese tea for exportation to the West. After being harvested, the tea leaves are rolled, fermented, and dried *(center),* before being taken to the quayside *(bottom left).* At the docks, workers trample them into chests, in preparation for weighing and selling to top-hatted Westerners. British imports of the leaf swelled more than fourfold in the course of the first thirty years of the nineteenth century, as tea drinking became increasingly fashionable in the Western world.

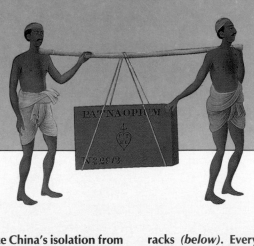

The trade that broke China's isolation from the West had its roots in the subcontinent of India. There, under the aegis of the East India Company, thousands of acres of fertile land were devoted to the cultivation of *Papaver somniferum,* the opium poppy. Sowed in November, the plants ripened in March, when the drug-rich sap was harvested through incisions cut in the seed heads. The grower delivered his wares to vast storehouses, where workers used brass cups to fashion the gum into balls weighing about two pounds each. Wrapped in poppy leaves, the round cakes were then dried on racks *(below).* Every day the cakes were turned and dusted with crushed poppy petals to ward off insects and mildew. Finally, the drug was packed in airtight crates.

Opium from the East India Company's own territory in Bengal was auctioned at Calcutta; that grown by native entrepreneurs in the hinterland—which the company subjected to profitable transit dues—was sold at Bombay. Chinese dealers, however, preferred chests that bore the company stamp—the produce of independent Indian sharecroppers was often adulterated with molasses or cow dung.

THE OPIUM INDUSTRY

lowed throughout the empire. "Opium," he declared, "is the common sink of all iniquity." His view was shared by the emperor, who called him to Beijing and, after a long series of personal audiences, appointed him imperial commissioner, with full powers to stamp out the opium trade.

The drug, once delivered at Linding, would usually enter the distribution network at Canton, and it was here that Lin duly arrived on March 10, 1839. Within a week, he had made clear his demands. First, all the opium held by foreigners, whether in the Canton warehouses, the Linding storage hulks, or the European supply ships, must be immediately handed over for destruction. "There must not be the smallest item concealed or withheld." Second, the barbarians must give a pledge never to bring opium into the country again and recognize that anyone breaking the pledge would "suffer the extreme rigor of the law"—decapitation. He also wrote to Queen Victoria exhorting her to play a part in suppressing the opium trade. "What it is here forbidden to consume, your dependencies must be forbidden to manufacture, and what has already been manufactured Your Majesty must immediately search out and throw to the bottom of the sea, and never again allow such a poison to exist."

The immediate reaction of the 350-strong foreign trading community, most of it British, was cynical disbelief. Other Chinese officials had made similar threats in the past, only to succumb to squeeze. However, as it became clear that the imperial commissioner meant what he said, the disbelief of the foreigners gave way to indignation. After two weeks of waiting for his demands to be met, Lin surrounded the foreigners' compound with soldiers and ordered their Chinese servants to leave.

Although they were now effectively hostages, the Europeans seemed unconcerned, passing the time with rat hunts, games of leapfrog, and cricket matches. As one of them later observed, "there was never a merrier

A contemporary engraving shows a crouching attendant preparing a fresh pipe for a disheveled patron of an opium den. Such haunts ranged from the primitive to the luxurious, although the method of taking the drug remained the same at either end of the scale: A small ball of opium, mixed with tobacco or incense, was placed in the bowl of a long pipe and ignited while the smoker inhaled. Rushing into the bloodstream, the drug produced a euphoric stupor. Each pipe provided just a few puffs—enough to affect a tyro, but of little consequence to addicts, who spent all day smoking.

community than that of the foreign merchants of Canton during their imprisonment. . . ." One who did not share the merriment was the superintendent of trade, Captain Charles Elliot. A former Royal Navy officer, now thirty-eight years old, Elliot was both forceful and ambitious. He was also a realist, and to him the situation appeared very dismal. In his view, the only sensible course was to give in, so on March 27, having committed the British government to indemnify the opium traders for their losses, he agreed to hand over their stocks to Commissioner Lin.

But Lin continued to insist on his second demand, and Elliot, on behalf of the foreign traders, was obliged to promise that they would never again bring opium into China. Over the next three months, Lin had some 20,000 chests destroyed, the contents decomposed with salt and lime, then sluiced into the Canton estuary. The stench was appalling, and Lin was moved to write and recite a supplicatory ode to the Spirit of the Southern Sea: "May the Spirit warn the fish in time, may its influence tame the bestial nature of the foreigners and teach them the Way."

On the face of it, Lin had won a great victory, asserting China's right to run its own affairs and firmly putting the Westerners in their place. The game, however, was far from over. Despite the promise made to the imperial commissioner, the opium traders were soon back in business, shipping supplies to new locations farther up the coast. Within nine months of Captain Elliot's submission, 8,000 new chests had been smuggled into China. Although Elliot deplored the resumption of a traffic "discreditable to the character of the Christian nations, under whose flag it is carried on," he was determined that Lin should pay for his act of "piracy" against Western traders. In a letter to the British foreign secretary, Lord Palmerston, Elliot denounced the recent blockade as "the most shameless act of violence that one nation has ever yet dared to perpetrate against another," and urged "powerful intervention" against "this rash man," Commissioner Lin.

In July, the murder of a Kowloon peasant by drunken British seamen added further fuel to the flames. Elliot refused to hand over the seamen for trial by the Chinese authorities, and Lin retaliated by cutting off all supplies to the British community. The situation deteriorated rapidly. On September 4, there was a skirmish in the Canton estuary between Chinese ships and the British frigate *Volage*. And two months later, the *Volage,* joined by a second frigate, the *Hyacinth,* scattered a fleet of twenty-nine war junks off the island of Chuanbi, sinking four vessels and inflicting heavy damage on several others.

Thus began what was to become known as the First Opium War. From England, where the reports of Lin's measures against British subjects had provoked much indignation, the government addressed a three-point ultimatum to the Chinese emperor. This demanded compensation for the 20,000 chests of opium destroyed, reparations for the imprisonment of the British merchants in Canton, and a guarantee of security for future British trade in China. To back up its ultimatum, the government dispatched an expeditionary force—4,000 troops carried in fifteen men-of-war and, ominously, five armed steamers, which arrived in the Canton estuary on June 21, 1840.

Although their navy was still powered entirely by sail and their soldiers armed with old-fashioned matchlock guns and bows and arrows, the Chinese remained sublimely confident of their military superiority. It was certain, declared Lin Zexu in a proclamation to the people of Canton, that the British fleet "will not venture to create disturbances." Sure enough, the fleet, after riding at anchor for a few days, sailed away again. But it was not returning home. Instead, it was heading north to attack the port of Dinghai, on the island of Zhoushan, seventy-five miles east of Shanghai. The expeditionary force reached its objective on July 4 and, having had its demand for surrender rejected, opened up a devastating nine-minute bombardment of the town.

Tattooed, hairy, and spouting clouds of smoke, a British sailor is depicted in the guise of a malign mythological monster in this Chinese caricature of 1839. Columns of text warn against the hirsute creature who "when it meets any one, it forthwith eats him." Such xenophobic representations were part of a Qing propaganda effort intended to evince distaste for the British.

With resistance shattered, the British troops swept through the smoking ruins searching for plunder. The inhabitants, noted a British officer, "in a thousand instances, received great injustice at our hands."

Leaving an occupying garrison on Zhoushan, the fleet resumed its progress northward, arriving at the mouth of the Hai He on August 15. The British were now only a few days' march from Beijing itself, and the emperor was becoming increasingly alarmed. By this stage, he had lost all confidence in the once-favored Lin—whom he described as "no better than a wooden image"—and replaced him with a new imperial commissioner, Qishan. Lin was exiled to Turkestan but later returned to Beijing. He was to achieve immortality modeling Chinese clothes, as a waxwork figure in the London showroom of Madame Tussaud.

Unlike his predecessor, Qishan had no doubts about the military effectiveness of the British forces. Their steamships, he advised the emperor, could "fly across the water, without wind or tide, with the current or against it." Moreover, the British armies were commanded by men trained in military affairs, whereas those of the empire were commanded by civil officials, who might be admirable calligraphists but who knew nothing of war. The first priority, declared Qishan, was to remove the threat to Beijing, which meant persuading the barbarians to sail south again.

In a British aquatint, a Chinese war junk goes up in a sheet of flame as an explosive volley from the steamship *Nemesis* finds its mark. The engagement, which took place in January 1841 during the First Opium War, at Anson's Bay in the Pearl River estuary, demonstrated the superior mobility and firepower of the British ships. In the course of a two-hour battle, eleven Chinese junks were lost, along with 500 of their crew; by contrast, only a handful of British sailors were wounded. Vessels such as the *Nemesis*—the world's first iron warship—were a key factor in Britain's victory over the Chinese navy. Heavily armed and drawing less than seven feet, the steamships could both outgun and outmaneuver their opponents in China's shallow coastal waters.

By contrast with the bellicose Lin, Qishan impressed the British as being both courteous and conciliatory, and they accepted his suggestion that it was better to negotiate at Canton, where the cause of the problem could be "investigated in detail and the culprits severely punished." However, after three months of fruitless discussion, the British decided to step up the pressure. On January 7, 1841, they captured the main defenses of the Canton estuary, the forts of Chuanbi and Taikoktow, killing an estimated 500 Chinese but suffering only a handful of casualties themselves. The lesson was not lost on Qishan. A few days later, he signed an agreement with Captain Elliot providing for, among other things, the payment by China of a six-million-dollar indemnity and the cession to Britain of a small fishing island, situated at the mouth of the Pearl River, called Hong Kong.

But the agreement pleased neither Lord Palmerston nor the Chinese emperor—the latter because it went too far, the former because it did not go far enough. "You seem," wrote the foreign secretary in a corrosive letter recalling Elliot to London, "to have considered that my instructions were waste paper." For Qishan, the consequences were rather more drastic. Stripped of his rank, his decorations, and his fortune, he was taken in chains to Beijing, where he was tried and sentenced to death. (In the event, he was sent into exile and later taken back into the imperial service.) There followed several months of sporadic fighting in the Canton area, culminating on May 24 in a British assault on the city. The next day, the emperor's cousin, Yishan, whom the Son of Heaven had sent south to "extirpate the barbarians," agreed, instead, to pay them the indemnity of six million dollars for not pressing their attack.

In the crowded environs of HMS *Cornwallis's* state cabin, representatives of the defeated Chinese emperor meet a British plenipotentiary to sign the Treaty of Nanjing on August 29, 1842. The humiliating settlement—the first to be signed by China with a foreign country in more than 150 years—ended the First Opium War and was the first in a series of treaties that forced the nation to abandon its isolationist stance and open its markets to foreign trade.

In August 1841, the British expedition, joined by fresh detachments from India, resumed action, seizing a string of coastal towns as it advanced northward again. Despite their antiquated weaponry and inferior training, the local troops sometimes fought back with impressive bravery. "The Chinese themselves are a very powerful race," observed one British officer. "They would make such perfect soldiers if taken properly in hand." On March 10, 1842—the Day of the Tiger in the Chinese calendar—the Chinese launched a counteroffensive, striking at the port of Ningbo, where the British had dug themselves in for the winter. Seeing that one of the city gates was open, thousands of the attackers rushed forward—straight into a well-laid minefield. Other Chinese who forced their way into the city were confronted by British artillery firing from a distance of less than 165 feet. The narrow streets were soon blocked with corpses, which the British were obliged to clamber over in pursuit of the now retreating enemy.

In May, the British reached Zhapu, south of Shanghai, where the garrison was made up of Manchu warriors, noted for their fierce courage and fanatical loyalty to the emperor. Resistance ceased only when the temple that had become their final stronghold caught fire. However, rather than submit, many of the defenders killed their wives and children, and then cut their own throats. The way was now clear to Shanghai, which fell to the British in June. From here, they turned inland, up the Yangtze River, and took Zhenjiang a month later. Again, the defenders were mainly Manchus, and they repeated the scenes that had greeted the British in Zhapu, massacring their families before taking their own lives. "It may be said that the Manchu race in this city is extinct," reported the British military commander, General Sir Hugh Gough. "I was glad to withdraw the troops from this frightful scene of destruction." Looting, both by British and by Chinese, added to the town's misery and made Gough "sick at heart of war and its fearful consequences."

The fall of Zhenjiang marked the end of Chinese resistance. On August 8, with British naval guns now trained on Nanjing, a team of Chinese officials went on board the flagship, HMS *Cornwallis,* to begin negotiations with the "red-bristled barbarians." The British had already drawn up a treaty, and it was made clear to the Chinese that they were required to sign the document as it stood. If they refused, warned Captain Elliot's successor, Sir Henry Pottinger, the expeditionary force, after taking Nanjing, would advance to take Beijing. This provoked an emotional outburst from the leader of the Chinese delegation, Zhang Xi. "You kill people everywhere, plunder goods, and act like rascals; that is very disgraceful; how can you say it is not like bandits? You alien barbarians invade our China, your small country attacks our Celestial Court; how can you say you are not rebellious?" As Zhang warmed to his theme, banging on Pottinger's desk and spitting on the floor, the Indian sentries posted outside the cabin unsheathed their swords in preparation for bloodshed.

Eventually, Zhang regained his composure, and the British agreed to hold up the bombardment of Nanjing while he conferred with his superiors—three commissioners appointed by the emperor. Having listened to Zhang's account, they reported to the Son of Heaven that the time had come "to ease the situation by soothing the barbarians," who would otherwise "run over our country like beasts, doing anything they like." On August 29, 1842, the Treaty of Nanjing was signed and the First Opium War came to an end. As the *Cornwallis* thundered out a twenty-one-gun celebratory salute, the commissioners were unable to contain their alarm, and one of them, according to an English observer, showed "deep consciousness of fallen power."

The primary provisions of the treaty were the cession of Hong Kong in perpetuity as a Crown Colony to Britain, the payment of a $21-million indemnity, and the opening to British trade and residence of the five ports of Canton, Xiamen, Fuzhou, Ningbo, and Shanghai. To compound China's loss, a supplementary treaty was signed the following year, recognizing Great Britain as a "most-favored nation"— automatically entitled to receive all rights that other countries might subsequently succeed in obtaining. The shrewdness of this move soon became apparent, as other Western powers hurried to take advantage of China's weakness. Within a few short years, Britain was benefiting from treaties signed with China by the United States, France, Belgium, and Sweden.

One matter not dealt with was opium. Although the commissioners had raised the issue of opium smuggling during the negotiations, Pottinger had declared that the problem was one for the Chinese themselves to solve. To the commissioners' plea that Britain prohibit the cultivation of the poppy in India, Pottinger had retorted that to do so "would merely throw the market into other hands." The trade continued, therefore, growing at an even faster rate than before.

For the first time, China had been defeated by the West, and the Treaty of Nanjing was the symbol of the Celestial Empire's humiliation. The West, however, was not the only danger to China: The country was also beset by economic chaos and social upheaval. The 100 years since 1741 had seen a massive growth in population—from around 140 million to some 400 million—which far outstripped the increase in agrarian production and created a chronic food shortage. "Not a year passes in which a terrific number of persons do not perish of famine in some part or other of China," wrote a French observer in the 1850s. "Many fall down fainting by the wayside and die before they can reach the place where they had hoped to find help. You see their bodies lying in the fields, and at the roadside, and you pass without taking much notice of them—so familiar is the horrid spectacle."

The peasants gave vent to their desperation through violence, attacking landlords and government officials, and forming numerous secret societies with the aim of spreading rebellion. Popular discontent, fanned by the monarchy's inglorious surrender to the foreign devils, was further inflamed by a series of natural disasters that followed in the wake of the war. Both the Yellow River and the lower Yangtze burst their banks, inundating vast areas and drowning millions of people. At the same time, many provinces were devastated by drought, epidemic, and pests. As China reeled before the onslaught, yet another rebel leader, Hong Xiuquan, hoisted his standard. However, Hong was quite unlike any of the other peasant dissidents, and his followers were to engage the Manchu dynasty in the longest and bloodiest struggle of its existence.

Born in 1814 to a farming family near Canton, Hong had suffered a severe breakdown after repeatedly failing the state examinations that would have set him on the road to advancement. In his delirium, he had seen himself in a vast palace where there appeared an old man with a golden beard. The old man had handed him a sword telling him to use it to kill demons—a task in

Taken back to England as a souvenir in 1803, this extravagantly carved ivory model of a mandarin's river barge ran on wheels powered by clockwork. In past centuries, the Canton workshops where this vessel was made had produced fine lacquerware and ivory objects for a discriminating clientele of wealthy Chinese. During the nineteenth century, however, the workshops' output was increasingly geared to Western tastes, and designers strove to present their foreign customers with stereotyped versions of Eastern exoticism.

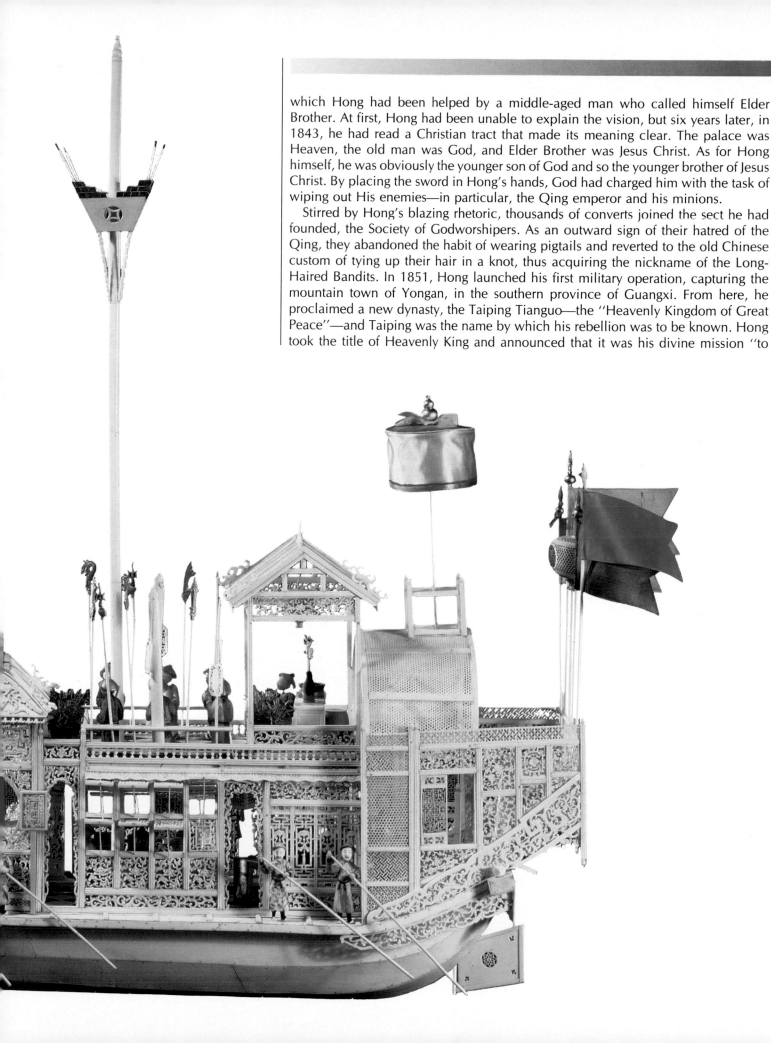

which Hong had been helped by a middle-aged man who called himself Elder Brother. At first, Hong had been unable to explain the vision, but six years later, in 1843, he had read a Christian tract that made its meaning clear. The palace was Heaven, the old man was God, and Elder Brother was Jesus Christ. As for Hong himself, he was obviously the younger son of God and so the younger brother of Jesus Christ. By placing the sword in Hong's hands, God had charged him with the task of wiping out His enemies—in particular, the Qing emperor and his minions.

Stirred by Hong's blazing rhetoric, thousands of converts joined the sect he had founded, the Society of Godworshipers. As an outward sign of their hatred of the Qing, they abandoned the habit of wearing pigtails and reverted to the old Chinese custom of tying up their hair in a knot, thus acquiring the nickname of the Long-Haired Bandits. In 1851, Hong launched his first military operation, capturing the mountain town of Yongan, in the southern province of Guangxi. From here, he proclaimed a new dynasty, the Taiping Tianguo—the "Heavenly Kingdom of Great Peace"—and Taiping was the name by which his rebellion was to be known. Hong took the title of Heavenly King and announced that it was his divine mission "to exterminate all idolaters generally, and to possess the empire as its True Sovereign."

Although Hong's followers were drawn originally from the poorer sections of society, they soon came to include a whole variety of anti-Manchu dissidents—from farmers and businessmen, overwhelmed by spiraling tax demands, to scholars and students, sickened by official corruption and ineptitude. Under the regime imposed by Hong, complete equality was the rule and all goods were considered common property. Alcohol and tobacco were forbidden; prostitution was outlawed; and rape, adultery, and opium smoking were made punishable by death. Also proscribed was the ancient and painful custom of foot-binding for women, who were treated as the equals of men. Women even served in the Taiping army, though no contact of any kind was allowed between them and their male colleagues.

Hong's enclave was both a threat and an insult to the authorities in Beijing. Not only had the rebel leader declared his intention of overthrowing the Qing dynasty; he had also chosen yellow, the imperial color, for his banner. However, government forces were unable to capture the Taiping stronghold, and in 1851, Hong and his 10,000 followers broke out of Yongan into the open country. Gathering recruits as they went, they gradually advanced the 750 miles northward to Nanjing, which they occupied in March of 1853. They celebrated their victory by slaughtering wholesale the Manchu garrison and their families—approximately 25,000 men, women, and children—and then throwing their bodies into the river.

By now the Taipings were 500,000 strong, with a fearsome reputation for battlefield discipline. Troops who showed any inclination to either retreat or desert were immediately killed

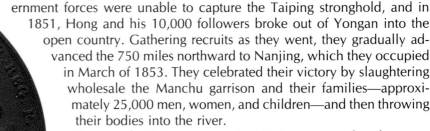

A painting executed in 1860 mirrors the view represented on the Great Seal of Hong Kong *(inset),* struck in 1842 when the island was ceded to Britain. Located near the Pearl estuary, the colony enjoyed rapid growth as a center of commerce. It also won a reputation as an unruly and sometimes dangerous place, whose cosmopolitan population of freebooters paid little heed to the law. As one prelate of the newly completed cathedral complained, residents were exposed to "the cup of the poisoner, the knife of the assassin, and the torch of the midnight incendiary."

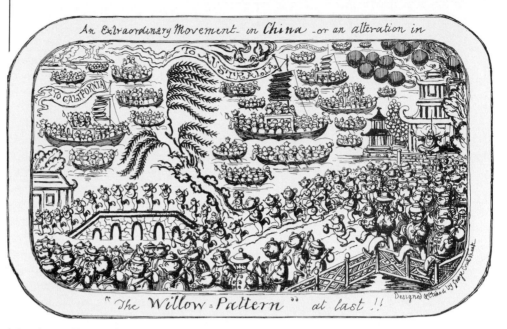

In an 1853 English caricature of China's famous "Willow-Pattern" plate design, Chinese emigrants throng to board boats bound for the gold-rush centers of Australia and California. In reference to China's principal export, the cartoonist has substituted teapots for the heads of the departing citizens. By the middle years of the century, the Chinese were becoming increasingly aware of opportunities outside their borders. Although initially small, the growing number of Chinese emigrants would soon be seen as a threat by nearby European settlements in the Pacific.

by their officers. The imperial forces, on the other hand, were little more than rabble, and it seemed only a matter of time before the Heavenly King entered into his inheritance. "The whole empire is in a ferment of excitement," noted an American missionary in July 1853. "Disaffection to the existing government is spreading rapidly, and signs of it are manifest in the open resistance to the oppressive demands of the mandarins in every direction. . . . The feeling is becoming universally prevalent among the people of all classes that the empire is destined soon to change hands."

It was while the Qing were thus engaged against the Taiping rebels that they found themselves embroiled in a second war with the British. The ink had hardly dried on the Treaty of Nanjing before the mutual recriminations began. On the one hand, the British accused the Chinese of failing to fulfill all their obligations under the treaty; on the other hand, the Chinese accused the British of ignoring the imperial government's ban on the importation of opium. The main cockpit of the dispute was Canton, where violent protest against the foreigners was common. One anonymous manifesto warned the "pigs and dogs" of Britons that "We are definitely going to kill you, cut your heads off, and burn you to death! We must strip off your skins and eat your flesh, then you will know how tough we are."

Such sentiments were encouraged by the imperial commissioner in Canton, Ye Mingchen, a man of ferocious temper who nursed a deep loathing of all foreigners. According to the governor of Hong Kong, Sir John Bowring, he was the "incarnation of ancient Chinese pride, ignorance, and unteachableness," and there appeared to be little doubt that one day his "insufferable conduct" would provide an opportunity for humbling him. The opportunity came in October 1856, when the Canton police seized the Arrow, a Chinese-owned but British-registered ship, and charged its Chinese crew with piracy and smuggling. Although Ye eventually handed back the prisoners, he rejected British demands for an apology. A naval bombardment of Canton having failed to change his mind, British troops were once again dispatched to the area.

This time they were joined by troops from France, which was out to avenge the recent murder of one of its missionaries in Guangdong province. Capturing Canton in December 1857, the French and British went on, the following June, to occupy Dagu, at the mouth of the Hai He. Eighteen years earlier, the arrival of Captain Elliot's expedition so close to Beijing had thrown Emperor Daoguang into a panic. Now his son, Emperor Xianfeng, was seized with similar misgivings, and the treaty signed by his representatives at Tianjin on June 26, 1858, was imposed, in the words of the British plenipotentiary Lord Elgin, "with a pistol at the throat." The treaty provided for the opening of ten more ports to foreign trade, the right of foreign merchants to travel freely in any part of the country, the right of foreign diplomatic missions to live in Beijing, and the payment of a four-million-dollar indemnity. It was also agreed that freedom of missionary activity should be guaranteed by the Chinese and that the trade in smuggled opium should finally be legalized.

The French, the Russians, and the Americans had also extracted favorable treaties from the Chinese at Tianjin, and now they and the British sailed thankfully home, well pleased with what they had accomplished. However, when the British and French returned in June 1859 to make a symbolic entry into Beijing for the ratification of their treaties, they were fired on by imperial troops at Dagu. The allies attempted to overrun the Chinese positions, but they were driven back with heavy losses. Neither government could ignore such a challenge, and in July 1860, another Anglo-French expeditionary force reached the mouth of the Hai He. Again, Dagu was occupied, and again the Qing entered into peace talks. However, far from reaching a settlement, the allied negotiators were taken prisoner, bundled into carts, and jailed as hostages.

Undeterred, the British and French pushed on to the fabulous Yuanming Yuan, the summer palace of the Qing emperors, on the outskirts of Beijing. Behind its walls, they discovered an oasis of peaceful luxury. Herds of deer wandered through more than seventy-five square miles of park; humpbacked marble bridges, ingeniously designed to form complete circles with their reflections below, arched across placid canals; brilliantly tiled pagodas shone above ornamental lakes; goldfish flashed in waters shaded by weeping willows and floating lilies; on embroidered cushions lolled panting lap dogs—brave, grotesque creatures of a kind then unknown to Europeans—that had been specially bred to represent a Chinese heraldic lion; and in some 200 fabulously decorated buildings, thirty of them imperial residences, lay riches beyond all dreams of avarice. Jewels, jade, ceremonial robes, the court treasures, bales of silk, and countless priceless artifacts represented the years of accumulated tribute placed before the Chinese emperors. There were splendid galleries of paintings and irreplaceable libraries. The Summer Palace was the quintessential treasure house of China. No such collection of wealth and beauty had ever existed anywhere else on earth.

Nor would it ever again. At 8:00 p.m., on October 6, 1860, a small party of officers entered the palace. Two hours later they emerged, their pockets bulging with valuables. The looting had begun. For three days, British and French troops rampaged through the palace's marble corridors and glittering apartments, smashing with clubs and rifle butts what they were unable to carry away. All discipline was lost as the men cavorted through this newfound plunderers' paradise. A British observer recorded that in one room "you would see several officers and men of all ranks with their heads and hands brushing and knocking together in the same box. . . . In another, a scramble was going on over a collection of handsome state robes . . . others would be

A pair of flying dragons flank neat Chinese ideograms on a title page from an edition of the Book of Genesis, printed by Christian Taiping rebels. The Taipings, who rose against the Qing dynasty in 1850, presented a religious as well as a military challenge to imperial authority. At one time, 500 followers were occupied in printing Chinese translations of the Bible, which their leader, Hong Xiuquan, intended to make the future textbook for state examinations. However, Western hopes that the revolt would promote Christian virtues in China were soon dashed as the Taipings showed themselves to be both violent and corrupt.

amusing themselves by taking 'cock' shots at chandeliers." Many managed to amass sizable fortunes before order was finally restored. The French general shrewdly set aside for himself the Chinese empress's jewel casket and its contents; while his British counterpart acquired "one of the handsomest pieces of booty"—a solid gold ewer, previously used for pouring rose water over the emperor's hands, which he thought might come in handy as a claret decanter.

Lord Elgin, who had been reappointed the British plenipotentiary, was appalled by such vandalism; but he was even more appalled when, after renewed peace talks, the Chinese returned only nineteen of the thirty-nine allied hostages they had seized. The other twenty, he learned, had been brutally tortured and murdered. To punish the Qing for their perfidy, he ordered that the recently plundered Summer Palace be burned down—"to mark, by a solemn act of retribution, the horror and indignation with which we were inspired by the perpetration of a great crime." Although the French objected, Elgin remained adamant, and on October 18, the Summer Palace, the symbol of imperial China's magnificence, went up in flames. In one outbuilding, the busy arsonists discovered a pair of mint-condition English riding carriages, an unused double-barreled shotgun, and two spotless artillery pieces bearing the London stamp "Woolwich 1782." Emperor Qianlong had, indeed, had no use for Lord Macartney's gifts.

The torching of the Summer Palace ended all resistance. After this blow to China's self-esteem, the signing of a new agreement presented no problem. Lord Elgin, carried in a large sedan chair by eight scarlet-clad Chinese porters—a privilege normally reserved for the emperor—made his triumphal entry into Beijing on October 24. And later that day, in the Hall of Ceremonies, having been humiliatingly forced to wait for two and a half hours, the emperor's representatives confirmed the Treaty of Tianjin. They also bowed to all of Elgin's other demands: the adding of Tianjin to the list of ports to be opened to foreign trade; the ceding of Kowloon to Britain; and the increase of the indemnities to $16 million. The French repeated the same scene on the following day. Emperor Xianfeng, who had fled in shame to Jehol, died just ten months later without ever returning to his capital.

The Second Opium War may have ended, but China's troubles continued. In the northeast, the Russians, through a mixture of guile and force, had wrested away immense tracts of territory adjoining the Amur and Ussuri rivers; along the western frontier, millions of the empire's Muslim subjects were in revolt; in the eastern plains, another formidable uprising had cut communications and claimed millions of lives; and in the south and the center of the country, the Taiping rebels, in spite of bloody dissension within their own ranks, continued their campaign to overthrow the Qing dynasty. But help for the Manchus against the Taipings was now to come from the opponents they had just been fighting—the Western barbarians.

At first, the West had been inclined to favor the avowedly pro-Christian Taipings, and one British official returned from a visit to the rebel capital of Nanjing convinced that "more political and commercial advantages were likely to be obtained from the insurrectionists than . . . from the imperialists.'' The Taipings, however, had long lost their earlier idealism. Venomous rivalry among the Taiping leaders—all elevated to the rank of king, the increasing despotism of the Heavenly King himself, and the propensity of the rebels to massacre the population of any town that offered resistance, soon led the Europeans to revise their opinion. As the British representative in Beijing later observed, there was little hope of ''any good ever coming of the rebel movement. They do nothing but burn, murder, and destroy.''

Now, in the wake of the Second Opium War, the Europeans wanted to protect the concessions they had won—and this meant supporting the Manchus against the Taipings. Arms and money were funneled to the imperial forces, and a contingent of

Flying large red standards, the massed troops of the imperial army lay siege to a flooded Taiping stronghold in a battle scene commissioned by the Qing court. The Taiping forces advanced to within seventy miles of Beijing before the imperial army forced them to retreat. It was only with the help of European troops, however, that the rebel movement was finally crushed in 1864.

Western mercenaries was formed. Strengthened with Chinese soldiers and commanded by a young British officer of exceptional ability, Major Charles George Gordon, this so-called Ever-Victorious Army fought successfully until its disbandment in 1864, by which time the Taipings had been driven back into Nanjing.

On July 19, after a six-week siege, imperial troops managed to break through the walls of the Heavenly Capital, burning and sacking the city. The Heavenly King, according to one report, took his own life in characteristically grand manner by swallowing a lethal quantity of gold leaf. He was buried in the grounds of the splendid palace he had built for himself, and several of his concubines hanged themselves in the trees above his grave. The other inhabitants of Nanjing—around 100,000 men, women, and children—also died, either at their own hands or at those of their conquerers. After thirteen years, and at a total cost of more than 20 million dead, the revolt of the Taipings was finally over.

But the reign of the Qing dynasty was equally doomed. The last fifty years had been a period of unmitigated disaster for imperial China. The nation had proved itself utterly incapable of withstanding the might of the industrial West. And the added humiliation of asking their new foes to assist in quelling the Taiping rebellion had cost the Chinese dear. In return for defeating the rebels, the British had insisted that the opium trade be legalized.

For all its vaunted past achievements, the Middle Kingdom was now firmly controlled by foreign interests. By 1880, the number of chests of opium entering the country each year had reached 150,000. In the same year, the Chinese bought some 448 million yards of British cotton. Throughout the country, French missionaries were proselytizing their foreign faith. Western legations were installed in Beijing, the very heart of China. "Barbarian" architecture was beginning to sprout along the Shanghai waterfront. And to despairing Chinese traditionalists, the area around the Pearl River estuary seemed frankly to be a lost cause.

A few forward-looking individuals saw that the only way to compete in this new society that had suddenly overtaken them was to imitate the ways of the Western world. To the orthodox majority, however, that road could only lead to disaster. One imperial tutor claimed that "If talented scholars have to change from their regular course of study to follow the barbarians . . . it will drive the multitude of the Chinese people into allegiance to the barbarians. . . . Should we further spread their influence and fan the flames?"

In subsequent years, there were a few halfhearted attempts at reform. But these were cut short by the ruthless and reactionary Empress Dowager Cixi, who remained the real power behind the Celestial Throne until her death in 1909. Under Cixi's iron rule, the regime tottered along much as before—too weak to withstand the foreigners, and too autocratic to heed its own people. It was forced to yield up ever more trading concessions within China. It lost great tracts of formerly dependent territories: Burma and, on a ninety-nine-year lease, mainland territory off Hong Kong went to the British; Vietnam to the French; Taiwan (Formosa), Korea, and the Ryukyu islands, including Okinawa, to the Japanese. Inevitably, resentment, xenophobia, and popular disgust at the Qing increased.

The Chinese had lost their place in the world. Not until 1911, when the Qing dynasty was finally overthrown by the nationalist leader Sun Yat-sen, would China's frustrated populace finally set out to regain its self-respect.

THE QUEST FOR KNOWLEDGE

For centuries past, Europeans had sallied forth—driven by dreams of discovery or conquest—to explore the globe of which they knew so little. But by the dawn of the nineteenth century, a new breed of voyager had emerged: adventurer-scientists whose main goal was the accretion of knowledge. Setting out to record their journeys in words and pictures, they reported geographical data, described the customs of indigenous peoples, and classified new plants and animals.

There was plenty for them to do, for at the beginning of the century, many blanks still remained on the world map. The interior of Africa was largely unknown, while inland Australia and Antarctica were a complete mystery. Despite early European colonization of the Americas, knowledge of the southern continent remained sketchy; and a practical overland route across North America had yet to be discovered. The explorers of the early industrial age began to systematically refine the rough constructs of world cartography.

Unlike their predecessors, travelers in the nineteenth century were often spon-sored in their endeavors by privately fund-ed learned societies rather than by govern-ments. The Africa Association, for example, was established in London in 1788 to pro-mote "the discovery of the interior parts of Africa." Others dug into their own pockets: The German aristocrat Baron Alexander von Humboldt spent a third of his capital on a fact-finding mission to South America.

The cost of knowledge was counted as much in suffering as in money. Tropical dis-eases, hostile tribes, and extremes of cli-mate took a heavy toll. Scurvy was painful-ly commonplace, and starvation was an ever-present threat: British naval officer Sir John Franklin became known as the "man who ate his boots" because of the priva-tions he endured in the frozen Arctic.

Nevertheless, the reports of these early travelers—whether describing disappoint-ment or triumph—were to initiate a lasting trend of scientific exploration. And some, inadvertently, would also show the way for later colonialists, whose interests lay more in economic exploitation than in the ad-vancement of knowledge.

Surrounded by specimens
and scientific instruments,
the German naturalist Al-
exander von Humboldt
(*seated*) and the French
botanist Aimé Bonpland
are pictured in their jungle
hut amid the lush forests
along the Orinoco. During
their five-year exploration
of South America, the two
men made many findings
in subjects ranging from
medicine to vulcanology.

AFRICAN ODYSSEYS

Long familiar to Muslim traders from North Africa, the secrets of the Sahara and the territory that lay beyond—in particular the Niger River and the fabled city of Tombouctou—attracted explorers from Europe like a magnet.

The lure of the Niger was scientific: Not only was its 2,500-mile course uncharted but even the direction of its flow remained a mystery. In 1796, the Scottish explorer Mungo Park caught his first glimpse of the river, "flowing slowly to the eastward," but nine years later, Park and his party were wiped out trying to follow its course to the sea—a task that was achieved only in 1830 by the Englishman Richard Lander.

Tombouctou exerted a different kind of fascination, for it was rumored to be a glittering oasis of wealth and culture. In 1828, the French explorer René Caillié became the first white man to return alive from the city—only to report that it was "nothing but a mass of ill-looking houses, built of earth."

In an engraving from his book *Travels in the Interior Districts of Africa*, Mungo Park watches Gambian Africans operating a smelting furnace.

Hidden in a litter covered with rugs and ostrich plumes, a Saharan bride is conveyed to her husband. The illustration is taken from a book by Captain George Lyon, the sole survivor of an 1818 expedition to the Sahara.

Seated under a sunshade in the stern of a boat, Richard Lander and his brother travel down the Niger to meet a local ruler, as illustrated in a book published by another member of the party. A humble servant on an earlier expedition, Lander journeyed successfully to the river's mouth in the Gulf of Guinea three years after his master's death.

SAHARA

Tripoli•

Tombouctou•

Niger River

Lake Chad

Gulf of Guinea

Explorers Dixon Denham, Walter Oudeney, and Hugh Clapperton met these musicians on a trans-Saharan journey. Starting from Tripoli, the Britons were the first Europeans to reach Lake Chad.

The modest town of Tombouctou is depicted in Caillié's journal, published in 1830. To avoid the hostile attentions of Tuareg horsemen, Caillié posed as a Muslim, hiding his notes in a copy of the Koran.

An oasis sketched by Hugh Clapperton was one of the few places where he and his two companions could refresh themselves on their crossing of the Sahara. Shortly after reaching this spot, rivalry between the team members grew so intense that they separated: Clapperton, on his own, eventually reached Sokoto, on the upper reaches of the Niger.

SURVEYS IN SOUTH AMERICA

During the nineteenth century, South America came under the spotlight of scientific inquiry through the work of Alexander von Humboldt and Charles Darwin.

Between 1799 and 1804, Humboldt and his partner Aimé Bonpland traveled more than 3,700 miles through rain forest and mountain range, collecting some 12,000 specimens, many of them new to science. Humboldt's geographical findings were equally significant; among other achievements, he discovered the cold Pacific current that bears his name and established the magnetic equator.

For Darwin, South America was a fount of ideas. His theory of evolution by natural selection was not published until 1859, but much of his evidence was collected in 1832 in Patagonia, where he discovered fossil mammals similar to living species, and three years later on the Galápagos Islands, where he found related species that had adapted differently to the separate conditions on each island.

Four species of Galápagos Islands finch, each with a beak adapted to a different food source, appear in Charles Darwin's *Journal of Researches*.

1. *Geospiza magnirostris.*
3. *Geospiza parvula.*
2. *Geospiza fortis.*
4. *Certhidea olivacea.*

FINCHES FROM GALÁPAGOS ARCHIPELAGO.

Orinoco River

MOUNT CHIMBORAZO

A N D E S

Galápagos Islands

PATAGONIA

Tierra del Fuego —

A watercolor shows Darwin's vessel, the *Beagle*, being greeted by a boatload of locals off the southern island of Tierra del Fuego. The *Beagle* carried three native Fuegians whom its commander, Robert Fitzroy, had taken to be "civilized" in England on an earlier trip in 1828. Duly returned to their compatriots, they soon reverted to their traditional lifestyle.

Humboldt's rough sketch of his pet black-headed cacajao monkey (*far left*) served as a model for a polished illustration (*left*) in a book describing the expedition's findings.

In a scene from Humboldt's book *Vue des Cordilliers*, a figure—possibly the author—picks plants at the base of Mount Chimborazo, in the Peruvian Andes. On June 23, 1802, Humboldt and Bonpland made a historic ascent of the volcanic peak, reaching a measured height of nearly 19,700 feet—the highest recorded altitude ever attained by humans up to that time.

AUSTRALIAN ADVENTURES

At the dawn of the nineteenth century, the continent of Australia was just a vague outline on the map, but in 1801, the British Admiralty sponsored Commander Matthew Flinders to survey its entire coastline. In the course of his successful circumnavigation, he discovered many natural harbors, which were soon settled.

The new colonies at first remained marooned amid huge tracts of unexplored country. But in 1813, the land-hungry settlers of Port Jackson (modern Sydney) breached the barrier of the Blue Mountains, thus opening a route into the uncharted interior. In the late 1820s, a young army officer, Captain Charles Sturt, ventured deeper still, tracing the course of the Murray-Darling river systems for more than 600 miles. A subsequent expedition in 1844 in search of an imaginary inland sea proved less successful; Sturt found little but a desert that now bears his name.

Painted in 1816, three years after the first crossing of the Blue Mountains, this view shows the eucalyptus-covered hills that had blocked further exploration inland for twenty-five years after Australia was settled.

Examples of Australia's unique fauna disport themselves on the shores of Kangaroo Island, off the south coast of Australia. Discovered by Flinders, the island was illustrated in his 1814 book.

Aborigines are shown spearing fish in a painting by Joseph Lycett, a convict transported to Australia for forgery. Lycett's pictures of the new land were so popular that he was granted a full pardon.

Paintings such as this study of koalas by the English zoologist John Gould introduced Europeans to Australia's unique marsupial wildlife.

BLUE
MOUNTAINS

STURT
DESERT   Murray

Darling   • Port Jackson

Kangaroo Island

The frontispiece of Sturt's published account of his 1844 expedition shows team members taking bearings in featureless sand hills near the salt marshes of Lake Torrens. Several hundred miles farther north, the party was marooned by drought for six months at a camp called Depot Creek, where temperatures in excess of 120° F. caused thermometers to burst.

A TRANSCONTINENTAL TRIP

When Meriwether Lewis and William Clark left Saint Louis with an expedition of forty-three in May 1804, they carried with them a commission from the third president of the United States, Thomas Jefferson, "to explore the Missouri River" and find "the most direct and practicable water communication across the continent, for the purposes of commerce."

After traveling northward up the Missouri, mostly by boat, they wintered in North Dakota, then moved on, making a portage of the Great Falls, before crossing the Rocky Mountains on foot and on horses they had bartered from local Indians. After voyaging down the Snake and Columbia river systems, the expedition reached the Pacific in November 1805. Retracing their steps, they divided on the way home for Clark to explore one of the Missouri's tributaries, the Yellowstone.

It was a singularly successful mission. Lewis and Clark collected valuable information about tremendously large tracts of previously unknown territory, established good relations with a number of Indian tribes, and demonstrated the viability of a commercial route to the West.

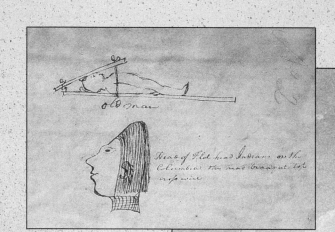

Clark's journal depicts Flathead Indians, who for beauty's sake, distorted their heads. They did this by tying a piece of wood to a newborn infant's skull for a year.

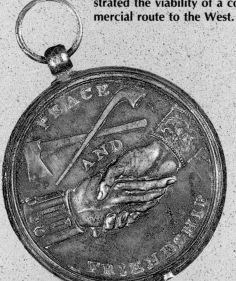

This silver medal was one of many gifts carried by the Lewis and Clark expedition to establish friendly relations between Indian tribes and the United States government.

A woodcut executed by the expedition's carpenter shows a member of the team escaping a grizzly bear. "I had rather fight two Indians than one bear," wrote Lewis.

This buffalo was painted by the artist George Catlin, who retraced Lewis and Clark's journey in 1830. The explorers saw buffalo in huge numbers on the Great Plains, where the Indians hunted them by tactics such as stampeding herds over cliffs.

Painted by Karl Bodmer, another of the artists to follow in the expedition's footsteps, this Indian village was the site of Lewis and Clark's winter camp in North Dakota. The boats, used for short journeys on the Missouri, were made of basketwork and covered by buffalo skins.

ORDEALS IN THE ARCTIC

Melville Island

Boothia Peninsula

Baffin Bay

Beaufort Sea

Bering Strait

King William Island

Hudson Bay

After the Napoleonic Wars, the prestige branch of Britain's Royal Navy became the one that was involved in the dangerous task of exploring the Arctic—a region that was claimed by the British but was largely unknown territory. Chief among the Admiralty's goals was to find the Northwest Passage—a seaway linking the Atlantic and Pacific oceans.

With a government prize of £20,000 for the first ship to chart the route, competition was keen. In 1820, Sir William Parry received £5,000 for reaching Melville Island, more than halfway through the passage. Nine years later, Captain John Ross survived a record-breaking four winters at the Boothia Peninsula—but, forced to abandon his icebound ship and retreat overland, he never penetrated as far as Parry. And between 1847 and 1848, tantalizingly close to victory, veteran explorer Sir John Franklin and his crew of 129 perished after two icebound winters off King William Island.

Over the next twelve years, the numerous rescue parties sent after Franklin filled more gaps in the Arctic map. It was not until 1906, however, that the passage was successfully navigated.

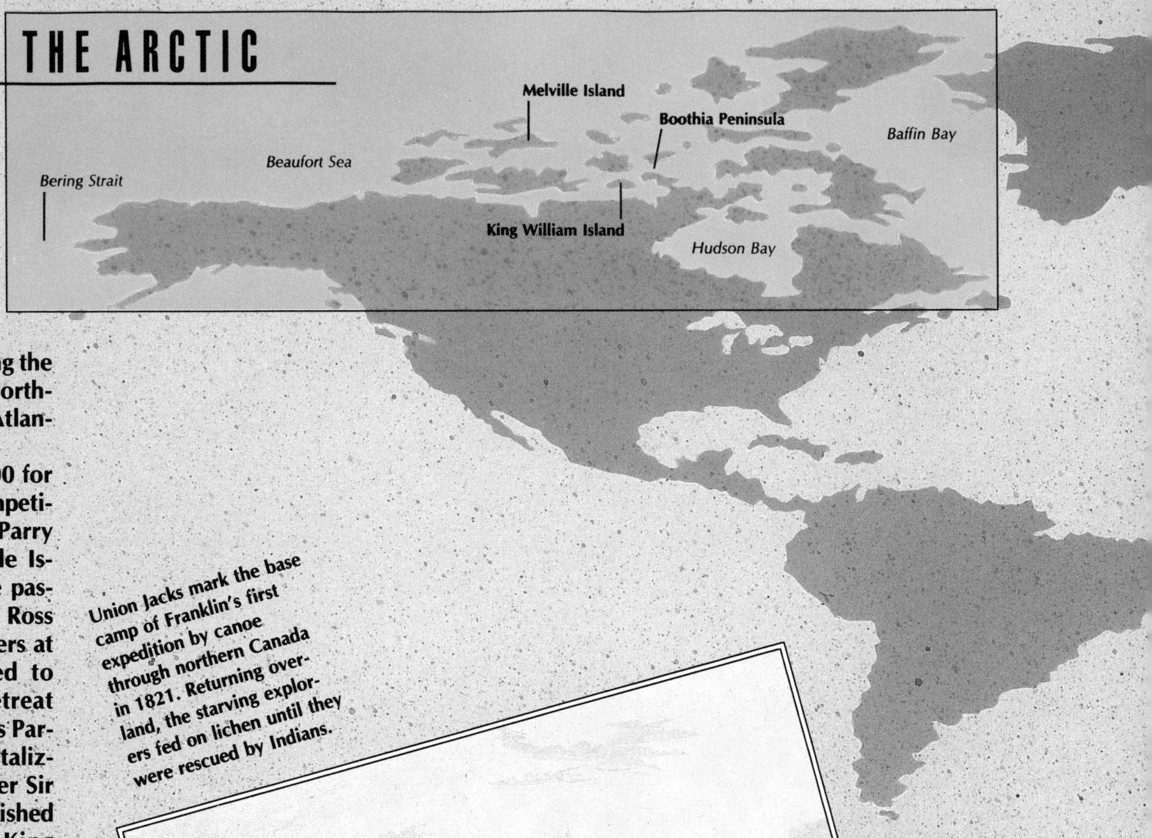

Union Jacks mark the base camp of Franklin's first expedition by canoe through northern Canada in 1821. Returning overland, the starving explorers fed on lichen until they were rescued by Indians.

Battened down for winter, their upper decks roofed with canvas, Parry's ships *Hecla* and *Griper* lie fast in the ice off Melville Island. To keep his men amused during the months of frigid darkness, Parry organized plays and started a ship's newspaper.

As illustrated in Ross's notebook, an Eskimo victim of a polar-bear attack sports a wooden leg fitted in 1829 by the carpenter of Ross's ship Victory.

A picture by Ross portrays a scene in the captain's cabin on the Victory, as Eskimos draw a map to demonstrate that his 1829 expedition has reached a dead end.

Ross's notebook depicts the first encounter between Eskimos and the Victory's company. Friendly relations were later established, and visits from the native hunters enlivened the crew's four-year sojourn trapped in the ice. With dogs borrowed from the Eskimos, a party led by Ross's nephew sledged overland to successfully locate the site of the magnetic North Pole.

5

On September 18, 1828, an Englishman named Nathaniel Isaacs left the African settlement of kwaDukuza for Port Natal, on the southeastern coast of Africa. His mission: to secure a bottle of Rowland's Macassar Oil, England's premier hair dressing, to darken the greying locks of Shaka, leader of the powerful Zulu nation. For this lotion—a compound of oil of origanum and olive oil—Shaka offered not only a herd of cattle and as much ivory as he could muster but also his scrawled signature on a deed granting about 2,500 square miles of territory to Isaacs himself.

In Britain, under English law, this document would have entailed freehold possession to a huge tract of land, making Isaacs one of the wealthiest men in the realm. But this was Africa. To the Zulu king it merely signified the right to use a small portion of his vast domain. It was a grant that implied fealty to Shaka and that would expire on the death of one of the signatories. Besides, unbeknown to Isaacs, Shaka had already granted the same piece of land to two other Europeans.

Shaka did not live to test the powers of Rowland's famous oil; his reign ended in assassination before the month was out, and Isaacs left the region three years later having failed to secure his promised territory. But the encounter was typical of the clash of cultures that echoed tragically throughout southern Africa during the first half of the nineteenth century. Ignorant and contemptuous of African laws and customs, Dutch and English colonists—themselves at loggerheads—pushed northward and eastward into the unknown continent. By the middle of the century, they had carved out substantial areas of southern Africa, including the richest grazing and agricultural lands, as their own exclusive territory. Along the way, they overran African peoples whose prior claim to the country was swept aside by the might of firearms and the weighty edifice of European legislation. The white man's path to conquest was strewn with misunderstandings, broken treaties, and ill-informed philanthropy; his ideology was an incompatible mixture of racism, rapacity, and genuine good intentions; his legacy was a land suffused with enmity, division, and bitter resentment.

The country molded by the events of the early nineteenth century is now the modern Republic of South Africa. At its heart lay the highveld, a great ocean of grass, broken only by an occasional tree or the flat-topped hillocks known as kopjes. Watered by the Orange River, which, swollen by its tributary the Vaal, meandered westward for almost 1,250 miles to the Atlantic, the highveld was home to immense herds of game—springbok, blesbok, wildebeest, zebra, quagga, and hartebeest—that roamed freely before the coming of men with firearms. Bellying around this abundant plateau was an escarpment of mountains, rising in the east—at heights of 10,000 feet—to the precipitous Drakensberg range. Below these jagged peaks lay Africa's southern boundary with the Indian Ocean, a narrow, semitropical strip that dropped down

The pelts and plumage of Africa's exotic wildlife bedeck the warlike figure of Utimuni, nephew of Zulu king Shaka, in this colored lithograph by a European artist. Part of an ancient and complex civilization, the Bantu-speaking Zulu were just one of many black peoples encountered by white settlers as they spread throughout southern Africa during the first half of the nineteenth century. Incomprehension between the black and white cultures was at first mutual, but by 1850, enslaved and dispossessed, most Africans understood only too well the motives that drove the white man.

First established at the Cape of Good Hope in 1642, Dutch settlers had steadily fanned out into adjoining regions of southern Africa, appropriating the land and cattle of the indigenous San and Khoikhoi peoples. By 1806, however, their eastward progress was blocked at the Great Fish River by the powerful Xhosa nation. In that year, Britain assumed control of the Dutch colony and fresh impetus was given to white expansion. In 1835, much of the Xhosa territory was annexed as British Kaffraria; and in 1843, Britain assumed control over Natal, once part of the Zulu kingdom. A dozen years later, white rule in southern Africa would comprise not only British possessions *(shaded green)* but also the independent republics of Transvaal and the Orange Free State *(shaded yellow)*, founded by Dutch-speaking migrants in 1852 and 1854 respectively.

from the present-day province of Natal to meet the continent's temperate tip around the Cape of Good Hope.

It was an ancient land. Some of its mountains were cold even before the earth's shifting crust had thrust up the Alps or the Himalayas. But its very existence was entirely unknown to Europeans until 1488, when a Portuguese seafarer named Bartolomeu Dias rounded the continent searching for a route to India. When the fabulous wealth of the East Indies was revealed early in the following century, a steady procession of ships began to ply Dias's route through the stormy waters of the southern hemisphere. By the dawn of the nineteenth century, however, Europeans were still mostly ignorant of what lay behind the surf-flecked coastlines visible from their ships. The Portuguese had established themselves as early as 1507 on the east coast at Mozambique and Delagoa Bay, site of the modern city of Maputo. But these steamy, disease-ridden outposts did little to excite expansionist urges, offering only slaves and a trickle of gold and ivory from the interior.

Still less was known of the lands a little to the south. Here, the dangerous shoreline lured countless ships to their doom. By the mid-seventeenth century, some 3,000 souls had been stranded on the coast, of whom barely 500 had struggled to the safety of Delagoa Bay. The survivors' stories excited some interest among traders, however, and in the eighteenth century, a number of ships touched at a small, oval bay near the mouth of the Mgeni River. Its inhabitants called the spot *iTeki*, "One Testicle,"

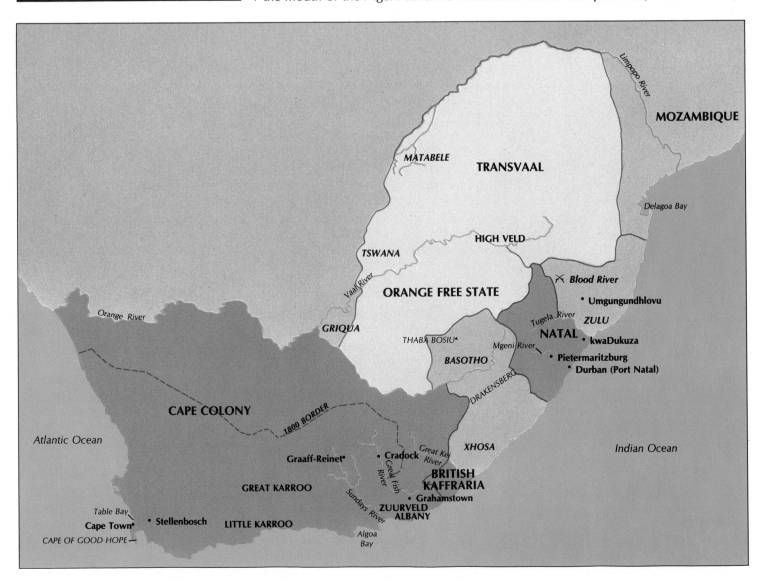

because of its shape. The Europeans knew it as Port Natal, from the name the Portuguese navigator Vasco da Gama had given the surrounding region after first sighting it on Christmas of 1497. There they exchanged trinkets in return for ivory and slaves, but few stayed to settle. One caller to the bay in 1718 noted the presence of "a penitent Pirate, who sequestered himself from his abominable Community and retired out of Harm's Way." And in 1790, a search party looking for shipwrecked mariners found a community whose 400 inhabitants of mixed blood were descended from three white women, survivors of an earlier wreck. But apart from such instances, the region saw little prolonged contact between Europeans and Africans.

But farther south at the tip of the continent, the situation was very different. In 1652, three ships from Holland had cast anchor in Table Bay, just north of the Cape. On board were employees of the Dutch East India Company, commissioned to build a fortified settlement providing water, fresh meat, fruit, and vegetables for Dutch merchants making the six-month run to the East Indies. It was a pleasant spot, sunny most of the year, overlooked by the steep-sided Table Mountain, upon which a layer of cloud cover testified—even on an otherwise clear day—to the fresh sea winds that cleansed the atmosphere. It was also isolated: A few hours' journey brought one to the tip of the world, where the cold waters of the Atlantic met the warm currents of the Indian Ocean in a confluence stretching out toward the Antarctic.

The company had at first no intention of founding a colony at De Kaap—"The Cape"—as the tiny outpost was known. Its aim was simply to provide a service for passing merchantmen. Within a few years, however, the settlement was expanding. To maintain a supply of fresh meat and vegetables, the company was forced to allow a few employees to become independent farmers, or Boers, outside the immediate confines of De Kaap. These pioneers were still very restricted as to how and where they could sell their provisions, and to escape the company's irksome regulations, some began to drift northward and eastward away from the settlement.

Seminomadic cattlemen possessed of a Calvinistic religion and a fierce sense of independence, these *trekboers* soon turned their backs on the restrictive controls of the Dutch East India Company. Always on the fringes of European settlement, they harnessed their oxen—often sixteen or more to a wagon—whenever the laws and taxes of civilization threatened to catch up with them. Some crawled northward through steep mountain passes to the Karroo, first of the great, semiarid plateaus stepping up to the highveld. Others pushed east along the coast, altering their course where crags or formidable river crossings obstructed their route. So long as there was fresh water, pasture for their cattle, and the prospect of unhindered journeys ahead, the trekboers enjoyed what they called the *lekker lewe,* the "sweet life."

Their needs were simple: a big iron cooking pot, a wooden chest, a bed with buffalo thongs supporting a woolen or feather mattress, perhaps a few chairs. Whole families could live in a three-room "hartebeest hut" of mud and reeds, or they could shelter in their wagons. They did without wine, bread, or beer, although there was generally room in the wagon for a cask or two of spirits. Meat, milk, and sometimes honey were the staples of their diet. Game abounded wherever the trekboer traveled, and he was a practiced marksman, who could load and fire his rifle at the gallop.

Religion was central to this scattered community. The stern God of the Old Testament, who led his chosen people out of Egypt, seemed particularly close to the trekboers' fugitive, often dangerous lives. Yet frontier families might go for weeks without so much as seeing a church. As often as not, the wagon was their place of worship, although families would travel many miles to reach a *predikant,* or minister, for such important events as christenings. While back in civilization, they would take the opportunity to trade their own produce—sheep and cattle, hides, soap, beeswax, and ivory—for essentials they could not manufacture: gunpowder, cloth, or iron farming implements. And few would return without brandy, coffee, and tobacco—prime luxuries of the frontier.

In the wake of the trekboers, the heavy hand of company administration stretched out over the settled areas. The Cape authorities charged a small annual fee for the "loan" of land within its territory, but collecting rent from the far-flung farmers was an administrative nightmare. If demands for payment were pressed, they could easily—and did frequently—move off in search of new pastures. Accordingly, the frontier was in a constant state of expansion, as the trekboers fanned out to escape the restrictions of company policy. And if there was one thing greater than the trekboer's desire for independence, it was his appetite for land. When a man finally found a place that tempted him to build a permanent farm, he would measure the extent of his territory by riding his horse at walking pace for half an hour toward all four points of the compass in turn. This ensured him an area of about ten square miles. He might, of course, need a second farm of equal size for summer grazing, and his sons would require farms of their own when their turn came to establish homesteads. Land was essentially for the taking. And to speed their conquest, or defend their gains, settlers joined together in *kommandos*—mounted bands equipped with firearms and sustained on long forays by strips of biltong, or dried meat.

Against these kommandos, the original occupants of the land could do little. One group were the Khoikhoi. "Men of men," they called themselves, although the Dutch referred to them as Hottentots, in imitation of their clicking speech, "a sudden retraction or clacking of the tongue, not unlike the noise of a hen in a farmyard." Fine boned and pale skinned—the color "of a faded leaf," according to one traveler—with high cheekbones, pointed chins, and widely spaced eyes set beneath tight, peppercorn curls, they were a pastoral people. Since ancient times they had kept sheep, but cattle were their principal wealth, providing milk, meat, transport, and even, when stampeded before Khoikhoi warriors, a military weapon.

Closely related to the Khoikhoi were the San, scattered among the hills to the north of De Kaap. Nomadic hunter-gatherers, the San stalked their prey with poisoned arrows, supplementing the meat with roots, berries, honey, caterpillars, and the larvae of termites and locusts. They were an artistic people, decorating ostrich eggs or the walls of their caves with representations of animals and hunts. And at night, they could dance for hours, often in imitation of the animals they had spent the day pursuing. They too spoke with the clicking speech characteristic of the Khoikhoi, and they were similarly slight in build, but because of their elusive habits and impermanent dwellings, the Dutch knew them as *bosjesmans,* or Bushmen.

Official policy was to trade fairly with the Africans, but the Boers often succumbed to the temptation to take advantage of these relatively defenseless people. Armed with lightweight throwing spears, or assegais, they were no match for a determined kommando. And when the Khoikhoi refused to sell their cows and oxen, impatient Boers used threats, took hostages, or resorted to theft. Just as often, however, the Khoikhoi succumbed to the allure of tobacco, brass wire, beads, and low-grade local brandy in payment for their cattle. Periodic government efforts to prohibit trade between Boers and Africans were flagrantly ignored. Stripped of their cattle, the Khoikhoi became impoverished and demoralized. Some slipped into a life of vagrancy and theft on the fringes of white settlement; a lucky few escaped with their stock into the hinterlands. But many more took low-paid work as laborers on white farms, effectively enslaved by a hated law requiring them to hold passes—only reluctantly issued by their masters—authorizing them to be absent from their place of work.

Any pretense the Khoikhoi had of an independent coexistence with the whites was shattered in 1713, when a load of infected ship's laundry triggered a devastating epidemic of smallpox. All of Cape society was struck, but the Khoikhoi were the worst affected. ''The Hottentots died in the hundreds,'' wrote a clergyman who witnessed the disaster. ''They lay everywhere on the roads, cursing the Dutchmen, who they said had bewitched them.''

The San, who did not keep cattle, were at first regarded as little more than a nuisance. But when they took to killing stock, the Dutchmen turned on their diminutive enemy with a vengeance. They hunted down the San like vermin, often using Khoikhoi trackers to speed up their work. Many were exterminated; a few survived by retreating northward into the arid Kalahari Desert, where they alone could eke out a subsistence; and wagonloads of San children were ''apprenticed'' as slaves.

From the earliest days, slavery had been well established in De Kaap and the longer-settled western regions, and by the nineteenth century, bondmen far outnumbered the white population. East African slaves provided agricultural labor, and Malays from the Dutch East Indies brought valuable building skills and the Islamic faith. Slaves also provided a sexual outlet for the largely masculine population of De Kaap in the early years of the settlement. The hour from 8:00 to 9:00 p.m. was open house at the company's notorious slave lodge. The result was a rapidly expanding population of mixed parentage. Some of this group were maintained as slaves and household servants; many merged imperceptibly with the white population; others

A patriotic engraving depicts British warships arriving in Table Bay on January 8, 1806, to seize the strategically vital Cape settlement from French-dominated Holland. Commanding the sea route to Britain's Indian possessions, Cape Town—as the British named the port—was one of the nation's chief prizes of the Napoleonic wars. The expeditionary force met little resistance: The town's population of 16,500—10,000 of whom were slaves—was barely double the number of troops sent to capture it. Intended mainly as a supply station, Cape Town had little wealth or comfort to recommend it to its new owners. Later, however, when peace had been restored to Europe, the British paid £6 million to the Dutch in compensation for their lost territory.

Pursued by white farmers, San warriors escape into the mountains after a successful cattle raid, as depicted in a watercolor of 1836. Ill-defined official frontiers meant little either to European settlers or to Africans: Neither recognized the territory or property claims of the other, and cattle rustling was a constant activity.

escaped northward, along with other outcasts, to form their own communities. Some of these migrants settled at the confluence of the Orange and Vaal rivers where, along with mixed-race Khoikhoi, they formed a powerful state temporarily beyond the law of the European colony. *Bastaards,* the members of this band called themselves, until one shocked clergyman persuaded them to accept the appellation of Griquas—on the presumption that most were descended from a family of that name.

By 1800, the Cape settlement was beginning to assume a nebulous identity of its own. At the end of the seventeenth century, an influx of Huguenots, Protestant victims of religious persecution in their native France, had enriched both Cape society and, by their establishment of vineyards, the Cape economy. Apart from the French, however, and a number of Germans who were among the company's early employees, there had been little immigration from Europe. As a result of their isolation from the Old World, the Boers began to develop a distinctive culture, with their own Dutch Reformed Calvinist church, their own hybrid Dutch dialect, to which slaves and

Khoikhoi made their contributions, and a bloodline that showed distinct traces of intermarriage with indigenous races. In his blue shirt, sheepskin trousers, and wide-brimmed straw hat, with a prophetlike beard and a pipe clamped permanently in his mouth, the frontier Boer seemed to travelers to belong to a race apart. One British visitor dismissed him as "unwilling to work and unable to think; with a mind disengaged from every sort of care and reflection." But more charitable travelers found the Boer courageous, independent, and unfailingly hospitable.

De Kaap was still, however, largely dependent on maritime trade, and its economy did not prosper consistently. On occasions the wheat crop failed completely, forcing the colony to survive on imports of rice from the East Indies. With one or two exceptions, De Kaap's vineyards produced wines that were scorned by the connoisseurs of Europe. Cattle were periodically subject to pests and diseases. Attempts to cultivate indigo, silk, cotton, coconuts, sugar, rice, olives, and several other products failed. Repeated efforts to breed sheep came to nothing. Periods of glut alternated with times of shortage. The demand for Cape produce varied with the number of ships putting in for provisions at Table Bay, and this fluctuated depending on the world's political situation. With an uncertain market and all the best agricultural land near De Kaap under cultivation, it was no wonder that many settlers turned to a self-sufficient life on the poorer, emptier lands of the colony's frontiers.

By 1800, however, the lekker lewe was becoming increasingly difficult to find. Barring Boer expansion, 500 miles east of the Cape on the Great Fish River were the Xhosa, a powerful and prosperous group of black Africans. The Xhosa were a Bantu-speaking people whose ancestors had drifted south out of central Africa many centuries earlier. One strand of this migration was already well established on the highveld by the eleventh century. Another, to which the Xhosa belonged, was pushing southward along the coast of Natal three or four centuries before the Portuguese rounded the Cape. Muslim traders had encountered these people on the east coast of Africa and had called them Kaffirs, or infidels, a name that was adopted by settlers in southern Africa.

In both appearance and social organization this race was strikingly different from the Khoikhoi and the San. "Tall, muscular, and robust," said the enthusiastic English traveler William Burchell of their men: "Good nature and intelligence are depicted in their features." Of the women he conceded, "Though of a color nearly approaching to black, their well-constructed features, their beautifully clean teeth, and their eyes dark and sparkling combine to render many comparatively handsome."

While an African servant fans flies away from the food, a frontier family of Boers, or Dutch settlers, listens to the local preacher reading from the *Zuid Afrikaan* journal in this watercolor of the mid-nineteenth century. Life for the isolated Boer farmers was never comfortable: Many farmhouses consisted merely of mud walls covered with a reed thatch, and even in more ambitious dwellings the floors were normally of clay treated with cow dung. In these scattered, largely self-sufficient homesteads, preachers played a crucial role in passing on news of the outside world and providing children with the rudiments of an education.

The Xhosa nation consisted of several chiefdoms, each comprising a number of loosely related clans. Their well-developed legal and political systems contributed to the generally peaceful conditions of Xhosa life. Public debate, rather than the dictates of a tyrannical chief, determined a group's actions, and political oratory was a respected accomplishment. Under Xhosa law a man was innocent until he was proven guilty. If found guilty, he was ordered to pay a fine of cattle or sentenced to death; there were no prisons.

Xhosa religious life revolved around numerous spirits, which appeared in virtually any form—animals, plants, mountains, rivers, or the weather—and which required propitiation with endless ritual. Protracted ceremonies, involving the ritual slaughter of cattle, were required on such important occasions as harvest time and the death or investiture of a chief. A warrior who had slain a foe was considered liable to contract a serious illness resulting in insanity if he did not undergo an elaborate cleansing process. The first step was to slash open his victim's abdomen to permit his spirit to escape. The victorious warrior then had to eat and sleep apart from his fellows until he had passed on the contagion, through sexual intercourse, to another. Ritual experts, or "witch doctors," both male and female, were employed to literally smell out evildoers, a procedure sometimes exploited by unscrupulous chiefs who feared a rival or coveted his cattle. Witchcraft itself was a capital offense.

The Xhosas' economy and much of their culture were centered on cattle. Xhosa men trained their cows to respond to whistles and calls; they bent the beasts' horns into elegant shapes, paraded them at dances and festivals, used them in payment for marriages, composed poems and songs to them, rode them, raced them, and sacrificed them to their ancestors. It was an important event when, at the age of about ten, the young boys of a clan became fit to carry out herding duties. Their ears were pierced in a mass ceremony, and they subsequently formed an *iNtanga,* a group of similarly aged males who would move through all the major events of life together— the most important being the ceremony that marked their transition from herders to full-fledged adults and warriors, capable of owning their own cattle.

The girls were gathered in similar age sets. But cattle-tending was strictly forbidden for women; they were not even allowed to wash the milk pails. To them fell the task of growing crops: the sorghum, maize, millet, sweet potatoes, beans, peas, and melons that supplemented the milk and occasional meat of the Xhosa diet.

Xhosa villages, or homesteads, were roughly circular arrangements of round, windowless huts, often built on a ridge. Central to each homestead was a circular brushwood kraal, or enclosure, for nurturing calves or containing animals when danger threatened. Otherwise, cattle ranged freely in the surrounding pastureland.

Shown in an oil painting, British settlers leave their ships' dinghies in April 1820 for the larger surf boats that will carry them on the last stage of their arduous sea voyage—a harrowing run through the mighty breakers of Algoa Bay to the African shore. Tempted by government grants of land and free passage, the 3,500 passengers on this fleet doubled the region's British population at a stroke—yet with 43,000 Dutch-speaking inhabitants in the Cape Colony, the British were still a minority. The newcomers were woefully ill-informed about the life that awaited them: Only after they landed did they realize that the government intended them to police the troublesome eastern frontier.

Clad in Western-style clothes, a young herder of mixed Khoikhoi and European parentage holds a whip made of hippopotamus hide in a colored lithograph. In poorer, more remote areas, miscegenation between European farmers and Africans was commonplace, although such unions were rarely officially recognized. In the early days of white settlement, some Boers who married Khoikhoi women adopted African customs and clothes. Generally, however, the movement was in the other direction: Children of mixed blood adopted Western manners and dress, and those whose skin was pale enough to pass muster entered Boer society.

The Xhosa were not strictly nomadic, but they often had to move between so-called sourveld and sweetveld pastures, for winter and summer grazing respectively. They also traditionally moved on to new land, deserting their old village, when the head of a homestead died.

They were puzzled by the trekboers. Did they wear clothes to conceal their unhealthy bodies? Why would they not integrate into Xhosa civilization, intermarry, and share the land? All they seemed interested in was Xhosa cattle.

The Xhosa were not a warlike people, but they were quite prepared to fight and were not the least intimidated by the Boers. Neither their technology nor their tactics, however, were equal to their confidence. Their armies comprised loose bands, or *impis,* in which there was little internal organization, save for a certain degree of support between members of an iNtanga. In battle the Xhosa carried cowhide shields and assegais, light spears with wooden shafts about four feet long bearing iron heads forged by their own blacksmiths. They hurled these weapons at their enemies before closing in to fight with the tapering wooden clubs the Dutch called knobkerries. It was an unequal struggle against the mounted Boers, who were equipped with firearms and occasionally aided by regular soldiers. By 1800, the Xhosa had been driven back across the shallow waters of the Great Fish River with the loss of 5,300 precious cattle. For a time, an uncomfortable truce was maintained, with the Xhosa to the east of the river and the *amaqwanga*—or "pale beasts," as they called the whites—to the west. There, with each tempted by the other's cattle and land, both sides began to nurse the grievances that would lead to future conflict.

Far from the war-torn frontier, the Cape settlement was beginning to feel the effects of European political maneuvers. In 1795, France had invaded the Low Countries and the exiled Prince William appealed for British assistance. Britain obligingly took over the administration of the Cape, then peacefully relinquished it again in 1803 to the Batavian Republic, as the Netherlands was briefly known. Three years later, Britain—now at war with the Batavian Republic—invaded the Cape with sixty-three ships and 6,700 troops, easily overwhelming a small defense force of burghers and Khoikhoi. The settlement was renamed Cape Town; Britain had acquired a new and troublesome possession.

Cape Colony, as it was now called, had a population of about 25,000 Europeans and nearly 30,000 black slaves, while a substantial number of Khoikhoi and people of mixed race put the whites in a significant minority. It was divided into four districts, each under a landdrost, or commissioner, but administration was never clear-cut in a country with such arbitrary and ever-changing frontiers.

Only in the southwestern region was there a semblance of colonial comfort and prosperity. Here were the most fertile grain farms and the vineyards whose disparaged wines nevertheless brought in a steady income. Cape Town itself, according to a French visitor, was "formed of neatly aligned white houses, which from a distance look like little houses of cards." The castle, the Commercial Hall, the Masonic Temple, and a few other imposing buildings gave it the air of a colonial capital. The streets were broad and tree lined; beside many of them flowed little streams—which stank abominably in the dry season. Basic food was cheap, and William Burchell noted that "Eating, drinking, smoking, and sleeping constitute the chief employments of the majority of the inhabitants."

Beyond the capital there were few substantial towns. Stellenbosch, just twenty-five miles east of Cape Town, was a leafy provincial center. Capital of the frontier district was Graaff-Reinet, some 400 miles to the northeast, which boasted twenty-two tradesmen in 1812, many of whom sold imported European goods. Other settlements were unpretentious collections of shops and thatched houses of unplastered brick. A Dutch Reformed Church, a wheelwright, a smithy, and perhaps a municipal building and a jail faced a central market square where pigs and poultry foraged in the dust.

On assuming control of this backwater, the British had no intention of making work

In an oil painting of 1850, Europeans browse among the trophies of British trader David Hume at Grahamstown market. During the first half of the nineteenth century, the plundered wealth of Africa's wildlife came to play an increasingly important part in the Cape's economy: By 1835, it counted for a quarter of the colony's exports. Traders journeyed deep into the continent, as far afield as the Limpopo River, buying tusks, hides, and ostrich plumes from professional hunters—both African and European—for resale with attractive profits at frontier centers such as Grahamstown.

for themselves by overturning the pattern of Cape life. Britain saw southern Africa's value largely in strategic terms, for the Cape station was crucial to its growing eastern empire. So middle-ranking Dutch officials continued at their posts, while British administrators sought merely to keep the colony peaceful and self-contained.

It was a vision doomed to failure. A vociferous wave of liberal-minded missionaries—the conscience of the British empire—began to champion the rights of the Khoikhoi and of slaves. They met head-on opposition from the increasingly angry and frustrated white farmers, blocked in their eastward migration by a wall of Xhosa. Mission stations, established on the colony's frontiers, were seen by Europeans as a drain on the source of cheap labor—mainly Khoikhoi—who took refuge there. The abolition of the slave trade in 1807 further frightened Boers into believing that their way of life was on the verge of collapse.

Britain's response rocked the boat even more dangerously. In an attempt to ensure a supply of frontier labor, the Cape government insisted that all Khoikhoi carry passes and declare a fixed address. As a concession to the liberals' plea for evenhanded justice, however, Britain permitted Khoikhoi to make legal claims against violent or unjust employers. This extension of rights to a despised people further inflamed Boer antagonisms, particularly when it became clear that the authorities were prepared to use military might—specifically, Khoikhoi soldiers—to enforce their ruling. As the years wore on, it became clear that a British administration would never restore to frontier Boers the unlimited labor force and lands of their dreams.

But shortage of land was an even greater problem for the Xhosa. Already far more populous than the Europeans, the Africans had never seriously regarded the Great Fish River as a border, or the Cape government as exercising any authority over them. As the competition for grazing land increased, disturbances broke out among the eastern chiefdoms, forcing thousands of Xhosa across the Great Fish. They spilled into the zuurveld—the land between the Great Fish and the Sundays rivers, eighty miles to the west. Here the conflict was continual, with raids and counterraids escalating into open warfare between Boer and Xhosa. "The country is on every side overrun with Kaffirs," reported a British officer, who considered the only solution to be immediate "decisive and hostile measures."

Cape Town's governor, Sir John Cradock, had come to the same conclusion. In 1811, he ordered one Lieutenant Colonel John Graham to drive all Xhosas east across the Great Fish. Graham took to his task with alacrity. Determined to "attack the savages in a way that I hope will leave a lasting impression on their memories," he laid waste villages and crops. Dawn raids destroyed gardens and huts; herds of oxen, driven in front of the soldiers, trampled fields of grain and vegetables into the ground. The tactics worked as intended. Early in 1812, thousands of Xhosa fled across the Great Fish, many to face lingering death by starvation.

Resolved to maintain a border along the Great Fish River, Governor Cradock ordered the construction of military blockhouses and established two new villages, called Cradock and Grahamstown. But the zuurveld was far from secure. The population of the Xhosa was steadily increasing, and in 1819, they swept across the Great Fish, almost capturing Grahamstown in a rash daylight assault. Again the British drove them back, now creating a no man's land, known as the ceded territory, to the east of the Great Fish, where neither white nor black would be permitted to settle.

In December 1820, the first of about 5,000 British men, women, and children, many of them desperately poor, put ashore at Algoa Bay near the mouth of the

Sundays River. They had been lured to Africa by accounts of the rich empty land that was theirs for the taking. Britain, in the midst of an economic depression, was delighted to get rid of them, and offered free passage and a plot of land. The Cape authorities saw an influx of settlers as a sure way to secure the war-torn Albany region—as this part of the zuurveld was reassuringly called. The men could help police the land by serving on local militias. The newcomers were, for the most part, sublimely ignorant of their destination. William Burchell, it was true, had written a pamphlet for emigrants, in which he warned of a "misunderstanding" with the Africans, but failed to mention the years of violence that had bloodied the region's history.

Inexperienced, ill-equipped, and absurdly hopeful (one immigrant complained that his grand piano was out of tune on arrival), the new settlers built rough shelters and bravely attempted to grow crops in a semiarid land that was suited primarily for grazing. Rust and locusts devastated their wheat for three successive years. Only those with capital could survive on their original 100-acre allotments. The rest straggled into towns and settlements, where those with useful skills could make a living. Others subsisted in miserable poverty. "You told me true," wrote one immigrant to his former employer, "when you said I might as well blow my brains out as come upon this expedition."

Though a failure in human terms, the Albany settlement increased the European presence on the eastern frontier by perhaps 50 percent. And those immigrants who survived the early disasters eventually made an important contribution to the colony's economy by successfully breeding merino sheep—an innovation the Boers had stubbornly resisted. Before the middle of the century, wool had overtaken wine as the Cape's chief export. By then, however, the entire political and economic complexion of southern Africa had irrevocably altered.

It was not the white man alone who was forcing change upon the country. Hundreds of miles from the disputed eastern frontier there erupted a terrible civil war among the African people throughout Natal and the highveld. The Africans called it the *Mfecane*, the "Crushing," and with good reason, for during its course, up to one million souls perished and millions more were left desperate and dispossessed.

It began in Natal, where the Bantu-speaking peoples were densely settled on a land that could ill support all their cattle. A severe famine at the beginning of the nineteenth century forced many clans to form larger groups in order to protect their grain stores and consolidate their grazing. Seeing the advantage of centralized control, an innovative leader named Dingiswayo organized his warriors into an army composed of several disciplined regiments, each wearing distinctive clothes and carrying similarly colored shields. With this war machine at his disposal, he conquered or intimidated most of his neighbors and emerged as ruler of a federation of chiefdoms.

Among Dingiswayo's most respected officers was Shaka, leader of the Zulus, one of the many subjugated Bantu-speaking clans. Shaka exulted in battle and, while serving under Dingiswayo, successfully initiated new methods of fighting that revolutionized African warfare. He based his regiments on existing iNtangas, insisting

Dressed in full battle gear and sporting the single crane's feather of a Zulu king, Shaka presents an imposing spectacle in this portrait by a visiting European artist. The tyrannical ruler, who from his accession in 1815 led the Zulu nation to dominion over much of the southeastern part of the continent, was notoriously vain, and this portrait—which is known to have delighted its subject—may well be more flattery than fact. All observers agreed, however, that Shaka, well over six feet tall and supreme in athletics and weapons-play, was a striking figure.

that they remain celibate until given permission to marry—generally not until they were thirty or older and then only to a female of Shaka's choosing. He ordered his warriors to discard their oxhide sandals and drilled them at running barefoot until they could cover up to forty miles a day—twice the distance the average European army could achieve. A troop of boys followed Shaka's warriors with cooking pots, extra weapons, and water. He dismissed the traditional assegai as a mere bird-scarer and developed instead a stabbing spear with a short shaft and broad blade—the *iKlwa,* named after the sound its blade made when pulled from a body.

Battle tactics also changed. When advancing toward the enemy, Shaka's army fell into a four-part formation whose sections were named to suggest a charging buffalo. In the center was the chest and behind it the loins, while two curved horns spread out along the flanks. As the chest rushed into battle, the horns encircled the enemy until their tips met. The men of the loins, who served as a reserve force, were instructed to sit with their backs to the fighting so as to remain emotionally detached until required for action.

On Dingiswayo's death in 1818, the warlike Zulu nation rose to power, inheriting his policy of conquest and expansionism. But while Dingiswayo had shown some tolerance for subordinate rulers, Shaka ruthlessly exterminated the ruling families of other chiefdoms, including their women and children, to form an aggressive, land-hungry Zulu state.

The turmoil in Natal had far-reaching effects. Not all chiefdoms were willing to accept the sovereignty of Dingiswayo or the despotic Shaka. Fleeing from the long arm of the expanding Zulu state, dispossessed Africans zigzagged through the densely populated hills of Natal, stealing cattle and overrunning weaker chiefdoms. By the early 1820s, several groups had escaped west over the Drakensberg and rampaged down into the veld, whose inhabitants had been living in relative harmony.

The Mfecane now became a streaming mass of terrified humanity, as one panicking group after another careered over the veld in search of land. Starvation as well as warfare took a heavy toll on the migrants. "I met two children," recalled one survivor of the Mfecane, "One was dead. The living one was eating the flesh of the dead one. I passed on." This period of anarchy had the effect of partially depopulating the veld. Not until 1828 did the desolation cease. And fifteen years later, Africans were still drifting back in search of their ancestral homelands.

Among those who never returned was Mzilikazi, a trusted subordinate of Shaka, who had been harried over the Drakensberg on the suspicion of cheating his chief of cattle. As it plundered its way across the veld, Mzilikazi's band swelled, taking prisoners and absorbing other refugees, until Mzilikazi had an army of followers calling themselves Ndebele or Matabele. Eventually, he was able to establish a huge domain in the northern veld, and with a disciplined army of about 5,000 warriors, became absolute master over an area of approximately 30,000 square miles.

Farther south, the years of destruction consolidated another nation around the figure of Moshoeshoe. The son of a village headman, Moshoeshoe emerged during the chaos of the Mfecane first as a warrior and then as a statesman of outstanding capacities. Seeking to avoid depredatory hordes such as those under Mzilikazi, he led his people safely from their homeland on the veld and settled them in the western Drakensberg on a flat-topped hill called Thaba Bosiu, or Mountain of Darkness. Situated in a deep valley, with 150 acres of pasture and a good spring on the summit, Thaba Bosiu offered an impregnable refuge. Access to the top was restricted to three

Shield

Throwing spear

Stabbing spear

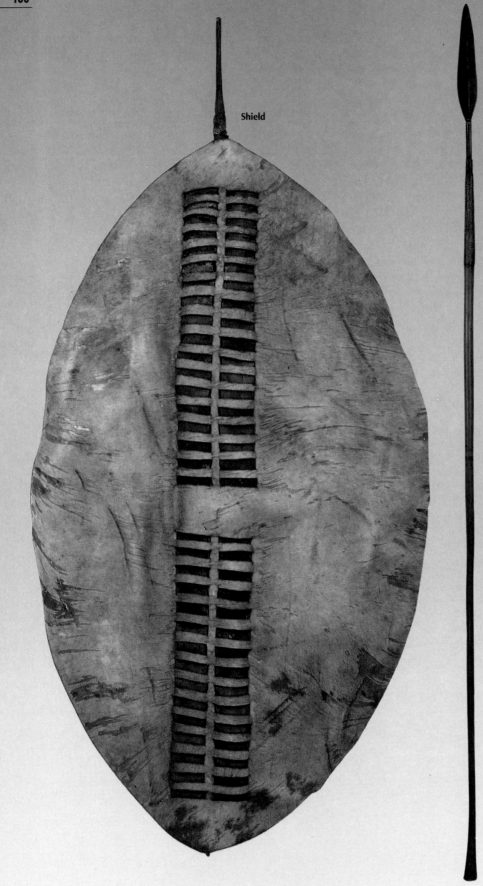

A Zulu warrior displays his combat skills in a traditional war dance. His *isi-Coco*, a waxed ring of head hair, indicates that he has been given permission to marry—a privilege granted only to proven veterans of battle.

THE ZULU WAR MACHINE

The source of Zulu ascendancy over neighboring peoples in the early nineteenth century lay in the military innovations devised by their ruler Shaka. In an age when African warfare was typified by loose, ritualized skirmishing, Shaka's changes transformed his army into a ruthlessly efficient killing machine.

The king introduced four-foot-high oxhide shields, much taller than those in use previously, and augmented the traditional armory of throwing assegais and knobkerrie cudgels with short stabbing spears. And he instructed his men on the use of their new equipment: Held in the left hand, the shield was hooked behind that of an opponent, who was then swung around with a backhand sweep to receive a deadly blow to his unprotected left side.

Shaka also understood tactics and strategy. Dividing his forces—15,000 strong by 1824—into well-ordered regiments, he trained them to move barefoot at speed through the bush, covering forty miles in a day. On sighting the foe, his regiments would adopt a battle formation modeled on the charging buffalo—a closely packed chest of seasoned veterans in the center, loins of reserves in the rear, and spreading horns of younger fighters on either side who quickly outflanked enemy forces.

Knobkerrie

narrow trails, and the hill's security was further enhanced by a rumor that it grew to an immense height at night, only subsiding to its actual 300 feet during the day. By offering sanctuary to all the human debris thrown up by the Mfecane, Moshoeshoe managed to piece together the BaSotho nation and successfully repelled the attacks of all warring factions. Sometimes this was done with uncommon good grace: Mzilikazi's hordes, for instance, received a gift of cattle as consolation for one failed assault. Later, in response to threats from Boers and British alike, Moshoeshoe acquired guns and horses for his men and became proficient in the skills of European warfare. He also "purchased," as he put it, missionaries from the Paris Evangelical Missionary Society, who clearly regarded him with reverence. "I felt at once," wrote one missionary, "that I had to do with a superior man, trained to think, to command others, and above all himself."

The same could no longer be said of Shaka, whose 20,000 or more beef-fed, celibate warriors had turned all Natal into a large, centralized Zulu state. Military success had not mellowed him; his vanity and cruelty increased with power. Still in his thirties, he held his subjects under the thrall of a fearsome dictatorship and tested his authority with daily acts of capricious violence. At the slightest cause for irritation—from a surly look to an ill-timed sneeze—an offender in his entourage might be hauled away and executed. Shaka was little kinder to women than to men. He never fathered a child (for fear of a successor, he insisted) but was insanely jealous of his 1,000-strong harem. On one occasion, returning unexpectedly from a journey, he had 170 young men and women put to death for suspected adultery.

Shaka took a benevolent interest in white settlers, who were clearly no threat to his dominion. These people first came to his attention in 1824, when a small band of Englishmen and Khoikhoi—among them Nathaniel Isaacs, who was later to receive Shaka's promise of land—began their struggle to establish a trading post at Port Natal. With few resources and no official assistance from Cape Colony, they were largely dependent upon favors from Shaka, such as grants of land and cattle. In return, they assisted the Zulu regiments on some of their military campaigns, their firearms making short work of Shaka's remaining enemies.

The Port Natal settlement grew steadily, almost assuming the status of a separate chiefdom. Its 1,000 inhabitants included white traders and ivory hunters, renegade Zulus, refugees from the Mfecane, and people of mixed African and European blood. They possessed their own kraals and cattle, but the omnipresence of patrolling Zulu regiments reminded them that they existed only on Shaka's sufferance. The Zulu leader showed an interest in western artifacts, and at one point, he dispatched Isaacs on an abortive diplomatic mission to conclude an alliance with Britain's King George IV. But the settlers knew that his caprice could turn against them at any time.

In 1827, one Englishman witnessed the unquestioning obedience the Zulu king commanded when his subjects gathered to bewail the passing of Shaka's mother.

> *Before noon, the number had swelled to about 60,000. . . . Shaka ordered several men to be executed on the spot; and the cries became, if possible, more violent than ever. . . . As if bent on convincing their chief of their extreme grief, the multitude commenced a general massacre. . . . Those who could no more force tears from their eyes . . . were beaten to death by others who were mad with excitement. Toward the afternoon, I calculated that not fewer than 7,000 people had fallen in this frightful, indiscriminate massacre.*

The violence of Shaka's reign ended abruptly in 1828, when two of his half brothers stabbed him with assegais as he received a visiting delegation. One story claimed that Shaka, in his dying breath, turned to his murderers and gasped, "You will not rule this country, the white people have already arrived." It would not be long before his assassin and successor, Dingane, learned the truth of this statement.

The white people of Cape Colony's eastern frontier were particularly resentful in the year of Shaka's death. The British, the Boers believed, were destroying their traditional culture. A new law, known as the 50th Ordinance, gave Khoikhoi the right to own land and abolished the pass laws that had tied them to frontier farms. The year 1828 also saw the emergence of a free press as censorship laws were relaxed, the reorganization of justice along British lines, and the adoption of English as the official language. There was even a hunt, organized along English county lines, whose scarlet-clad members hallooed after jackals and gathered at annual hunt balls. Land was becoming increasingly difficult to acquire on the eastern frontier: British settlers with vast flocks of sheep were beginning to occupy the once-wild territory west of the Great Fish, and the Xhosa continued to block the coastal route east. Many Boers now began to talk of hitching up their oxen once more and trekking north.

A further threat to the Boer's way of life arose in 1834, with the abolition of slavery throughout the British empire. Although a transition period kept the "freed" slave in virtual bondage for another four years, the end was in sight. It was not so much the

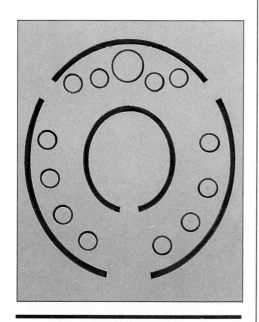

In this colored lithograph of 1849, beehive-shaped huts, fashioned of grass woven onto frameworks of branches, make a backdrop for Zulu women preparing beer. As the diagram above shows, a typical homestead, or kraal, consisted of several such huts within a circular stockade, themselves ringing a central enclosure where the cattle, which grazed on the surrounding grasslands during the day, could be penned at night for protection from thieves and wild animals. Most kraals housed the members of a single extended family, whose head lived in the large hut farthest from the main entrance.

loss of labor that appalled the Boers as the threat of what one called the "ungodly equality" between black and white. Compensation totaling £1,250,000 sterling was offered to slave owners, but the money had to be collected in London. This meant either a three-month trip to England or the payment of a substantial agent's fee. In the end, many Boers received no compensation at all and felt not only wronged but robbed. In the year of abolition, three advance parties of trekkers, horrified at what they considered to be their bleak prospects, left the eastern territories to report on the land beyond the Orange River. They returned the following year to find war raging between colonists and Africans.

The Missionaries' Message

From the early years of the nineteenth century, the Cape Colony became a center for the activities of European missionaries bent on introducing Africans to Christianity and Western ways. For some sixty years, the field had been dominated by the Moravians, a German Protestant sect, who had established the first mission as early as 1737. But by 1815, some 2,500 Africans were living in settlements established by evangelists from all over Europe. As the century progressed, the missionary message would reach thousands more.

White settlers had ambivalent feelings about missionary work. While they hoped that the churchmen would, as the authorities urged, make the black population "serviceable to the Colony," many farmers believed that the easier working conditions at mission stations merely attracted labor away from the farms and produced a pampered, insubordinate work force.

Some missionaries, such as Robert Moffat, were content simply to spread the word of God in remote areas. Others, however, found it impossible to separate their vocation from the politics of race. One such, John Philip, spoke out so vehemently against exploitation of the Africans that his name entered Boer vernacular as a byword for troublesome meddling.

Robert Moffat preaches to the Tswana people, among whom he lived, north of the Vaal River, for fifty years.

The fact was that true peace had never settled upon the eastern frontier. The ceded territory was constantly violated by both colonists and Africans, who could not resist so much unclaimed land. And as these two cattle cultures came in contact, the vicious cycle of theft and reprisals began again. Population was growing on both sides of the border, swelled in the east by an influx of refugees from the Mfecane.

The Xhosa had reached the breaking point. They bitterly resented a law that permitted Boer kommandos to follow the spoor of stolen cattle to African kraals and take Xhosa cattle if their own were not evident—a right that was easily abused. Xhosa chiefs, they complained, were treated like criminals by colonial authorities; one had been shot dead while ill. A terrible drought, which had driven numbers of Xhosa and Boers into the ceded territory in 1829, exacerbated the conflict still further.

The war that broke out at the end of 1834 was unlike any of its predecessors. It began quite suddenly when 12,000 Xhosa poured into colonial territory, frustrating

Clad in Western fashions, African families gather outside their cottages at the mission station of Genadendal in the 1840s. Situated on the site of the first Moravian settlement, ninety miles inland from Cape Town, Genadendal became the center of a growing network of Moravian missions and led the way for those of other denominations.

their opponents at first with the use of hit-and-run guerrilla tactics. Early in the action, a swashbuckling British colonel named Harry Smith rushed from Cape Town to the war zone, covering the 600 miles in six days, and to him went most of the credit for the inevitable victory of British guns over African spears. In fact, the Xhosa did not surrender but agreed to peace because they were tired of war. When Smith attempted to drive them east of the Kei River and extend colonial territory up to that river by creating Queen Adelaide Province, the Xhosa simply refused to leave.

It had been a costly and bitter nine months of conflict. The colonists had lost 456 farms and thousands of cattle, horses, and sheep. The Xhosa, too, had suffered badly. As Cape Town's new governor, Sir Benjamin D'Urban reported, "There have been taken from them also—besides the conquest and alienation of their country—about 60,000 head of cattle, and almost all their goats; their habitations are everywhere destroyed and their gardens and fields laid waste. They have been, therefore, chastised—not extremely but perhaps sufficiently." Most significantly, the Xhosa's paramount chief had been taken hostage by Harry Smith and shot while trying to escape.

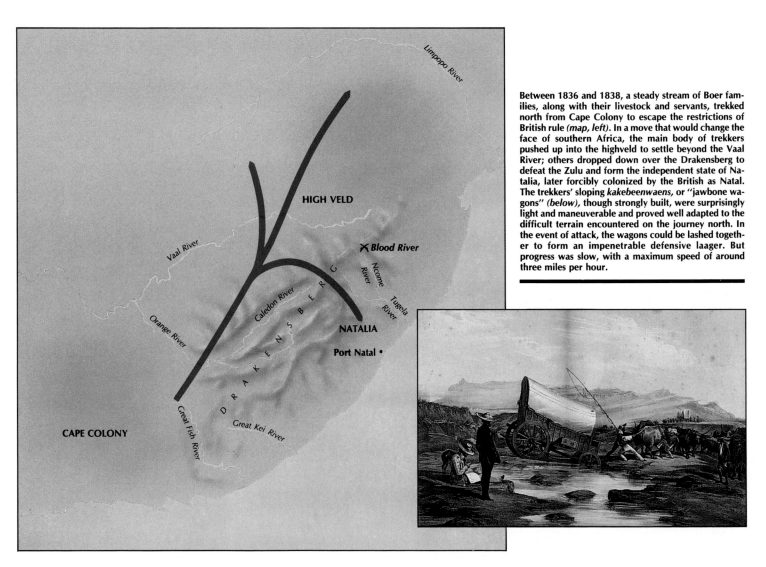

Between 1836 and 1838, a steady stream of Boer families, along with their livestock and servants, trekked north from Cape Colony to escape the restrictions of British rule *(map, left)*. In a move that would change the face of southern Africa, the main body of trekkers pushed up into the highveld to settle beyond the Vaal River; others dropped down over the Drakensberg to defeat the Zulu and form the independent state of Natalia, later forcibly colonized by the British as Natal. The trekkers' sloping *kakebeenwaens*, or "jawbone wagons" *(below)*, though strongly built, were surprisingly light and maneuverable and proved well adapted to the difficult terrain encountered on the journey north. In the event of attack, the wagons could be lashed together to form an impenetrable defensive laager. But progress was slow, with a maximum speed of around three miles per hour.

British soldiers cut off his ears as souvenirs, while others tried to gouge out his teeth with bayonets. It was an act of mutilation the Xhosa never forgave.

Yet the Xhosa were not the only malcontents. For the frontier Boers the frustration was insupportable. They had apparently won a war, but they had only burned-out farms to show for it. Then new hope arose with word that the trailblazing parties of trekkers had returned. One expedition, journeying to what is now Namibia, had found only a dry, inhospitable land. Another, however, had traveled the full length of the veld and enthusiastically described a limitless plain of sweet grass, much of it apparently empty. The third party had struggled over the Drakensberg to Natal, clearly the promised land. "Only heaven," asserted the expedition's leader, "could be more beautiful." For many Boers this was encouragement enough to set off for new lands on what became known as the Great Trek.

The first party of about 200 trekkers crossed the Orange River in February 1836, led by a belligerent and single-minded leader named Andries Hendrik Potgieter. A larger party set out the following year under Piet Retief, a prosperous former official of the eastern provinces. It was Retief who formally enunciated the trekkers' aims in a published manifesto. "We despair of saving the colony from the evils that threaten it," he wrote, "nor do we see any prospect of peace and happiness in a country thus distracted by internal emotions." His niece was later to express more precisely the trekkers' principal grievance. The emancipation of the slaves, she wrote, was "contrary to the laws of God and the natural distinction of race and religion."

In the wake of the groups led by Potgieter and Retief, a stream of ox-drawn wagons lumbered up to the veld. It was a slow haul. Encumbered with sheep and cattle, the wagons could move at a pace of only five to six miles per day. And the trekkers strictly maintained a Sabbath day of rest—even though they were not always sure which day of the week it was. Nevertheless, by 1839 from 5,000 to 6,000 Boers, along with thousands of Khoikhoi and black attendants, had trundled northward in a migration that would change the map of Africa.

The veld was as fertile as reported, but it was much more populous. The Ndebele, who considered the land their own, resented what they correctly judged to be a European invasion and killed a number of trekkers who strayed north of the Vaal River. The Boers' revenge was swift and conclusive. Released from the restraints of British supervision, they launched a savage campaign of reprisals. In the open land of the veld, they discovered, the mounted gunman was supreme; and no African army could breach a well-defended laager—a circle of wagons reinforced with thorn bushes. Led by Potgieter, a Boer kommando drove far into the northern veld against Mzilikazi. The campaign culminated in a nine-day bloodbath that accounted for an estimated 3,000 Ndebele casualties and pushed the remainder northward into what is now southern Zimbabwe. The Boers themselves suffered no casualties. "What was theirs is now ours," remarked one of their leaders with artless simplicity.

Having disposed of the only human obstacles on their way to the lekker lewe, Potgieter's Boers resolved to settle permanently on the highveld. Piet Retief, however, had his heart set on Natal. In the spring of 1837, he led a party of trekkers over the Drakensberg and down into a land he called the "most beautiful in Africa."

Still suffering from the aftermath of the Mfecane, Natal was relatively underpopulated. As more trekkers poured into this green and desolate land, Retief hurried to the Zulu capital of Umgungundhlovu, north of the Tugela River, to negotiate a settlement with Dingane. The Zulu leader greeted Retief's party with apparent warmth and agreed to cede territory to the Boers if they would prove their good intentions by recovering some stolen cattle from a nearby chief. Retief set out on this mission with a light heart, believing that the future was assured.

Dingane was, in fact, deeply suspicious and fearful of the Europeans. He had watched apprehensively the growth of Port Natal and had recently heard horrifying rumors of Potgieter's campaigns on the veld. White and black men were enemies, he had once remarked; "They do not like each other and never will." When Retief's party returned in January 1838, with 300 head of cattle, Dingane again welcomed the Boers enthusiastically. On the day of their departure, he invited them to a ceremony in their honor. Leaving their weapons outside as requested, the Boers obligingly watched a massed war dance of chanting Zulu warriors. Suddenly Dingane sprang to his feet and shouted above the din, "*Bulalani abtagati!*" "Kill the wizards!" The visitors were dragged to the hillside used for official executions and beaten to death with clubs and stones. In all, seventy Europeans and thirty Khoikhoi servants perished. Months later, Retief's fellow Boers would identify his desiccated body amid a tangle of corpses. Perfectly preserved in a leather pouch hanging from his shoulder was a document signed by Dingane, granting southern Natal to the trekkers.

Determined to drive all of the newcomers off his land, Dingane immediately launched a murderous night raid on the remaining Boers, who confidently awaited Retief's return. Nearly 300 trekkers—including 185 children—and 200 of their servants died in the massacre. "In one wagon were found fifty dead," recounted a survivor, "and blood flowed from the seam of the tent sail down to the lowest part."

Still coveting the country they had struggled so hard to reach, those Boers left alive drew their wagons together and appealed for reinforcements. Nine months later, Andries Pretorius, a prosperous landowner, rode over the Drakensberg with sixty horsemen and immediately called a kommando to attack the Zulu nation. On December 14, 1838, Pretorius formed a laager of sixty-four wagons on the banks of the Ncome River where, two days later, the Boers were attacked at dawn by a force of some 12,000 Zulus. The circular fortress blazed with continuous gunfire, and by midday the battle was over. More than 3,000 Zulus lay dead, as "thick on the ground as pumpkins on a fertile piece of garden land," noted the victors' preacher. So many corpses clogged the river that its waters turned red, and the Boers renamed it Blood River. None of the 600 defenders died and only three were wounded.

On the same day that Boer history was being made at Blood River, eighty British troops landed at Durban, as Port Natal was now called, and ran up the Union Jack. For years, British authorities had tried to ignore the growing settlement in Natal. Their policy was to discourage expansion, but now that the Boers threatened to create a disruptive presence so near the Cape Colony, they felt obliged to use force.

The taming of Natal was not a simple matter. Having temporarily subdued the Zulus, the exultant Boers declared the independent state of Natalia with its capital at the new settlement of Pietermaritzburg. They then joined forces with Mpande, half brother of Dingane, to drive the Zulu leader out of Natal. Dingane died in exile, and the amenable Mpande became paramount chief of an emasculated Zulu state north of the Tugela River.

Relations meanwhile worsened with the British, who disapproved of the Natal Boers' high-handed treatment of the African people. In addition, racial problems were exacerbated by an influx of Mfecane victims, who now returned to find white men occupying their traditional lands.

Captured in an oil painting, Boer horsemen pursue flee-ing Zulus at the battle of Blood River on December 16, 1838. Though heavily outnumbered, the Boers were well protected within a laager positioned with the Ncome River on one side and a steep ravine on another. This, coupled with their vastly superior firepower, al-lowed them to overwhelm their foe. After the attack, Boer sharpshooters easily picked off escaping Zulus as they waded across the Ncome or tried to hide in its shallows. While only three Boers were injured—none fatally—3,000 Zulus out of the 10,000 who went into battle were killed.

In 1843, Britain formally annexed Natal and began to impose the very regime that the Boers had gone to such lengths to escape. Particularly distressing for them was the decision by Theophilus Shepstone, Diplomatic Agent to the Native Tribes, to allocate reserves where the incoming African refugees could exist with a fair degree of autonomy. In 1848, the Boers wearily trekked back over the Drakensberg into the still-free veld. "I was almost paralyzed to see the whole of the population, with few exceptions, trekking," wrote Harry Smith, now Sir Harry, who had been appointed governor of Cape Colony the previous December. He could not persuade them to turn back. After just ten years, the chosen people had left the promised land.

The burst of energy that precipitated the Great Trek shattered the mold of southern African politics. Too late did Britain attempt to take its wayward colony seriously. From 1835 Britain had maintained a sporadic and increasingly precarious peace by a system of treaties, which recognized frontier chiefs as sovereign rulers. Now things were to change. "The British Authority is to be supreme and to be in all cases implicitly obeyed," wrote Lord Grey, secretary of state for the colonies. Sir Harry Smith was to be the champion of this new policy. Aggressive, theatrical, and incur-ably vain, he dashed to the eastern front within days of his appointment. There, on December 23, 1847, he announced to an assembly of chiefs that he would annex the land up to the Great Kei River as a separate colony, to be known as British Kaffraria. He then gestured to a covered wagon standing nearby. "Do you see that wagon, I say?" he shouted. The vehicle, which had been packed with gunpowder, exploded with a deafening roar. "There go the treaties. Do you hear? No more treaties!" The bemused chiefs got the message: Their sovereignty was gone.

Aside from the special effects, Smith's aim here, as on other frontiers, was to assimilate the warring factions into a British colony and its people into British culture. He would build schools for the Africans, and they would all learn English. "You may no longer be naked and wicked barbarians," he harangued. "You must learn that it is money that makes people rich by work, and helps me to make roads."

The eastern frontier was no longer the most urgent of Cape Colony's problems. Gradually the area known as Transorangia, which lay between the Orange and the Vaal rivers, had emerged as a tinderbox of racial and political unrest. For more than 150 years, the Orange River valley had been a refuge for people of mixed race, particularly the Griquas. The turmoil of the Mfecane had thrown warring African peoples into this already volatile region. And now the trekkers were swarming across the Orange, demanding an independent state. Unable to accept the rights of other races as equal to their own, the Boers appropriated Griqua and African territories with few formalities and with inevitably violent consequences.

Into this lawless country galloped Sir Harry Smith. His confident proposal for Transorangia was more or less the same—though minus the fireworks—as his solution for the eastern frontier: annexation. Accordingly, in 1848, Transorangia became the Orange River Sovereignty, a part of Cape Colony. The trekkers, led by Pretorius, were furious and rebelled. Smith attempted to calm his "children" as he called the Boers, while threatening them with the kind of biblical vengeance that he thought they would appreciate. "As I abhor war," he claimed in a manifesto, "so will I terribly wield its power if you drive me from your affections." The rebellion was quickly suppressed by British troops.

For all the sound and fury of his oratory, Sir Harry's policies ultimately signified

British troops and Xhosa forces confront each other watchfully while their leaders attempt to resolve a land dispute in 1846. Competition between white settlers and African farmers for scarce grazing land was intense, and Cape Colony's eastern frontier was a theater of almost continuous conflict. Though inferior to the British in both training and firepower, the Xhosa quickly learned to cope with European techniques of warfare. Moving at night to avoid detection, their guerrilla forces concentrated on disrupting supply lines and ambushing small groups of soldiers cut off from the main force. Their knowledge of the terrain allowed them to retreat into steep or heavily wooded country inaccessible to the cumbersome British formations. Ultimately, however, such resistance proved powerless to prevent British rule from expanding.

nothing without continued support from London. Wars continued in the annexed regions, and colonial wars were an expense that the British government only grudgingly met. The end of this brief flirtation with expansionism was not far distant: Under the Sand River Convention of 1852, the land north of the Vaal River—the domain of Andries Hendrik Potgieter and 15,000 or so fellow Boers—became the independent Boer republic of Transvaal; three months later, Sir Harry departed in uncharacteristic gloom for England; and in 1854, the Orange River Sovereignty was renamed the Orange Free State, a second Boer republic. The two new states had little in common. Transvaal, at the extremity of white expansion, retained much of the frontier spirit, with rugged Boer individualism prevailing over a weak central authority. The Orange Free State, on the other hand, influenced by the neighboring Cape Colony, was better organized, with its own constitution and Volksraad, or parliament. Both trekker republics, however, shared one portentous dictum: Whether in church or state, there was to be no equality between black and white.

The divisions inherent in South African society had been born. A few more decades would crystallize the region into its bitter twentieth-century composition.

The final blow for the Xhosa came in 1857. They had been defeated in war, and their lands had been taken from them. Now, to compound their misery, disease was decimating their herds. In such desperate straits, they were open to any remedy that might restore their lost fortunes. If only they slaughtered all their cattle and destroyed their grain, a young prophetess claimed, the Xhosa's dead ancestors would rise to sweep the white man from their land. The Xhosa duly slaughtered the cattle and destroyed the grain, but no help came from beyond the grave. Some 25,000 Xhosa were estimated to have starved. Many thousands more poured into the Cape Colony—to the delight of white, labor-hungry farmers, now armed with strict legislation against offending servants.

Ten years later, Moshoeshoe found himself in a fight for his life against the predatory Boers, to whom much of his land had been arbitrarily assigned when the boundaries of the old Orange River Sovereignty had been settled. The British reluctantly intervened in 1868, creating the British protectorate of Basutoland. It would be just short of a century before Moshoeshoe's once great kingdom received independence as the landlocked state of Lesotho.

Moshoeshoe, however, was more fortunate than most. By the end of the century, Britain had annexed the remaining chiefdoms between Cape Colony and Natal, as well as having viciously crushed the Zulus, who in 1879 had risen in desperation against British attempts to remove their independence. Their exiled chief wrote plaintively to the governor of the Cape: "I have done you no wrong, therefore you must have some other object in view in invading my land."

He had. Within the previous decade prospectors had unearthed the diamond-bearing blue volcanic plug at Kimberley in Griqua territory as well as the staggeringly productive gold reefs of Transvaal. Southern Africa was now at the forefront of imperial Britain's attention; and what the European wanted he eventually possessed. Any lingering hopes the African races may have entertained of sharing the region vanished. By the end of the century, deprived of their lands, reduced to the status of manual workers for white enterprises, and controlled by a rigid set of "native laws"—including, again, the hated passes—they were forced to witness Boer and Briton battling for possession of their country. They had become outsiders in their own land.

	1800-1810	1810-1820

CONTINENTAL EUROPE

1800-1810

Napoleon Bonaparte defeats Austria at Marengo (1800).

Britain and France make peace at the Treaty of Amiens (1802). War resumes the next year.

Napoleon is crowned emperor of France (1804).

Victory at Trafalgar establishes Britain's naval supremacy (1805).

Napoleon destroys a Russo-Austrian army at Austerlitz (1805). The following year he defeats Prussia at Jena.

France forms the Rhine Confederation (1806).

France invades Portugal (1807).

Napoleon defeats the Austrians at Wagram (1809).

1810-1820

Napoleon's heir, the "King of Rome," is born (1811).

French troops withdraw after an abortive invasion of Russia (1812).

A European coalition defeats Napoleon at Leipzig. The French are driven from the Iberian Peninsula (1813).

Napoleon abdicates and is exiled to the island of Elba (1814).

Napoleon returns from exile, only to be defeated at Waterloo (1815).

Napoleon is exiled to the island of Saint Helena (1815).

The Congress of Vienna restores France's monarchy and partitions post-Napoleonic Europe (1815).

GREAT BRITAIN

1800-1810

Combination Acts outlaw the formation of "combinations," early trade unions (1800).

Numerous Enclosure Acts begin to be passed to consolidate agricultural land into larger holdings (1800).

Gas lighting is introduced (1805).

Richard Trevithick exhibits the first steam-powered locomotive (1808).

1810-1820

Rioting workers smash factory machinery in the Luddite revolt (1812).

The Luddite uprising is quashed (1813).

In the slump following the Napoleonic Wars, the Corn Laws are passed to protect the interests of big landowners (1815).

At the Peterloo Massacre, mounted yeomanry injure 400 people demonstrating against the Corn Laws (1819).

SOUTHERN AFRICA

1800-1810

After eight years' administration of the Cape settlement during war with France, Britain hands control back to the Netherlands (1803).

Following the resumption of war in Europe, Britain seizes the Cape again (1806).

The abolition of the slave trade and the extension of legal rights to nonwhites in the Cape Colony cause discontent among the Dutch-speaking Boers (1807).

1810-1820

Tension increases on the eastern frontier between white farmers and the Xhosa people (1811).

British forces drive the Xhosa back beyond the Great Fish River (1812).

Shaka ascends the Zulu throne and begins a sweeping military reform (1818).

The Xhosa push westward across the Great Fish River but are driven back (1819).

LATIN AMERICA

1800-1810

A slave revolt in Haiti gains independence for that island from the French (1804).

A British expeditionary force occupies Buenos Aires, but is soon expelled (1806).

Francisco de Miranda leads an abortive rebellion in Venezuela (1806).

Following Napoleon's usurpation of the Spanish throne, Spanish officials are increasingly despised as French puppets (1808).

1810-1820

Creole juntas take power in Spanish America (1810).

Miranda and Simón Bolívar create Venezuela's First Republic (1811).

Spanish forces retake Venezuela (1812).

After a bloody campaign, Bolívar forms the Second Venezuelan Republic (1814).

Argentina declares its independence (1816).

José de San Martín and Bernardo O'Higgins join forces to liberate Chile (1817).

Bolívar defeats the Spanish at Boyacá. Liberated New Granada is united with Ecuador and Venezuela as the Republic of Colombia (1819).

CHINA

1800-1810

Some 2,000 chests of opium a year are exported to China from British India to offset an adverse balance of trade (1800).

Piracy becomes rife off the China coast (1807).

1810-1820

An uprising in south China is put down at the cost of 20,000 executions (1813).

Britain invades China's vassal state Nepal (1816).

A British embassy under Lord Amherst fails to negotiate a trade agreement with China (1816).

TimeFrame AD 1800-1850

1820-1830	1830-1840	1840-1850
Napoleon dies (1821). Full-scale rebellion against Ottoman rule breaks out in Greece (1821). The British poet Lord Byron, leading light of the Romantic movement, dies during the Greek War of Independence (1827).	Revolution in Paris replaces King Charles X with Louis-Philippe (1830). Belgium gains its independence from the Netherlands (1830). Greece gains its independence (1830). Russia puts down a rebellion in Poland (1831). Austria suppresses uprisings in Italy (1831). German states form the Zollverein customs union (1832).	Austria crushes an uprising in Galicia and occupies Kraków (1846). A rash of revolutions, fueled by nationalism, liberalism, and socialism, sweeps through Europe. Within a year they are all crushed (1848).
Combinations flourish underground so vigorously that the government legalizes them (1824). Britain's first passenger railroad opens between Stockton and Darlington (1825). George Stephenson's Rocket is chosen as the locomotive for a major new railway line between Manchester and Liverpool (1829).	The success of the Manchester-Liverpool line inaugurates an explosive period of railroad construction (1830). The Reform Act gives Britain's middle class greater representation in Parliament (1832). Philanthropist Robert Owen forms the Grand National Consolidated Trades Union. It collapses within a year (1833). Queen Victoria ascends the throne (1837). The Chartist movement is formed to agitate for political reform (1838).	The Mines Act is passed and is swiftly followed by a spate of legislation to improve working conditions (1842). The Corn Laws are repealed and an era of free trade begins (1846). The Chartist movement collapses (1848).
Some 3,500 Britons land at Algoa Bay as settlers and as guards for the troubled eastern frontier (1820). Zulu expansion sparks a massive African migration, the Mfecane (c. 1820). More than one million die in the ensuing havoc. A small band of settlers from the Cape set up a trading post at Port Natal, in Zulu territory (1824). Shaka is assassinated by two of his half brothers, one of whom, Dingane, takes the Zulu throne (1828). Even as press censorship laws are relaxed, English is made the official language and justice is reorganized along British lines; the Boers of the Cape Colony become increasingly resentful of foreign rule (1829).	The abolition of slavery in the British empire further threatens the Boers' way of life. Three advance parties of Boers set out to reconnoiter new lands (1834). Nine months of bloody warfare erupt between the Xhosa and the Cape Colony (1834). Boers begin to trek north to escape British rule (1836). Trekkers under Piet Retief turn south into Natal (1837). Dingane kills Retief and 400 trekkers (1838). Vengeful Boers massacre the Zulu at the battle of Blood River and declare the independent state of Natalia (1838).	Britain annexes the fledgling Boer state as Natal (1843). The British annex much Xhosa land as British Kaffraria (1847). The Natal Boers trek back to the highveld to escape British rule (1848). Britain brings Transorangia, a northern, Boer-occupied territory, within Cape Colony (1848).
With O'Higgins installed as dictator of Chile, San Martín sails to take Peru (1820). Spanish troops are finally expelled from Venezuela and Bolívar accepts the presidency of Colombia (1821). Mexico declares its independence (1821). Bolívar is appointed dictator of Peru (1823). The Spaniards are driven from Upper Peru, which becomes the independent state of Bolivia (1825). Portugal recognizes the independence of Brazil (1825). A congress intended to form a confederation of Central and South American states ends in failure (1826).	Simón Bolívar resigns his presidency as Colombia begins to disintegrate. He dies the same year (1830). Texas declares its independence from Mexico (1836).	The United States annexes Texas (1845). U.S. forces invade the territory of New Mexico (1846). Fighting ceases as American troops take Mexico City (1846).
Emperor Daoguang ascends the Chinese throne and issues stern decrees against the consumption of opium (1821). Opium imports reach 10,000 chests per year, causing a severe drain on China's silver reserves (1825).	The British government abolishes the East India Company's monopoly of trade with China. Western merchants flock to the Far East (1833). The aggressive stance of Britain's trade superintendent, Lord Napier, almost sparks a war (1835). The British are ordered to destroy their opium stocks. The First Opium War commences (1839).	The First Opium War ends with the Treaty of Nanjing, which cedes the island of Hong Kong to Britain and opens five major ports to Western trade (1842). Emperor Hsien-feng comes to the throne. Within a year, China is thrown into turmoil by the Taiping rebellion (1850).

ACKNOWLEDGMENTS

The following are reprinted with the publishers' permission: page 124: "Not a year passes . . ." and page 127: "The whole empire is in a ferment . . ." quoted in *The Dragon Wakes,* by Christopher Hibbert, London: Penguin Books, 1984. Page 161: "Before noon . . ." from *The Washing of the Spears,* by Donald R. Morris, London: Cardinal, 1988. The editors also thank the following individuals and institutions for their help in the preparation of this volume:

England: Bedworth, Warwickshire—Fred Phillips. Bradford—Ray McHugh, Senior Keeper, Bradford Industrial Museum. Brighton—Martin Leighton. Cambridge—Tim Blanning, Reader in Modern European History, Sidney Sussex College, Cambridge University. Dorking—Donald Payne. London—Judy Aspinall; BBC Radio 3; Stephen Bull, National Army Museum; Windsor Chorlton; Craig Clunas, Far Eastern Department, Victoria and Albert Museum; Patrick Conner, Martyn Gregory Gallery; Martin Hinchcliffe, Keeper of Weapons, National Army Museum; Vicky Leanse; Andrew Mackenzie; Beth McKillop, Department of Oriental Manuscripts, British Library; Caroline Manyon; John Orbell, Baring Brothers; Chris Rawlings, Photographic Service, British Library; Lynne Richards, Hayward Gallery; Alan Sked, Senior Lecturer in International History, London School of Economics and Political Science; Robert Sharp, Science Museum; Deborah Thompson; Clive Wainwright, Department of Furniture, Victoria and Albert Museum. Warwick—Richard Chamberlaine-Brothers, Warwickshire County Records Office. Windlesham-by-Sea, West Sussex—Ian Knight, Zulu War Group.
Scotland: Lanark—Lorna Davidson, Education Officer, New Lanark Conservation Trust.
South Africa: Cape Town—Poul Hansen, Don Nelson Publishers.

BIBLIOGRAPHY

GREAT BRITAIN
Allen, G. Freeman, *Railways.* London: Orbis, 1982.
Bagwell, Philip S., *The Transport Revolution from 1770.* London: Batsford, 1974.
Briggs, Asa:
The Age of Improvement. London: Longman, 1959.
Iron Bridge to Crystal Palace. London: Thames and Hudson, 1979.
Social History of England. Harmondsworth, England: Pelican, 1987.
Burton, Anthony, *Our Industrial Past.* London: George Philip, 1983.
Calder, Jenni, *The Victorian Home.* London: Batsford, 1977.
Chambers, J., and G. E. Mingay, *The Agricultural Revolution.* London: Batsford, 1966.
Clark, Ronald W., *Works of Man.* London: Century, 1985.
Clayre, Alasdair, ed., *Nature and Industrialization.* Oxford: Oxford University Press, 1977.
Crafts, N. F. R., *British Economic Growth during the Industrial Revolution.* Oxford: Clarendon Press, 1985.
Davis, Ralph, *The Industrial Revolution and British Overseas Trade.* Leicester: Leicester University Press, 1979.
De Vries, Leonard, *Panorama, 1842-1865.* London: John Murray, 1967.
Farnie, D. A., *The English Cotton Industry and the World Market.* Oxford: Clarendon Press, 1979.
Hartwell, R., ed., *The Long Debate on Poverty.* London: Institute of Economic Affairs, 1972.
Hollis, P., *Class and Conflict in Nineteenth-Century England.* London: Routledge and Kegan Paul, 1973.
Inglis, Brian, *Poverty and the Industrial Revolution.* London: Hodder & Stoughton, 1971.
Jennings, Humphrey, *Pandaemonium.* London: Andre Deutsch, 1985.
Marshall, Dorothy, *Industrial England.* New York: Scribner's, 1973.
Matthias, Peter, *The First Industrial Nation.* London: Methuen, 1969.
McKendrick, Neil, and John Brewer, *The Birth of a Consumer Society.* London: Europa Publications, 1982.
Mingay, G. E., *The Transformation of Britain.* London: Paladin, 1987.
Morgan, Bryan, *Early Trains.* New York: Golden Press, 1974.
Musson, A. E., *The Growth of British Industry.* London: Batsford, 1978.
Nock, O. S., *Railways Then and Now.* London: Paul Elek, 1975.
Parker, M., and D. Reid, *The British Revolution.* London: Blandford, 1972.
Perkin, H., *The Origins of Modern English Society.* London: Routledge and Kegan Paul, 1969.
Pike, E. Royston, *Human Documents of the Industrial Revolution in Britain.* London: Allen & Unwin, 1966.
Plumb, J. H., *England in the Eighteenth Century.* Harmondsworth, England: Pelican, 1950.
Porter, Roy, *English Society in the Eighteenth Century.* Harmondsworth, England: Pelican, 1982.
Reid, Robert, *Land of Lost Content: The Luddite Revolt.* London: Cardinal, 1986.
Richards, Dennis, and J. W. Hunt, *An Illustrated History of Modern Britain.* Harlow, England: Longman, 1983.
Sanderson, M., *Education, Economic Change and Society in England, 1780-1870.* London: Macmillan, 1983.
Taylor, A. J., ed., *The Standard of Living in Britain in the Industrial Revolution.* London: Methuen, 1975.
Thompson, E. P., *The Making of the English Working Class.* Harmondsworth, England: Pelican, 1968.
Trench, Richard, and Ellis Hillman, *London under London.* London: John Murray, 1985.
Unstead, R. J.:
Age of Machines: 1815-1901. London: Macdonald Educational, 1979.
Freedom & Revolution: 1763-1815. London: Macdonald, 1972.
Wood, Christopher, *Victorian Panorama: Paintings of Victorian Life.* London: Faber and Faber, 1976.
Young, G. M., *Portrait of an Age: Victorian England.* Oxford: Oxford University Press, 1953.

CONTINENTAL EUROPE
Barnett, Correlli, *Bonaparte.* London, Allen & Unwin, 1978.
Bergeron, Louis, *France under Napoleon.* Princeton: Princeton University Press, 1981.
Chandler, David G., *The Campaigns of Napoleon.* London: Weidenfeld and Nicolson, 1967.
Connelly, Owen, *Napoleon's Satellite Kingdoms.* London: Macmillan, 1965.
Connelly, Owen, ed., *Historical Dictionary of Napoleonic France.* London: Aldwych, 1985.
Cronin, Vincent, *Napoleon.* Newton Abbot: Readers Union, 1972.
Esposito, Vincent J., and John Robert Elting, *A Military History and Atlas of the Napoleonic Wars.* London: Faber and Faber, 1964.
Grandjean, Serge, *Empire Furniture.* London: Faber and Faber, 1966.
Herold, J. Christopher:
The Mind of Napoleon. New York: Columbia University Press, 1961.
The Age of Napoleon. London: Weidenfeld and Nicolson, 1963.
Horne, Alistair, *Napoleon, Master of Europe.* London: Weidenfeld and Nicolson, 1979.
Lefebvre, G., *Napoleon.* New York: Columbia University Press, 1969.
Mansel, Philip, *The Eagle in Splendour.* London: George Philip, 1987.
Markham, F., *Napoleon and the Awakening of Europe.* London: Macmillan, 1965.
Maurois, André, *Napoleon.* London: Thames and Hudson, 1963.
Thompson, J. M.:
Napoleon Bonaparte. Oxford: Blackwell, 1988.
The Letters of Napoleon. Oxford: Blackwell, 1934.
Tulard, J., *Napoleon: The Myth of the Saviour.* London: Weidenfeld and Nicolson, 1984.

LATIN AMERICA
Adams, W. J., *Journal.* Dublin: R. M. Tims, 1824.
Ades, Dawn, *Art in Latin America: 1820-1980.* London: The South Bank Centre, 1989.
Beals, Carleton, *Eagles of the Andes.* Philadelphia: Chilton Books, 1963.
Bethell, Leslie, ed., *The Cambridge History of Latin America,* Vol. 3. Cambridge: Cambridge University Press, 1985.
Bingley, William, *Travels in South America.* London: John Sharpe, 1820.
Bonnycastle, R. H., *Spanish America.* London: Longman, Hurst, Lees, Orme and Brown, 1818.
Boulton, Alfredo, *Historia de la Pintura en Venezuela.* Caracas: Editorial Arte, 1968.
Dominguez, J. I., *Insurrection or Loyalty.* Cambridge, Mass.: Harvard University Press, 1980.
Fitzgerald, Gerald E., ed., *The Political Thought of Bolivar.* The Hague: Martinus Nijhoff, 1971.
Lemos, Carlos, et al., *The Art of Brazil.* New York: Harper & Row, 1983.
Lynch, John, *The Spanish American Revolutions.* New York: Norton, 1986.
Masur, Gerhard, *Simon Bolivar.* Albuquerque: University of New Mexico Press, 1969.
Read, Jan, *The New Conquistadors.* London: Evans Brothers, 1980.
Salcedo-Bastardo, J. L., *Bolivar.* Richmond, Surrey: Richmond Publishing, 1977.
Walton, William, *Present State of the Spanish Colonies.* London: Longman, Hurst, Rees, Orme and Brown, 1810.
Worcester, Donald, *Bolivar.* London: Hutchinson, 1978.

CHINA
Beeching, Jack, *The Chinese Opium Wars.* London: Hutchinson, 1975.
Clunas, Craig, *Chinese Export Watercolours.* London: Victoria and Albert Museum, 1984.
Clunas, Craig, ed., *Chinese Export Art and Design.* London: Victoria and Albert Museum, 1987.
Collis, Maurice, *Foreign Mud.* London: Faber and Faber, 1946.
Conner, Patrick, *The China Trade, 1600-1860.* Brighton: The Royal Pavilion, Art Gallery and Museums, 1986.

Crossman, Carl L., *The China Trade.* Princeton: The Pyne Press, 1972.

Fairbank, John, *The Great Chinese Revolution.* London: Picador, 1988.

Hart, Robert, *These from the Land of Sinim.* London: Chapman & Hall, 1901.

Hibbert, Christopher, *The Dragon Wakes.* London: Penguin Books, 1986.

Holt, Edgar, *The Opium Wars in China.* London: Putnam, 1964.

Hsü, Immanuel C. Y.:
The Rise of Modern China. Oxford: Oxford University Press, 1983.
China's Entrance into the Family of Nations: 1858-1880. Cambridge, Mass: Harvard University Press, 1960.

Legouix, Susan, *Image of China: William Alexander.* London: Jupiter Books, 1980.

Michael, Franz, and Ch'ung-li Chang, *The Taiping Rebellion.* Washington: University of Washington Press, 1966.

Milton, Joyce, and Wendy B. Murphy, *Tradition and Revolt: Imperial China.* London: Cassell, 1980.

O'Neill, Hugh, *Companion to Chinese History.* New York: Facts on File Publications, 1987.

Rodzinski, Witold, *The Walled King-*
dom. London: Fontana, 1984.

Wakeman, Frederic, *Strangers at the Gate.* Berkeley and Los Angeles: University of California Press, 1966.

Waley, Arthur, *The Opium War through Chinese Eyes.* London: Allen & Unwin, 1958.

Warner, John, comp., *Hong Kong Illustrated.* Hong Kong: John Warner Publications, 1981.

Warner, Marina, *The Dragon Empress: Life and Times of Tz'u-hsi.* London: Weidenfeld and Nicolson, 1972.

Wright, Mary C., *The Last Stand of Chinese Conservatism.* Stanford, California: Stanford University Press, 1957.

Yap, Yong, and Arthur Cotterell, *Chinese Civilization.* London: Weidenfeld and Nicolson, 1977.

SOUTHERN AFRICA

Attwell, Michael, *South Africa.* London: Sidgwick and Jackson, 1986.

Bergh, J. S., *Tribes and Kingdoms.* Cape Town: Don Nelson, 1984.

Bryer, Lynne, and Keith S. Hunt, *The 1820 Settlers.* Cape Town: Don Nelson, 1984.

Burchell, William J., *Hints on Immigration to the Cape of Good Hope.* London: J. Hatchard & Son, 1819.

De Kiewiet, C. W., *A History of South Africa.* Oxford: Oxford University Press, 1941.

Denoon, Donald, and Balam Nyeko, *Southern Africa since 1800.* London: Longman, 1984.

Elphick, Richard, *Kraal and Castle.* New Haven: Yale University Press, 1977.

Elphick, Richard, and Hermann Giliomee, eds., *The Shaping of South African Society.* Cape Town: Longman, 1979.

Guy, Jeff, *The Destruction of the Zulu Kingdom.* London: Longman, 1979.

Hattersley, Alan, *An Illustrated Social History of South Africa.* Cape Town: A. A. Balkema, 1969.

Knight, Ian, *The Zulus.* London: Osprey Publishing, 1989.

Lacour-Gayet, Robert, *A History of South Africa.* London: Cassell, 1977.

MacMillan, W., *Bantu, Boer, and Briton.* Oxford: Oxford University Press, 1963.

Marks, Shula, and Anthony Atmore, eds., *Economy and Society in Pre-Industrial South Africa.* London: Longman, 1980.

Marks, Shula, and Richard Rathbone,
Industrialization and Social Change in South Africa. London: Longman, 1982.

Marquand, Leo, *The Story of South Africa.* London: Faber and Faber, 1955.

Morris, Donald R., *The Washing of the Spears.* London: Cardinal, 1988.

Oberholster, J. J., *The Historical Monuments of South Africa.* Cape Town: National Monuments Council, 1972.

Parsons, Neil, *A New History of Southern Africa.* London: Macmillan, 1982.

Peires, J. B., *The House of Phalo.* Berkeley: University of California Press, 1981.

Peires, J. B., ed., *Before and after Shaka.* Grahamstown, South Africa: Rhodes University, 1981.

Ransford, Oliver, *The Great Trek.* London: John Murray, 1972.

Tobias, Phillip V., ed., *The Bushmen.* Cape Town: Human & Rousseau, 1978.

Venter, C., *Great Trek.* Cape Town: Don Nelson, 1985.

Walker, Eric A., *A History of Southern Africa.* London: Longman, 1962.

Wilson, M., and L. Thompson, eds., *South Africa to 1870.* Vol. 1 of *The Oxford History of South Africa.* London: Oxford University Press, 1969.

PICTURE CREDITS

Mary Evans Picture Library, London. **129:** By permission of the British Library, London. **130, 131:** Wan-go Weng, Lyme, New Hampshire / Collection Chaoying Fang. **132, 133:** Map by Alan Hollingbery—*(inset)*, Deutsche Akademie der Wissenschaften zu Berlin. **134, 135:** Map by Alan Hollingbery—by permission of the British Library, London 681 e 21 Opp P252; Eileen Tweedy, London /by permission of the Royal Geographical Society, London; by permission of the British Library, London 147f. 4 Opp P122; by permission of the British Library, London 10095 i 3 Pl. 6—by permission of the British Library, London 20c 39 pl. II; by permission of the British Library, London 147 f.4 Opp PT VIII. **136, 137:** Map by Alan Hollingbery—by permission of the British Library, London; Staatsbibliothek Preussischer Kultur-

besitz, West Berlin; Eileen Tweedy, London /by permission of the Royal Geographical Society, London—The Royal College of Surgeons of England / The Charles Darwin Museum, Orpington, Kent; Eileen Tweedy, London /by permission of the Royal Geographical Society, London. **138, 139:** Map by Alan Hollingbery—Brian Bird Photography / Mitchell Library, State Library of New South Wales, Sydney; by permission of the British Library, London 462e 4 Pl. 14—National Library of Australia, Canberra—by permission of the British Library, London 455 c13 Opp P184; by permission of the British Library, London 2374 cl. 6 flp. **140, 141:** Map by Alan Hollingbery—by permission of the British Library, London 9605 K2 Opp P10; by permission of the British Library, London 1788 C7 Pl. 2 *(top right)*—P. Hollem-

beak / American Museum of Natural History, New York; by permission of the British Library, London 10412 a22 Opp P239; The Denver Public Library, Western History Department . **142, 143:** Map by Alan Hollingbery—Eileen Tweedy, London /from *Narrative of a Journey to the Shores of The Polar Sea* by John Franklin, 1823; Aspect Picture Library, London (2)—Eileen Tweedy, London / from *Journal of a Voyage for the Discovery of a North-West Passage from the Atlantic to the Pacific* , 1821; Aspect Picture Library, London. **144:** By permission of the British Library, London Cup. 652m 25 Pl. 13 **146:** Map by Alan Hollingbery. **149:** Courtesy the Director, National Army Museum, London. **150:** Africana Museum, Johannesburg. **151:** William Fehr Collection, Cape Town /courtesy Don Nelson, Cape Town. **152:** Albany Muse-

um, Grahamstown. **153:** By permission of the British Library, London, Cup. 652 m25 Pl. 7. **154, 155:** Albany Museum, Grahamstown. **156:** By permission of the British Library, London 104, 7h 1b Opp P58. **158, 159:** Michael Freeman, London /courtesy Ian Knight, Shoreham-by-Sea, Sussex (3); Eileen Tweedy, London / Royal Botanical Gardens, Kew, Surrey—Michael Freeman, London / courtesy Ian Knight, Shoreham-by-Sea, Sussex. **160:** By permission of the British Library, London, Up 652 m.25 Pl. XXVI. **161:** Art by Ian Bott. **162, 163:** Africana Museum, Johannesburg; by permission of the British Library, London, Up 652 m.25 Pl. 9. **164:** Map by Alan Hollingbery; Africana Museum, Johannesburg. **167:** The Voortrekker Museum, Pietermaritzburg. **168:** Courtesy the Director, National Army Museum, London.

INDEX